SOLDIER TO AMBASSADOR:

NORMANDY LANDING TO THE PERSIAN GULF

SOLDIER TO AMBASSADOR:
NORMANDY LANDING
TO THE PERSIAN GULF

A Memoir Odyssey
by

Charles W. Hostler, Ph.D.
U.S. Ambassador — Retired

San Diego State University Press
and
Institute on World Affairs
2003

Soldier to Ambassador, Normandy Landing to the Persian Gulf:
A Memoir Odyssey
by Charles W. Hostler, Ph.D.

is published by
San Diego State University Press
in conjunction with SDSU's
Institute on World Affairs
San Diego State University
San Diego, CA 92182.

FIRST EDITION

ISBN 1-879691-71-X

CONTENTS

ACKNOWLEDGEMENTS

My special thanks to Chin-Yeh Rose, whose love, support, vision of what this book could be, and attention to detail have combined to make this work possible.

My appreciation also to many other friends for their help and to SDSU Press Director Harry Polkinhorn, whose efforts and guidance aided the completion of this book.

Chapter One
Shaping Circumstances
(1919 – 1942)

Luck and fate are underrated. Looking back over my life, beginning as a newsboy in San Francisco during the Depression and until my service as U.S. Ambassador to the State (now Kingdom) of Bahrain in the Persian Gulf War, I saw that hard work, perseverance, and basic intelligence all contributed to success. But so did luck; so did fate. I have known my share of disappointments and failures, certainly, but I have also been blessed with an extraordinary amount of good fortune. More than a few of my successes appear to be the result of nothing more than a series of auspicious coincidences and a positive attitude toward them. I understand a person was strongly recommended to Napoleon to be a senior officer to lead an important and dangerous mission. Napoleon is said to have replied, "I am convinced about his abilities, but is he also lucky?" However, I believe the future is not completely in the hands of fate, but is also at least in part influenced by ourselves and our own initiative. Lucky people are usually willing to take risks for possible gain.

Perhaps this is a soldier's way of looking at things. I was among the thousands of U.S. troops who landed on the beaches of Normandy on D-Day in 1944, and, as an OSS intelligence officer, I moved across Europe in the Allied vanguard. I saw many of my comrades die on the battlefield, and, like everyone else, I knew of the many more who perished each day across Europe and in the Pacific. I was no more intelligent, hardworking, or persevering than those who were killed in action. I was just luckier. To suggest otherwise diminishes the memory of those men and the ultimate sacrifice they made for their country.

In a sense, my run of good luck began long before I was born. Each of my ancestors survived disease, starvation, exposure, and every other threat to human existence at least long enough to beget a new generation, passing along a unique set of genes in an unbroken chain that stretches back to the very beginning of life on this planet. Every person alive today shares this same good fortune, of course, so it cannot be said to be uncommon. It is, nevertheless, miraculous. I wonder sometimes how close my genetic chain came to being broken. Like every person alive today, I was just one misstep, one miscalculation, one particularly virulent germ away from never being at all. To be living now at almost 84 years old, the ultimate survivor in this unbroken chain of life, is a mind-boggling marvel. Perhaps, as Francis Bacon said, "Chiefly, the mold of a man's fortune is in his own hands," but I can't underrate luck in the balance.

Parental Influences

A more immediate stroke of fate involved the fortuitous meeting of my parents. This, too, is a miracle of human existence that every living person shares. The circumstances of my parents' meeting were extraordinary and even more wondrous. My wonderful mother, Catherine Marshall, was in the British women's auxiliary army corps (WAAC), and my father, Sidney Marvin Hostler, was an American army officer. They met in France during World War I. The confluence of these factors — war, Britain, France, and the United States — not only resulted in my begetting, but would shape my being and my future in other ways as well.

My parents had wartime comrades who remarkably met in France in parallel circumstances: a delightful British WAAC named Aimée and a fine American Officer, Warren Cranton. They married, lived in Chicago, and were life-long friends with my parents. My middle name of Warren memorialized this outstanding friendship.

My parents never mentioned it, but simple mathematics suggests that I was conceived in France. My parents traveled to England, as hastily as the war's conclusion would allow, in order to marry at my mother's home in Alston, Cumberland, on June 3, 1919. Shortly thereafter, they came to the United States, settling in Chicago (see photo #2) where my father's uncle, Sidney, owned a coal and coke trading company (not the Coke we now think of; coke was the residue of coal left after destructive distillation and used as fuel). My father went to work in the family business, and I was born a few months later on December 12, 1919 (see photo #1).

Thanks to the success of the Hostler Coal & Coke Company, my family lived comfortably during the 1920s. We had a pleasant house, automobiles, and enough money to make numerous trips to Europe. We visited my mother's family in England and also traveled to Belgium and France. This was my first exposure to French, the language that would help to shape my destiny.

On one of our visits to England, my parents, aunts, and uncles discussed the advantages of my attending a British boarding school. Arrangements were made, and in 1928 I enrolled in Sir William Turner's Coatham School for Boys in Redcar on the North Sea coast of England (see photo #3). My mother returned to the United States, and I was left under the caring and watchful eye of my British aunt and uncle, Mahoney and Cecil Crosthwaite. Mahoney had married into a fine and prosperous family, the Crosthwaites, who operated a fleet of large tugboats on the Tees River. I lived at Coatham School, but spent many weekends at my uncle's estate, Langbaurgh Hall, in Great Ayton, Yorkshire.

At Coatham School I had the advantage of studying a foreign language earlier than my American contemporaries. I enjoyed French and seemed to have a talent for it. The years I spent at Coatham School gave me a strong foundation in the language.

Along with that of many other persons, my family's prosperity came to an abrupt end shortly after the U.S. stock market crash of 1929. A financial moratorium was declared that froze the company's assets. Then came the Great Depression, and without the available money to buy coal, the Hostler Coal & Coke Company was instantly out of business and economic despair hovered over our lives like a plague. My parents sold their lovely home, packed up a few things, and in desperation headed West in an overloaded car (see photo #4). We became Illinois "Okies" seeking a new life and economic recovery. We ended up at the home of my father's sister, Loreene Sipp, in Marin County (on the outskirts of San Francisco), California. We lingered there for a number of months as my parents searched for work. Meanwhile, at the age of 12, I sought to do my part peddling magazines. Each day I crossed San Francisco Bay on the ferry, picked up a canvas saddlebag full of magazines at my employer's newsstand, and ventured into the crowds that gathered near the cable-car turn-arounds and trolley-car stops. There, I hopped onto trolleys and sold copies of *The Saturday Evening Post*, *Liberty*, and other magazines to the passengers—at least until the conductor chased me off. Even though I made only a few dollars a day, I was the family's sole breadwinner for many months. We learned to accept a future that played out one day at a time.

Eventually, my hardworking father found employment with the National Recovery Administration (NRA), a "New Deal" U.S. Government program. This event was a rescue from our dire financial situation, but this development later proved meaningful to me in other ways. Father joined what ultimately became the California State Employment Service, and the family relocated to Los Angeles and Hollywood.

One poignant event that still frequents my memory involves one of my after-school jobs in Los Angeles. At one period I worked as a paid helper for a charitable distribution program. When we were completing a Thanksgiving delivery schedule my boss noted that we had one turkey left in the delivery wagon I was pulling. He turned to me and asked, "Do you know any deserving family for this turkey?" I eagerly responded, "My family needs one." I was delighted and grateful when he concurred and quickly walked home carrying the gift, thinking how happy and pleased my father and mother would be. When I proudly offered the turkey, they burst into tears.

My mother acquired a real estate license and became one of the area's early female real estate agents. It was an enterprising move that ultimately improved our financial situation and gave me the direction for later successful investment in California real estate.

I attended Hollywood High School. Not surprisingly, I excelled in French, thanks to the years I had spent at Sir William Turner's Coatham School and traveling in Europe. Otherwise, I was an average student, distracted by family financial problems and chasing the pretty girls at Hollywood High. While my family was getting back on its feet, financial survival was still very much on our minds. I continued to work after school, parking cars at nights at the famous Hollywood Pantages Chinese Theater, the scene of many movie premieres. I was often tipped a dollar, a lot of money at that time. I also worked in a malted milk shop in the evenings after school. My cleaning job at the malt shop involved breaking up the milk slush that was delivered to the shop in frozen containers. The work was hard, but I felt well compensated because, in addition to my pay, I could have unlimited numbers of malted milks. I also managed to treat my young lady friends to malted milks whenever they stopped by to chat—a perk that did more than a little to enhance my standing with the fairer sex of Hollywood High.

UCLA, Douglas Aircraft, and the California Highway Patrol

After graduating from high school in 1938, I enrolled in the University of California at Los Angeles (UCLA). I joined Phi Kappa Sigma, the same fraternity that my father had belonged to when he was at Northwestern University. We were known as Phi Kaps. To support myself at university, I took a full-time night job at the Douglas Aircraft Company, located in nearby Santa Monica, not far from UCLA.

In 1939, war erupted in Europe, and, while American troops were not yet in combat, the Douglas plant was operating around the clock in preparation for the inevitable. I worked on the famous

DC3 transport aircraft, which the military called the C47. The rugged DC3 (or Dakota) was perhaps the most successful commercial aircraft ever built. President Dwight Eisenhower, whom I was to meet several times as one of his WWII subordinates, said the DC3 was one of the Allies' four key weapons. The others were the jeep, the bazooka and the atomic bomb. More than 18,000 DC3s were constructed with about 2,000 still in use some 65 years after their conception. I worked the graveyard shift, from midnight to 8:00 a.m., then hurried to UCLA for my 8:30 classes. Between being president of my fraternity for a year, and the active pursuit of girls, I struggled academically. However, even without adequate time to study, I managed to get by with passing grades.

I progressed through college without having any particular career in mind and majored in public administration, in part because my father worked for the government. Because of my interest in the military I joined the Reserve Officers Training Corps (ROTC) and took advantage of its scholarship benefits (see photo #5). As graduation approached, one of my public administration classes required students to take a civil service examination to better understand how the public bureaucracy worked. For no special reason, but with important consequences to follow, I took the written civil service exam for the California Highway Patrol (CHP). Apparently I scored well because I received a letter from the CHP inviting me to take the remaining qualification tests — an interview, a physical fitness test, and a driving test.

The physical fitness test was demanding, but not beyond my youthful capabilities. We had to run a certain distance within an allowable time, climb a rope, do chin-ups, the usual sort of thing. I passed, and moved on to the driving test. I had purchased my first car, a used "model A" Ford convertible, during my work at the malt shop, so I had plenty of experience driving a car. However, the same could not be said for riding a motorcycle, and, unfortunately for me, this made up the second half of the driving test.

Rather than risk disqualification and admit I had never ridden a motorcycle, I positioned myself towards the end of the line and watched. To my chagrin, the other fellows were all skillful. By the time it was my turn, I had formed an idea of what to do. I didn't say a word and just went up to the motorcycle, got on, and accelerated away. Everyone watched as I made a slow, wobbly circumnavigation of the course.

When I returned to the starting point, the officer in charge said, "You have never ridden a motorcycle before, have you, son?"

"No, sir, I haven't," I admitted.

He looked me up and down for a moment. "Well, at least you had the guts to try," he said as he scribbled something onto his clipboard. "I think you can eventually master it. You pass."

"Thank you, sir," I said, grateful for the lucky break.

Then came a momentous event that became etched in my memory. On December 7, 1941, about a month before I was due to graduate from UCLA, the radio in the fraternity house announced that the Japanese had bombed Pearl Harbor. It was inevitable that I would soon be called up to serve as a 2nd Lt. in the Army Air Corps. I just wasn't sure when. In that era before computers, processing the paperwork to call up troops required a great deal of time and took place in Washington, D.C. The Army Air Corps estimated that I would receive my orders and first assignment in about three months.

Three weeks later in January, 1942, I graduated from UCLA and simultaneously received my ROTC commission as a second lieutenant. I also received a letter from the California Highway Patrol offering me a position with the CHP. I wanted to accept the post but felt compelled to inform the CHP personnel office that I soon would be called into the armed forces. The CHP personnel officers understood, but there wasn't much they could do. I had qualified for the job, and it was mine for the taking. I certainly would not be the only CHP officer they would lose to the war effort, and they probably hoped that those officers would return to the CHP when the war was over. At that point, of course, no one had any idea how long the war would last.

On January 25, 1942, I reported to the CHP training school located in Northern California and received six weeks of intensive instruction. I learned valuable physical skills, such as the use of firearms, carrying out high-speed pursuits, and subduing suspects. I also gained precious understanding about the mental aspects of investigation, interrogation, and judgment under stressful situations.

My field service in the Highway Patrol was relatively brief but exceedingly useful. I was stationed along what was called the Ridge Route, a busy stretch of highway that crossed the San Bernardino Mountains between the Los Angeles Basin and the high deserts to the north. The weather along the Ridge Route could be treacherous, and soon I was forced to reckon with human injury and carnage along the road. The highway was also a major escape route for criminals fleeing from Los Angeles to points north, including the Nevada border and Las Vegas. Several times during my stay, we received police radio calls about absconding suspects, and we were there to apprehend them. I found the work challenging and rewarding—something I felt cut out to do.

The State of California only benefited from its investment in my training for another six weeks in the field after I graduated from the CHP academy. Then orders came to report for duty in the Army Air Corps. I like to think, however, that the state and indeed the nation profited indirectly from my law enforcement training, as I soon had ample opportunity to employ most, if not all, the learned skills in the battle against the Axis powers in Europe.

The U.S. Army Air Corps

In March, 1942, I received the package containing my orders from the Army Air Corps to report for duty, and so I acquired my second lieutenant's uniform. I showed my new uniform to my buddies at the CHP station, and my commander commented on the similarity between the CHP and Air Corps uniforms. He had me pose for "before-and-after" pictures next to my patrol car — one in my CHP uniform and one in my Air Corps version (see photos #6 & #7). He told me that I was always welcome to rejoin his unit and the CHP after the war, but he predicted that I would probably seek other challenges. As it turned out, after changing for the snapshots, I never wore the CHP uniform again.

My orders called for me to report for duty at a new Army Air Corps installation later called Hunter Air Base being established near Savannah, Georgia. As was customary before the wide use of airlines, the package containing my orders also included a one-way railroad ticket. I boarded the train in San Bernardino.

When I arrived in Savannah three days later, I made my way to the Army Air Corps base to report for duty. I entered the office of the Base Adjutant (at Hunter Air Base), who was hard at work behind stacks of paper piled high on his desk, strode up to his desk, snapped to attention, and gave him a brisk salute. As I stood there, erect, my hand lightly touching my brow, I had no idea that my life was about to change forever—that I was standing, as the saying goes, in the right place at the right time.

The adjutant looked up from his paperwork, sized me up, and groaned. "Aw, jeez," he said. "Not another young fellow right out of college." He half-heartedly returned my salute.

"I don't suppose you've ever done any real work, now have you, son?" he asked sarcastically.

"Oh, yes, sir," I countered. "I was an officer in the California Highway Patrol."

"You were?" he asked, his eyes lighting up. "That's great. Then you're officially a Base Intelligence Officer, the Police and Prison Officer, Fire Marshal, and in charge of garbage collection."

Those may not have been the most prestigious duties in the Army Air Corps, but to a twenty-two-year old youth who, six months before had no idea what to do with his life, they sounded pretty important. I was determined to make the most of them.

The base being new, its facilities were primitive, at best. Its military prison, for example, was nothing more than a barracks surrounded by a high fence topped with barbed wire. Even under guard, the compound was far from being escape-proof, and every now and then we had a breakout. Because the facility was surrounded by Georgia swampland, tracking the escapees was difficult. The local police had a contingent of bloodhounds, however, and the sheriff had offered us his assistance whenever we needed it. Off we would go into the swamp with hounds baying, just like a hunting expedition. Often as not, the human beings hunted, like their wild counterparts, would eventually clamber up trees to escape from the dogs, which is where we would "tree" them. Because of our close cooperation, the Sheriff of Chatham County, Georgia, made me an "Honorary" Deputy Sheriff in August, 1943.

One escapee made it across the swamp before being apprehended by the local authorities. I received a call from a local sheriff to come to retrieve the military prisoner, so I went after him. The local town jail in Waycross, Georgia, was then about as primitive as our military base brig. The male prisoners were held on the ground floor and female prisoners on the second level. After we had secured the prisoner in the car, the sheriff drawled, "Son, before you go, I want to show you something."

He led me back to the jail, and we started up a dimly lit staircase. It was summer, and, in those days before air conditioning, the wooden building was sweltering. The second floor was bare, but in the middle was a kind of cage, about thirty feet long on each side, with metal bars that ran from floor to ceiling. The female prisoners were held collectively in this single, large cell. There must have been twenty-five women crowded together, and for relief from the heat, they had stripped naked. Many of them had been arrested for prostitution. When they saw me with the jailer, they decided to have a little fun. "Hey, put that young one in here with us," one shouted. Some of the rest joined in, striking their best streetwalker poses and shouting out obscenities. This was an interesting situation for a very young lad who had never seen anything like it before, nor has he since.

While stationed in Georgia, I became acquainted with Martha Ann Cowan, the daughter of a senior base officer. Martha and I felt an immediate attraction and soon began to date. Although she was only nineteen, she had already been married and divorced. Her parents were eager for her to improve her situation with a better marriage so they encouraged the romance. We married in 1943 after a six-month courtship.

It was during this era that General William J. "Wild Bill" Donovan, one of the most highly decorated U.S. officers of World War I, began to assemble the Office of Strategic Services (OSS) at the behest of President Roosevelt. This became known to me through another of the strange coincidences that shaped my life. The U.S. was almost completely unprepared for the dangers and stresses of the 1940s in the field of covert special intelligence operations, as in so many others. It is almost a miracle that the U.S. built a fine war-time record with its OSS, which was later developed into the CIA.

The chance came from my uncle, Paul Sipp, the same uncle who had kindly provided a home for my family in Marin County, California, during the depths of the Depression. Uncle Paul had moved to New York City and had been a founding member of a successful municipal bond firm called the First of Michigan Corp. One of his colleagues on Wall Street was friendly with Donovan. In fact, General Donovan had selected this gentleman, a reserve colonel, to be the personnel officer for the fledgling OSS. When Uncle Paul learned that General Donovan was recruiting people for some sort of special overseas intelligence operation, he contacted me and asked if I might be interested in such an assignment. "Oh, boy, yes," I said, so Uncle Paul set the interviews in motion.

The leaders of the OSS were conceiving a variety of programs with different covert foreign intelligence and special warfare objectives even as they recruited new officers. D-Day was still many months away, but one of these secret programs called for American OSS agents to discreetly capture and control Nazi secret agent collaborators in Europe. For this particular assignment, the OSS was looking for a few aggressive young officers who were college graduates, fluent in French, willing to accept "hazardous duty," and preferably with an intelligence background. In retrospect, it seems as though I was predestined for this challenging assignment.

By the time the OSS opportunity arose, I had been promoted to the rank of Captain in the Air Corps. Neither my wife nor my parents-in-law in Savannah wanted me to take this position with OSS. None of us knew exactly what would be involved, but we could easily divine that I would not be sitting behind a desk in the U.S.A. My six-month-old marriage was already in trouble, and my wife added that she would divorce me if I joined this special OSS unit. I was very sorry that she felt as she did, but my desire to serve was firm and final. I asked my commanding officer for permission to transfer to the OSS, and he granted it. Subsequently, a marriage annulment was arranged.

I arrived in Washington in the winter of 1943. Alongside the reflecting pool between the Washington Monument and the Lincoln Memorial stood a row of temporary wooden buildings. Some of these housed the OSS. On reporting for duty, I was informed that I would have to undergo further selective evaluation and training at remote sites. I was instructed to report at a certain time to an obscure garage in Washington, D.C. At the garage, I was ordered to remove my officer's uniform and my watch, and to dress in military fatigues — the better to move about anonymously in the sea of GIs that had flooded the nation's capital. With about 20 other potential selectees I got into the back of a standard military truck and took a thirty-minute ride into the Virginia countryside.

We stopped at an elaborate country mansion owned by the Willard family, who had made its fortune operating the famous Willard Hotel in Washington. We were shown to our accommodations, given false names, and told not to divulge any information about our backgrounds. The OSS wanted to make sure that any of us who might be captured or not be selected, not only would not, but could not, provide any information about these potential OSS colleagues.

The OSS was America's first clandestine foreign intelligence organization, and as a discipline this type of secret intelligence operation was still in its infancy in the U.S.A. Considering that, the training, and testing, and assessment we received was quite sophisticated, thanks to men like Dr. John W. Gardner and Dr. Henry A. Murray. The Willard estate was staffed by a group of prominent psychologists and professors who had designed a battery of innovative tests to determine our appropriateness, mental acuity, and fitness. (See the pioneering book *Assessment of Men*.) For example, one by one we were led into a bedroom and told to determine quickly as much as possible about the person who had resided there. We checked the closet for clothing and shoes to estimate height, weight, and sex. We searched for clues through pockets, closets, drawers, and waste bins. Afterwards, we individually had to write everything down that we could discern and then offer our analysis concerning the former occupant. Another time, we were led in small groups down to a creek that ran through the grounds. We were stopped beside a large boulder and told to move it to the other side of the creek. The observers watched as the group interacted, formed a plan, and went about the work. The observers acted as though we were being timed, but what they were really interested in was our behavior: Who were the leaders? Who were the innovators? Who were the naysayers? In short, what was each man's potential for his specific future assignment?

The entire week was one long stressful observation period. Even when we were not involved in an exercise or being trained, we were being carefully scrutinized. How much would we reveal about ourselves? How did we behave when we were tired? One night, the observers made a conscious effort to get us drunk, just to see how we acted under the influence of alcohol and what we would reveal. At the end of the week we were required to write a detailed profile and analyses of each of our fellow potential recruits. The week's ordeal, known as the "psychological evaluation," was in some ways devious and innovative. But in field operations it indicated with reasonable accuracy the candidate's strengths and weaknesses and assuredly saved lives. Although we never spoke of it, by the end of the week it was clear that some of us would be selected and others would not. Fortunately, I made it, and became a part of the exclusive X-2 division of OSS, and a whole new and exciting phase of my life was about to begin.

Chapter Two
Deception and Counter-Espionage with OSS in WWII Europe (1943 -1 945)

OSS/X-2

The significant and closely-held joint activities of the X-2 section of the U.S. Office of Strategic Services (OSS), predecessor to CIA, which worked closely with the British MI 5 and MI 6 organizations, played an enormous role in saving Allied military lives and in confusing Axis military strategists during WWII. Six decades have passed since the landings in Normandy, and the need for continued secrecy has diminished. It is appropriate now to reveal more about the very successful and closely-guarded top-secret operations that helped greatly to deceive the Germans as to our true plans and thus reduced the number of Allied casualties. Many Allied troops owe their lives to an arsenal of cover and deception that was their "best kept secret." This deception turned into what many considered to be the greatest intelligence coup of WWII.

The OSS Headquarters was located at 24th & F Street, NW, Washington, D.C. After my extensive screening and final qualification for OSS beginning in December, 1943, I was sent for several months of specialized intensive training as part of X-2 (the Counter-Espionage Section of OSS) the Chief of which was a Washington. D.C. attorney,

James R. Murphy. The instruction involved a number of schools outside Washington, D.C. The OSS schools I attended included "S" (psychological evaluation), "A-3" (sabotage, SO, acronym for Special Operations), "E" (espionage, SI, Special Intelligence), "The Farm" (X-2, counter-espionage), and others. They concentrated on personalized instruction in enciphering and deciphering messages (including "one-time" encryption pads); how to send and receive Morse code; how to use explosives and weapons of all sorts; how to avoid booby traps; how to pick locks; how to install hidden microphones; how to conduct interrogations; how to resist giving critical information when you are interrogated; how to infiltrate enemy or unfamiliar territory at night; how to use direction-finding equipment; indoctrination courses on various enemy intelligence services; instruction in the manipulation of rumor; monitoring of enemy wireless; and the exploitation of double agents (see photo #8).

When the time arrived in March, 1944, for me to depart OSS Headquarters in Washington, D.C. for my assignment in Europe, I was given an extra weight allowance of 25 pounds for "special OSS equipment." I was provided with a number of items, which included:

(1) Leica camera with telephoto lenses
(2) Speed-o-copy lens for copying documents
(3) Pistol .45 caliber with holster and clips
(4) Pistol .25 caliber automatic "Zehna" with left-handed shoulder holster
(5) Lock-picking set

(6) Zeiss binoculars

(7) U.S. carbine, caliber 30, with folding stock (parachutist)

(8) For bargaining purposes, building good will, and obtaining information outside the continental USA:

(a) 2 dozen, nylon stockings, popular sizes

(b) 2 dozen, rayon stockings, popular sizes

(c) Lipsticks, popular shades

(d) Compacts

(e) Lighters and cigarettes.

The latter items were informally described as "for feminine appeasement" — and "will bring joy abounding."

Training with British MI-6

After completing my stateside training in the U.S., I received "clearance" from British Intelligence to proceed to Section V of MI-6 for their specialized instruction. One British question in the clearance process was, "Do you have any Irish connections?" (which I did not). I left Ft. Hamilton, New York, in March, 1944, and crossed the Atlantic to Scotland on the Queen Elizabeth. The luxury liner had been converted into a troop ship, with as many as 18 junior officers in bunks in a single stateroom, dodging U boats (German submarines), and eating the available two meals per day (which were necessarily divided into five-group sittings per meal). I shared my cabin with three other officers and two civilians. Personalities on board included

Joe Louis (then a Staff Sgt. and Heavyweight Boxing Champion of the World), and another person whom I remember was the Undersecretary of State Stettinius (who was later to be Secretary of State).

After five days at sea we disembarked in Glasgow to the stirring strains of a Scottish bagpipe band. We then sat up all night on a blacked-out troop train to Addison Roads, London. The Londoners were suffering through relentless Nazi bombers and V 1 and V 2 missile attacks and existed on a very reduced standard of living. This was a grievous time of death, disruption, and privation for Londoners. Grosvenor Square (nicknamed "Eisenhower Platz") and the surrounding area were almost completely occupied by American organizations. The U.S. Senior Officers' Mess was at 45 Park Lane and had the best food in town (for Majors and above, though OSS Captains could obtain entry cards). The British troops who were away from the U.K. had a well-known, justified lament about the flood of about two million American G.I.s who were "oversexed, overpaid, and over here."

I began close orientation training from March until June, 1944, with our experienced British counterparts, Section V of MI 6, the counter-espionage element of the British Foreign Military Intelligence Service. This joint effort took place primarily at a building innocently labeled "Charity House" at 7 Ryder Street, near St. James Street. The U.S. OSS/ SCI units later had a field training exercise entitled "Exercise Larry" near Horsham, England, at the end of April, which gave us simulated experience in capturing and "converting" enemy agents. While in London, I was quartered much of the time at the Normandie Hotel in Kensington.

Among the talented members of MI 6 at that time (many of whom were college professors from Cambridge and Oxford) was the noted British author Malcolm Muggeridge, who has written "Oh, those first OSS arrivals in London! How well I remember them . . . arriving like 'jeune filles en fleur' straight from a finishing school, all fresh and innocent, to start work in our frowsty old intelligence brothel. All too soon they were ravished and corrupted, becoming indistinguishable from seasoned pros who had been in the game for a quarter century or more." Those talented individuals included the brilliant, cranky Oxford historian Hugh Trevor-Roper, who later wrote the best-seller *The Last Days of Hitler,* author Graham Greene, and its chief, Felix Cowgill.

Another one of the senior staff of Section V who trained us in counter-espionage techniques in London was the infamous double agent, Kim Philby, a long-serving and treacherous senior officer in British intelligence, who was later branded as a traitor for the Soviets. I crossed paths again with Philby in two foreign locales in future years. The first was in 1948, to 1949, during his period as the British Secret Intelligence Service's Station Commander in Istanbul, while I was providing U.S. military intelligence training to the Turkish Air Force. The second time was in Beirut, Lebanon, in the early 1960s when he was a "stringer" for the weekly *Observer* and the *Economist,* and I was employed in that city as the Middle East Director for the Douglas Aircraft Company. He was drinking very heavily then. Once, at a Beirut cocktail party, he unsteadily lurched over to me, and, in a friendly but wicked way, whispered with his usual stutter, "Still playing the 'old game,' Charley?" Philby was apparently convinced that my then legitimate employment with Douglas Aircraft was a "cover" for continued service to OSS/CIA. On another of his drinking sprees in a Beirut bar (I believe it was at the well-known "Kit-Kat Club"), Kim made the caustic and unfair observation, "The Arabs are the only people I know of who combine ignorance with arrogance." He defected on the night of January 23, 1963, and fled from Beirut over the Eastern Turkish border to Moscow, where he later died.

The OSS/X-2 organization (the name was probably derived from the British "Double-Cross Committee") was created by OSS's General Donovan to satisfy Prime Minister Winston Churchill's insistence that the U.S. intelligence services be able to maintain exacting security standards before the British would reveal their incredible decoding and counter-espionage successes. Paramount among those success stories was cracking the German Enigma ciphering machine. Their resulting product was known as "Ultra" and involved the British accomplishments at Bletchley Park, outside of London. The code-breakers were mischievously sometimes referred to by their colleagues as "voyeurs" (a French word twisted to imply those who lasciviously engage in "key-hole peaking"). The British were primarily interested in decoding German messages about troop movements and order of battle. But, as a "by-product" they deciphered material leading to the detection and co-opting of German agents operating in the U.K. Among them was the agent code-named "Garbo" and the infamous Eddie Chapman, a patriotic crook made prominent by the book and the 1967 British-French movie entitled "Triple Cross" featuring British actor, Christopher Plummer. Other German agents, who were meticulously arrested, were given a choice to either work for the British MI 6 or be hanged as spies.

The "Ultra" secret was one of the most closely-held intelligence coups of the war. Although eventually over ten thousand individuals knew in part about this precious enigma, the general public did not learn the full story until about 30 years after the war when the first book on the subject appeared in 1972, which was the prelude to many other books. Without exaggeration, Ultra was called "The most comprehensive and effective system for penetrating an enemy's mind that has ever been evolved."

There is a wonderful story told regarding the need for ironclad discretion that involved General Sir Stewart Menzies, the "C" or director of the British Secret Intelligence Service (SIS) or MI-6. King George VI once jokingly pressed Menzies to reveal details about the Service.

"Menzies," said the King, "what would happen if I were to ask you the name of our man (or agent) in Berlin?"

Menzies replied, "I would have to say, Sir, that my lips are sealed."

"Well, Menzies. supposing I were to say, off with your head," said the King.

"In that case, Sir, my head would roll with the lips still sealed."

I was a part of a small American OSS X-2 liaison group sent to England to exploit counter-espionage data based on Ultra traffic. Between 1943 and 1945, the OSS accumulated information on enemy espionage agents and cover organizations. There was some overlap with FBI files, which concentrated on agents operating *within* the U.S., and the British registry, which was older and larger. The OSS/X-2 collection by the end of WWII consisted of cards (largely 3" by 5") on over 300,000 individuals. My official OSS code name was "Poplar" (a genus of slender, quick-growing tree).

In cooperation with our Allies, chiefly the British, the OSS contributed to the apprehending of many sensitive enemy agents in military zones rendering ineffective some primarily German controlled stay-behind networks. These were usually indigenous French persons who were Fascist sympathizers trained to function after being overrun by the Allies, working from behind Allied lines and reporting to their *Abwehr* (German Military intelligence) controllers. The Ultra decryptions were essential to our work, since they enabled us to judge enemy intentions and movements. This, together with general intelligence data, augmented by direction-finding specialists, was used to pinpoint the location and characteristics of the enemy stay-behind agents in occupied France. Our dangerous and time-sensitive mission was to race ahead (or in some few cases to parachute) urgently and discretely to control or geld these agents before Allied troops might unwittingly kill or disrupt them.

Once we had these agents under our influence, we would attempt to "convince" them of the hopelessness of their situation and insist on their immediate and complete "cooperation." We rarely used force, but often used threats with lethal implications. If the agent hesitated or equivocated, we would mention our fine French liaison officers (such as the distinguished Colonel Louis Douin) and make it clear that our French colleagues were aching to promptly take custody of such traitors to France. Recognizing their vulnerability, they usually complied, although French Resistance members sometimes discovered these individuals and settled scores with the agents in their own way.

We were in a race against time to assure that the new fully-interrogated double agent was sufficiently converted, psychologically committed, and placed back on the air with his Morse code transmitter, hopefully, in time to satisfy his established schedule with his German controllers. We had to use caution and empathy to assure that double agents did not introduce a word or signal indicating that they were under our control. We also had to master details of the enemy agent's wireless transmission style and wrist rhythm (or "fist") in sending messages so that if the agent "died" or an Allied stand-in was necessary, we could continue transmissions without being detected by the German controllers.

When agents were successfully doubled, we assigned a case officer or handler, who attempted to fully understand and to introduce himself almost completely "into the skin" of the agent. Then, as quickly as we could do so confidently, we proceeded to send judicious mixtures of accurate and false data to the *Abwehr* listening posts. Messages planted with the Germans had to be cautious and clever, believable, utilizing the kind of information an agent in his (or her) location might be expected to obtain. We transmitted factual messages whenever possible, often introducing only marginally contradictory data since agents frequently would be expected to learn different things about Allied movements and units. Using a "one-time pad" encryption system, we obtained key deception strategy emanating from SHAEF (Supreme Headquarters Allied Expeditionary Force). We inserted carefully crafted deceptions into the messages reflecting the views and concepts that Allied headquarters meant to use to confuse the Germans and distort the reality. Above all, our messages should never compromise the Ultra secret itself. Our primary objective was to penetrate the enemy by exploiting its own agents.

By the early spring of 1944, it was clearly impossible to hide the fact that the major Allied cross-channel invasion would come somewhere between the Cherbourg peninsula and Dunkirk. The true preparations could not be completely disguised, and the distance from the bases at which fighter cover could be supported helped to define the limits. The initial overall deception plan (code named "Fortitude") was dictated by these circumstances and, therefore, resulted in a general scheme of three points in relation to Normandy: first, to postpone the date of the main attack in the minds of the Germans; second, to indicate that the invasion would come in the east rather than 170 miles away in the west of the threatened area; and third, to suggest that after the real attack had begun it was only a first blow and that another, even heavier assault would follow in the Pas de Calais area.

Double-Cross agents were only a part of the Allied machinery of deception. The cover plan was developed in the Germans' minds also by using bogus wireless deceptions (the Y Service), by visual deception (for example, dummy assault craft), by the actual movement of troops in England, and by promoting the existence of notional divisions and armies, and so on.

Our work was conducted in great secrecy. Perhaps no secret was more closely held. Had the Germans at any point suspected that one, much less most, of their agents had been "turned," and that German intelligence was sending its sensitive queries directly to us, the *Abwehr* certainly might have abandoned all their presumed agents, changed their codes, and tried to send in new agents. These new agents in turn would have had to be detected and doubled (or executed), and the Germans would quite likely have realized that their Enigma ciphers were being routinely read. Thus, we were engaged in the most intense work of all intelligence, a deception that, once entered upon, simply *had* to succeed.

The British used doubled German agents ("Garbo," et al.) in England to plant lies about British plans and morale on the home front. But those lies were of use only if we could know how the Germans responded to them. Ultra transcriptions and other intercepted traffic made this possible.

There were seven broad objectives, as laid out by Sir John Masterman, the British Chairman of the Double Cross (XX or Twenty) Committee:

1. to control the enemy's systems;
2. to apprehend enemy agents;
3. to learn as much as possible about the personalities and methods of the *Abwehr* and other German intelligence units;
4. to make the German codes and ciphers reveal their secrets;
5. to study the questions asked by the Germans of their agents as evidence of their intentions;
6. to influence their plans by the answers sent back; and
7. to deceive the enemy about Allied plans.

Special Counter Intelligence (SCI) units were set up in both the U.S. and British headquarters at the Army level. Our mission was to use our initiative and special training to deal with the stay-behind networks and border-crossers in France once the invasion had been launched. The objective was to eliminate enemy intelligence assets and to manipulate with deception those agents who were permitted to survive. A great U.S. SCI colleague I met during our Ryder Street training was Akeley P. Quirk, then a Lt. Commander, USNR. After the war he became a Los Angeles attorney and wrote a fine memoir entitled *Recollections of World War II* (OSS SCI Unit 6th U.S. Army Group).

"The Great Crusade"

On the early evening of "D-Day," June 6, 1944, because of the urgency of the intelligence mission, our OSS/SCI unit was sent across the stormy English Channel and debarked with several jeeps into the water from an LST at Utah Beach. The jeeps were kept moving forward in the water, thanks to their added "snorkel" devices, which replaced the disconnected exhaust pipes and exited their fumes a foot above the windshield. We had been exceedingly fortunate to disembark at Utah Beach—while the troops who had landed on Omaha Beach six miles east of us had run directly into well-trained German units who hit U.S. troops with devastating fire from the bluffs. Those landing on Utah Beach met comparatively light resistance, thanks in part to the earlier parachute and glider landings of the U.S. 82nd and 101st Airborne divisions. The U.S. 4th Division, for example, bravely suffered less than three hundred casualties that day at Utah Beach. The carnage of D-Day and after was horrific, but the objectives given to us were precise and well-defined.

Our OSS/SCI unit advanced carefully and apprehensively through the beach obstacles and the debris of war. We cautiously made our way inland about five miles on a road leading through flooded meadows and marshland, which showed the scars of battle. We ultimately camped in an apple orchard and dug in with slit trenches, slept in pup tents, and concealed our jeeps under camouflage nets. We collapsed into our uncomfortable slit trenches in a jumble of exhaustion, excitement, and gratitude at having survived that far.

Subsisting on C rations, we were instructed not to take nourishment from the French economy because it would aggravate the food shortage of the local population. After time, however, we did occasionally enjoy the robust local Normandy cuisine (and their hearty Calvados cider brandy) by bartering our cigarettes and rations. Our task was promptly to gain control of the targeted enemy agents *before* Allied ground forces could over-run or disrupt them. Thus, we tried always to arrive at the time an identified agent's town or village was about to be captured. We would take under control any stay-behind agents, as well as captured key German intelligence personnel and files.

My initial objective was a painful and memorable one. Our target was a French wholesale grocer located in the general vicinity of the town of

Ste. Mere Eglise. He was high on our priority list for being a Fascist sympathizer and having an intelligence commitment as a stay-behind agent to the *Abwehr*.

Anxious not to excite the suspicions of his neighbors, I knocked lightly on his door, and he answered. Asking him if we could enter, I sensed he was immediately suspicious and apprehensive. Attempting to deal with him in a composed and civil manner, I didn't directly point my carbine or .45 pistol at him. He swiftly struck me heavily in the head with the blunt end of a meat ax grabbed from the table behind him. My enlisted driver leaped to my rescue and finally subdued him. We hastened to push him inside and to convince the Frenchman to cooperate. In fact, he had little choice. My forehead wound was bleeding heavily. I was later treated and temporarily bandaged by a roadside U.S. Army medical corpsman. I declined to go to a U.S. field hospital because of apprehension about the security of our sensitive mission; I did not want to delay the successful handling of my first stay-behind agent. This painful wound qualified me for a Purple Heart award, but at the time our concerns were elsewhere, and I later continued to get treatment along the roadside from military first aid stations. As a result, it took several excruciating weeks to heal, and I carry the mark of the wound to this day with a visible dent on my forehead. It was an honor later to receive the Purple Heart.

German military resistance was still strong in the vicinity of Cherbourg, which precluded entering that important port until later, so we headed south. The OSS headquarters in London, meanwhile, believed that to increase prompt effectiveness, parachute training was needed for a few of us, so we could jump into target areas that might otherwise be inaccessible or delayed.

I was sent back to Britain for five days of parachute training at the famous Ringway Airport in Manchester, Cheshire. Instruction was at the elite British Special Training School (STS) Number 51 and involved six parachute jumps including three from a Whitley bomber at 700 feet and three 700-foot night jumps from a tethered balloon. It was always an exhilarating moment when the jump master signaled "go." I sat on the edge with my legs dangling and slipped down through the open "Joe" hole in the bottom of the British bomber, tumbling into space. This special course prepared us with "insertion techniques" as they were called. British, U.S., and other allies (Poles, French, and others) trained side by side in STS 51 under personalized, intense instruction. A British Lord was among the students. He was accompanied by his burly "batman" (or personal military servant) on each of his jumps. My graduation was accompanied by a written commendation from the British school commandant stating that I had jumped with "confidence and determination." Upon returning to France, my OSS superior looked at the document referring to my "confidence and determination" and wisecracked, "What, no parachute?" (see photo #9).

My OSS unit focused actively on our deception mission, pursuing the list of German controlled stay-behinds. We urgently wanted to reach our targets before the Allied troops or resistance forces found or dislodged them. Many of our targets were the so-called "Milicien" or pro-German French fascists, who were appropriately regarded as traitors to France. The Resistance forces continued to receive weapons from the Allies, and as the German forces disintegrated in any locale, the French patriots became correspondingly more aggressive. They had a lot of scores to settle. Occasionally, we found French corpses. French justice was swift. Hence, we had to be at our target punctiliously at the proper moment. This often put us ahead of our own front-line troops.

We moved on to Vannes, Carentan, and then with the First U.S. Army SCI Unit, proceeded to Cherbourg around mid-July, 1944, as the German military opposition finally caved in under Allied military pressure. The Germans destroyed the port of Cherbourg before surrendering. One area that they did not completely demolish was a tunnel with a grotto-like interior filled with many barrels and cases of high-quality French liquors and wines that the Germans had collected. For me, one of the highlights of Cherbourg involved the "liberation" of two barrels of fine French Armagnac brandy that had been reserved for high-ranking German officers in a large cellar within those fortified walls of

Cherbourg. Certain early arriving American troops were quick to relieve the storerooms of the great Armagnac. Hurriedly, we located bottles and smaller containers to empty the contents of one barrel. The other barrel was buried in a field outside of Cherbourg. Thus, in the following weeks, some OSS teams never lacked for libation. The German stay-behind agent code-named "Dragoman" was used to relay deceptive information concerning Allied progress in reconstructing Cherbourg harbor.

With the arrival in Normandy of General George Patton on August 3, 1944, our OSS/SCI unit was attached to the headquarters of the U.S. Third Army. I carefully kept his G2 staff informed of our activities and coordinated with Third Army movements, but our operational directions came from OSS/X2 in London by encrypted radio messages. Third Army G2 Col. Oscar Koch later issued an official commendation for my "assuming command of Special Counter Intelligence operations for Third Army when combat operations were in progress . . . and the excellent results attained . . . are to be most highly commended." (I still attend the Third Army Staff Reunions for the "Lucky Few of World War II," which are organized by the dedicated former Assistant G1 Coy Eklund.)

When I reached the heavily fortified and defended town of Rennes in early August, I came upon a most rewarding goal. Rennes, the capital of Brittany province, was an interesting city and was the headquarters of the "Free Brittany" independence movement. Many countries in Europe had local political groups that wanted to sever themselves from their central governments. The large Gestapo and *Sicherheitsdienst* headquarters in Rennes were located purposely and judiciously in a former girls school, right in the middle of a hospital complex upon which large Red Crosses were painted on the roofs. This helped to protect them from Allied air strikes, however "surgical" the U.S. bombings were intended to be.

On my arrival in Rennes the German military forces were still actively in the process of evacuating buildings and burning documents. There was an exchange of gunfire, and a few of the remaining Gestapo made their escape. I was able to capture several personally including a key German Gestapo major whose interrogation was very fruitful. In this Gestapo headquarters we discovered voluminous files and many incriminating materials. In the interrogation room, I found a large assortment of devices used for torturing prisoners, who included resistance members and allied military. There were thumb screws, a variety of whips, and rubber hoses filled with nails which were designed to rip the flesh from victims. Instruments that were used to crush fingers and other parts of a person's body gave a clear picture of the brutality of the Gestapo. I took extensive photos for use later in the Nuremberg war crimes trials. A medieval atmosphere seemed to permeate the offices which contained these sadistic devices.

The Liberation of Paris

As the Allied forces approached Paris, it was obvious that Paris, the French capital, was a sensitive and rich area for intelligence. Lt. General Omar N. Bradley's 12th U.S. Army Group prudently organized in advance a "Paris Task Force" to focus on certain very critical targets utilizing seasoned key Allied intelligence personnel. In the mid-weeks of August, 1944, special teams were assembled near the small town of Rambouillet, about 35 miles from Paris. We operated with the help of the personnel of U.S. CIC teams (Counter-Intelligence Corps) and other Allied French-speaking groups to deal with a multiplicity of targets.

The "Paris T-Force" (abbreviation for "Task Force") team leaders were carefully selected and assigned to cover certain key parts of Paris. I was named as Target Team Commander responsible for the 5th (Pantheon) and 6th (Luxembourg) arrondissements on the Left Bank of the Seine River. These were districts of Paris which contained many important targets. My assigned priorities included (1) the facilities of the Sorbonne University which were engaged in nuclear research and had been originated by the late famed Mme Curie; (2) the Hotel des Monnaies to assure that the Germans did not carry off the French monetary engravings in order to disrupt the French economy with counterfeit money (as they had done successfully earlier in the U.K. with high-quality forged British bank notes, with superb paper); and (3) the "controlling" of stay-behind agents located in these districts. The Hotel Lutetia, which was the Gestapo Headquarters for France, yielded a great deal of useful documentation.

We entered Paris on the morning of August 25th. We had been positioned and instructed to arrive in Paris before the front-line troops. It was before the last vestiges of the 11,000 German military (many of whom were headquarter personnel, not combat troops) and German civilian workers had left the city. Hence, we found ourselves racing down streets and passing German vehicles going and coming in various directions. We often drove alongside of them. It was almost comical. We didn't bother them, and they didn't bother us. We had important work to do, while they were running for their lives. Their trucks and other vehicles were piled high with luggage, wine, and looted acquisitions as they headed east dodging gunfire from the French Resistance. Those German troops who were taken prisoner were taken to a temporary detainment area in the Bois de Boulogne.

The excitement of being among the first troops to liberate Paris was unforgettable. The deliriously happy French people crowded the streets touching our jeeps, kissing us, offering bottles of wine. However, many scurried about settling scores with German collaborators and Fascist *Milicien* in small private wars. The *Milicien* were hunted throughout Paris and summarily shot (or women who had consorted with the Germans had their heads shaved)!

The main headquarters of the Paris Task Force was placed in the famous Petite Palais, near the Champs d'Elysees. I situated my unit's headquarters in the Mairie (mayor's office) of the 5th arrondissement at 21 Place du Pantheon, just across the street from the historic Pantheon where the tombs of Victor Hugo, Voltaire, Rousseau, and Zola are located. The mayor himself had vanished, and it was locally said that he may have been a German sympathizer.

On the afternoon on Saturday, August 26th, French General Charles De Gaulle made his triumphant procession through Paris. De Gaulle had an uneasy relationship with many of the Allied commanders. At the time of the Normandy landings there were initially differences over the question of installing an Allied military government in liberated France, not a French one as De Gaulle wished. My jeep was in his entourage as it proceeded down the Champs Elysées to the Hôtel de Ville and to the great Cathedral of Notre Dame (dating from 1163). As we arrived outside the Cathedral shots were apparently fired down from a sniper on one of the Cathedral's towers. In the confusion two French tanks stationed in the square opposite the Cathedral opened fire on the towers with .50 caliber machine guns. The rounds dislodged one of the famous stone gargoyles of the Cathedral, which came tumbling down almost grazing my nose and landing at my feet. When I regained my composure, I picked up the remnants of the gargoyle and placed them in my jeep and then followed De Gaulle into the Cathedral. When I came out, the gargoyle had been taken from my vehicle. I still think from time to time of what a wonderful conversational piece that gargoyle would have made in my garden.

General Bradley kindly cited me for "conspicuously meritorious and outstanding performance . . . displaying a high degree of initiative and tact in directing the operations of his Target Team . . . in its successes" (see certificate, p. 50).

Nancy and Metz

On September 7, 1944, after our work with the Paris Task Force was completed, we hurried off toward eastern France and Germany to continue our core activities, which were then focused around the provincial capitol areas of Nancy and Metz (but also included work in Toul, Verdun, St. Avold, Thionville, Esch, Saverne, Diekirch, and Arlon).

In combat, the lines of engagement between enemies often are ragged and loose. Whole regions sometimes were free of contact. Often, our OSS teams raced into these voids aiming at stay-behind agents in small French towns and were occasionally shocked by running into pockets of retreating German troops.

One morning my jeep driver and I were speeding along a road in rolling countryside in the vicinity of Nancy. We came up a slight hill, and just over the crest was a distressed German tank with mechanical problem, and its engine was smoking. We had no time to avoid it and we were in its field of fire. It was useless to attempt immediately to turn around. We drove up to the tank and circled around it rapidly. Luckily for us, the startled four-man, black-clad German tank crew was out of the tank lying among some bushes off to the side of the road. We exchanged alarmed glances. We were armed, but were in no mood to get into a shooting match. We and the Germans were equally surprised at meeting under such circumstances, and at that moment they were apparently more interested in survival than combat. I am sure the Germans were as relieved as we were when we raced back over the hill. The Germans may have thought that there was a large contingent of American troops coming right behind us.

We arrived in the Metz, the largest town of northern Lorraine, on the day of its liberation. The mayor and jubilant townspeople invited us to join them for a celebration in the evening at the Hotel de Ville (Town Hall). Towering above this building in the heart of the town is the Cathedral St-Etienne, which was built in the thirteenth century and is one of the tallest cathedrals (137 feet) in France.

The fun-filled party at the Town Hall was full of rejoicing French citizens celebrating their freedom. The refreshments were flowing freely. One particularly exuberant young lady lurched toward me and thrust an open magnum of champagne into my mouth. Her well-intended move was so fast and uncontrolled that she broke off a large part of my upper front tooth and caused my lips to bleed painfully.

The bleeding was easy to stop, but there were no readily available dental facilities to make a tooth cap so for quite a long time, I kept up my duties with a big gap in my front tooth. It was ultimately capped months later by a dentist in Rumania.

In October, 1944, in the beautiful and elegant town of Nancy, I was assigned quarters in an apartment at 18 Rue Isabey, which had been occupied by the recently departed Gestapo. It involved as well a young, pretty French girl who had fallen in love with a Gestapo officer. Her father was the owner of a nearby popular bistro, which was a favorite for the local French as well as the occupying German officers and men. This young lady worked as a bar-girl for her father, and romance in this case had transcended traditional Franco-German hatred.

Asked why she had not accompanied her lover back to Germany, she said she was afraid to leave her parents, and she also believed with them that Germany had lost the war. She attached herself to me. I was now security for her. As a 24-year-old bachelor, I didn't resist sufficiently, I must confess. Later, she came to me in a panic. The French authorities wanted to make an example of her and other French women who had consorted with the Germans. She wasn't a danger politically, just an attractive and vulnerable French girl.

"The mayor has threatened me," she told me as a torrent of tears gushed forth. He wanted to have her head shaved and for her to be paraded through the town with other women who had fraternized with the Germans. She pleaded for me to go to see him. I shouldn't have done it, but I did. I told the mayor that she was now helping the Allies. It was somewhat of a distortion, of course. He responded, "First, she is with the Germans and now with the Americans." He was disgusted, and I didn't blame him.

Battle of the Bulge

On December 16, 1944, German Panzer units made a bold and surprising counter-offensive into the Ardennes. It was aimed toward the huge Allied supply dumps around Liege and then to press onward to capture the important port of Antwerp.

Eisenhower ordered General Patton to change the direction of his offensive in the Saar and to assemble a major counter-blow toward Bastogne by December 23, 1944. The Germans had organized a special unit of English-speaking German soldiers, fitted them in Allied and U.S. Army uniforms and with captured U.S. jeeps, trucks, and tanks. They were under the command of the daring SS Commando leader Otto Skorzeny (on September 16, 1943, Skorzeny had led an airborne task force which had rescued Mussolini from confinement in the Gran Sasso mountain resort).

They penetrated through the Allied military front and tried to issue false orders, to dash ahead to capture bridges on the Meuse River and road junctions, and to spread defeatism in the Ardennes region. The fear spread that one of their intentions was to assassinate General Eisenhower. The SHAEF Headquarters became highly conscious of the danger, and throughout the area the security was tightened. Military Police stopped passing jeeps and often ignored rank and credentials by asking the occupants unusual questions on American customs or slang to test their true U.S. credibility.

Third Army's G-2 utilized our OSS/X-2 teams' talents and resources, along with Counter-Intelligence Corps (CIC) teams, to join the effort against the German Skorzeny commando threat. It was fairly quickly eliminated by tight Allied security screening measures. Patton's Third Army began its thrust, which by December 26 carried them into Bastogne and lifted the seige. The German counter-offensive in the Ardennes was overcome after about ten horrible days, thanks in part to the ability to resume Allied air attacks.

My unit later went with Third U.S. Army forces through the Sigfried German defense line to Trier and Cologne, across the German border (see photo #10). I realized that the SCI units and my French-speaking skills weren't going to be as useful and exciting in Germany where the struggle was winding down, so I began to inquire with my superiors about an alternate assignment. I got a break, as I so often have in my life. I was selected by OSS to proceed to Bucharest, Rumania, where there was a serious problem with a key OSS officer who was involved with a beautiful Rumanian woman with a shady and treacherous past.

For my work in the Third U.S. Army area of operations, I was awarded the Legion of Merit. The citation application (originally classified Secret) for this U.S. decoration says in part: ". . . Lt. Col. Hostler was in charge of the entire Special Counter-Intelligence program throughout the area covered by, and in the path of, the Third U.S. Army. The implementation of this program, directed toward the penetration of the German Intelligence Service, involved complex and dangerous counter-intelligence operations which were of the greatest significance to military operations. . . . The effectiveness with which he carried out these tasks is indicated by the fact that during the campaigns of Normandy, Northern France, the Rhineland and the Ardennes, Lt. Col. Hostler was directly or indirectly responsible for assisting in the apprehension and exploitation of approximately 43 enemy agents. . . . The Special Counter-Intelligence program promulgated by Lt. Col. Hostler contributed immeasurably to the rendering ineffective of the German Intelligence Service, and thus to the success of the military operations of the Third U.S. Army, and to the ultimate Allied victory."

After the war, the German military archives were thoroughly examined by Allied intelligence analysts to verify how well these secret operations had succeeded. They found that the Germans were never aware of the extent to which they had been penetrated and misled by our efforts. The Double-

Cross system permitted us successfully to deceive and control the German espionage network in France during a crucial period of the war. Western authorities concluded that these secret operations contributed substantially to the Allied military success and probably saved many thousands of Allied lives. General Dwight Eisenhower himself said after the landings in Normandy that the OSS's covert contributions had been worth the equivalent of a military division in Europe. This made it all worthwhile.

HEADQUARTERS TWELFTH ARMY GROUP, APO 655

EUROPEAN THEATER OF OPERATIONS UNITED STATES ARMY

This

CERTIFICATE OF MERIT

is awarded to

Captain CHARLES HOSTLER, 0442428, United States Army

IN RECOGNITION OF CONSPICUOUSLY MERITORIOUS AND OUTSTANDING PERFORMANCE OF MILITARY DUTY

Citation

As a Target Team Commander, "T" Force, Twelfth Army Group, from 25 August 1944 to 7 September 1944, he displayed a high degree of initiative and tact in directing the operations of his Target Team. The information gathered was of great importance to the success of the "T" Force mission.

O. N. Bradley
O. N. BRADLEY
Lieutenant General, U.S.A.,
Commanding

Chapter Three
Adventures in WWII Rumania
(1945 - 1946)

Italian Intermezzo

After successfully accomplishing my part in OSS/X-2's exciting deception and counter-espionage program in Western Europe during WWII, I was selected by OSS London on instructions from the head of OSS, "Wild Bill" Donovan, for assignment to Bucharest, Rumania. It was March, 1945, and the Allies had by then penetrated into Germany as far as Aachen.

In connection with my transfer and en route to Rumania, I was given my first two-week leave or Rest and Recuperation (R & R) since my arrival on the war-time continent. I traveled by jeep via Cologne (in ruins) to Luxembourg and Paris (staying at the requisitioned exclusive Hotel George V) and flew by military aircraft to London for a briefing by OSS on the problems related to my new and complex assignment in Rumania, and then on to Marseilles. The U.S. military had taken over a number of deluxe hotels along France's international playground, the Riviera, for R & R purposes. It was a delight to stay in Cannes on the Boulevard de la Croisette at the famous Carlton Hotel and the Majestic Hotel and then to move on to Nice, on the Promenade des Anglais, the undisputed Queen of the Riviera. An opportunity arose to accompany a U.S. Air Corps pilot colleague from Marseilles on an interesting military flight via Algiers, Cairo, Athens, and ultimately to my destination, Naples, arriving about mid-April, 1945. I reported for interim assignment to the headquarters of the 2677th Regiment OSS (Provisional). It was attached to the Allied Headquarters for the Mediterranean Theater of Operations, located in the magnificent former Italian Royal Palace designed in 1752 for the Bourbon King, Charles III. With its grand cascades, in Caserta, outside of Naples it is often called the Versailles of the Kingdom of Naples. The palace has about 1,200 rooms, and this site had the great advantage of being a relatively short drive from such dream visiting spots as Rome. I had an audience at the Vatican with Pope Pius XII (who was Pope from 1938 to 1958) on April 29, 1945, when he received a group of U.S. military officers. Other memorable sites were Positano, Amalfi, Sorrento, Sicily, Pompei, and of course the Isle of Capri.

It happened that General "Wild Bill" Donovan, with his fine connections, had chatted in New York with serial divorcee and best-dressed icon, Mrs. Mona Williams, former wife of New York utilities magnate, Harrison Williams. Mrs. Williams had rejoiced with Donovan over the exciting accomplishments of OSS's "heroic boys" in the European campaigns. In her enthusiasm she offered General Donovan the use of her magnificent Villa La Fortino in Capri and said that "When the Isle of Capri is liberated from the Axis forces, OSS can utilize my fully staffed Villa La Fortino as an R&R

site for selected, deserving personalities." It turned out that the Villa La Fortino had been carefully preserved by the German military hierarchy, and its wine cellar, furnishings, and staff were beautifully intact. Mrs. Williams had maintained a long-time romance with and ultimately married the famous German Count Von Bismarck, and the villa included a glorious bedroom overhanging the sea, which had been the focus of their rendezvous.

Cecil Beaton had photographed her studied elegance, Cole Porter wove her into song lyrics, Dali painted her (facetiously in rags), and Bette Davis opened the play *Skeffington* by sweeping down a staircase and saying to herself, "You're Venus and Mrs. Harrison Williams combined — you're just too beautiful to live." *Vogue* magazine praised her and her pure white diamond ring, which was over an inch long (see James Birchfield's 1997 book).

I had great times as an OSS guest on several stays on Capri and remember sharing this beautiful site with OSS friends including Kermit "Kim" Roosevelt (see photo #12), Maria Gulovich (the OSS heroine of Slovakia), and later visitors including Mr. and Mrs. Roy Melbourne (Deputy Chief of the U.S. Legation in Rumania).

My work with the 2677th OSS Regiment (Provisional) in Italy involved participating in the Po Valley military campaign in northern Italy (see photo #11) and in carrying out classified X-2 assignments. James Jesus Angleton, the legendary X-2 Chief for Italy (at the age of 27), a good friend from my days at Ryder Street in London with MI-6 and OSS/X-2 London, was strengthening his intricate control over the various Italian security and intelligence networks during this chaotic period. I was pleased to be of assistance to Angleton in Italy while waiting for my move to Rumania. Jim later became the enigmatic Director of Counter-Intelligence at the Central Intelligence Agency.

Rumanian Scene

OSS's director, Major General William J. Donovan, tenaciously tried through the spring and early summer of 1944 to send a team to Rumania to gather intelligence and to aid imprisoned American pilots. The chief obstacles were the scarcely veiled hostility of the British and Soviets to the project, but there were also fears on the part of the U.S. State Department that the OSS would become embroiled in an Anglo-Soviet feud over the Balkans. Events overtook the plan for covert penetration of Rumania. On August 23, 1944, young (23 years old) King Michael ousted the pro-German dictator Marshal Ion Antonescu and dramatically turned his country from being Germany's partner over to the side of the Allies. The new Rumanian government immediately signaled its desire to release all Allied prisoners of war, thereby providing the OSS with an opportunity to enter the country openly. The Fifteenth Air Force's Air Crew Rescue Unit, manned in part by the OSS, sent a team to Popesti airfield near Bucharest on August 29, 1944, to arrange for the repatriation of about 1,125 American POWs. Major Walter M. Ross of the OSS planned and directed this operation. Members of the OSS's Research and Analysis Branch accompanied the Air Crew Rescue Unit and proceeded to the oil fields at Ploesti to gather information on the effects of Allied bombing, which was later used by the United States Strategic Bombing Survey. A second group of intelligence personnel went to Bucharest to establish a city team. While the Soviets had already seized the German legation, Bucharest's chief of police helped the U.S. unit enter offices of the Luftwaffe, the headquarters of the Gestapo, the offices of an export-import firm with ties to German intelligence, and the German passport-control office. The Bucharest OSS team was joined on September 2, 1944, by Lt. Commander Frank G. Wisner, USNR, who arrived by air from Istanbul. Frank Wisner later helped to establish and lead the Office of Policy Coordination (OPC), the clandestine arm of the CIA. Sadly, he later committed suicide, but his distinguished name is carried on by his very able son, Frank G. Wisner, who served brilliantly as Under Secretary of State, U.S. Ambassador to India, Philippines, Egypt, and other key assignments. He is now Vice Chairman of the vast insurance conglomerate AIG, Inc. in New York City.

The Soviets did, however, figure prominently in Wisner's orders from Donovan. Brief instructions sent to Wisner on August 25, 1944, stated that requirements for political intelligence had been "prescribed by the State Department" and that the first priority was to determine "the intentions of the Soviet Union regarding Rumania." Detailed follow-up instructions, dated October 14, concentrated almost entirely on the Soviets, and the first of six paragraphs of intelligence objectives focused on the Soviet military. The second paragraph dealt with the nature and extent of Soviet control over Rumania, while the third fixed on the Allied Control Commission (ACC), nominally the body through which the "Big Three" (Britain, U.SA., and the Soviets) supervised Rumania, but which was actually dominated by the Soviets. The fourth paragraph specified questions about military geography, most of them related to locations in the Soviet Union. The fifth and sixth paragraphs dealt respectively with local political and economic questions, and the Germans were mentioned only marginally.

Soviet-American relations had not yet begun their steep decline. In 1943 President Franklin D. Roosevelt had virtually banned the gathering of intelligence on the Soviets. In August, 1943, when first seeking the approval of the Joint Chiefs of Staff for operations in the Balkans, Donovan had stressed the importance of establishing "relatively stable non-Communist but not anti-Soviet governments in the Balkans."

Conforming both to Soviet demands and to the spirit of his instructions from the JCS, Donovan provided the Soviets with a list of the OSS personnel sent to Bucharest about a month after (September, 1944) the city team had reached the Rumanian capital. In the meantime the OSS unit had won the gratitude of the local Soviet military commanders by getting the American Fifteenth Air Force to perform air strikes that aided the advance of the Second Ukrainian Army into Hungary. The essentially political concerns of the OSS's "American Military Unit" (AMU) were somewhat masked by two ostensibly military objectives: the repatriation of the remaining American POWs and the assessment of bomb damage.

When he reached Bucharest, Wisner accepted the hospitality of a local beer magnate, Mitu Bragadiru (informally known as the "Beer Baron of Bucharest"), and moved with his OSS team into the Bragadiru mansion where they stayed for several months. Bragadiru's wife soon became Wisner's mistress, and she, Princess Alexandra ("Tanda") Caradja Bragadiru, was reportedly later recruited as a Communist agent. The presence of the OSS in Rumania was unusually uncovert, and in an attempt to solve the problem of cover in mid-December the AMU was attached to the American (USMR) delegation to the ACC. This arrangement, which remained in force until the OSS/SSU left Bucharest, did not deflect sharp questions from the Soviets about the continued presence of the OSS in Bucharest.

Until the arrival on November 11, 1944, of Burton Y. Berry, the American Political Representative, Wisner was the senior American official in Bucharest. He remained the senior American military officer until the arrival on November 25, 1944, of the fine Brigadier General Cortlandt Van Rensselear Schuyler, U.S.A. Schuyler was head of the USMR, which consisted of approximately 50 U.S. military personnel, who were essentially observers (as were a comparable British Military Representation in Rumania). Both units worked together closely to keep informed primarily on the activities of the large Soviet Military Representation under General Vinogradov, which then encompassed over 500,000 Soviet troops in Rumania. In principle, the OSS worked harmoniously with Berry and Schuyler, but initially there was friction about the scope of the OSS's activities. The most potentially serious of these was with Berry, who in late December, 1944, proposed that the OSS turn its sources over to him and close shop. Donovan adamantly refused to do this. Schuyler, who supported Wisner and the OSS against Berry, was bothered by the duplication of effort entailed in the OSS's meeting with sources already in contact with Berry's staff or his own. Of the opinion that the OSS should concentrate "on intelligence fields not otherwise available to the War and State Department missions," General Schuyler restricted OSS to unofficial (but not exclusively) clandestine contacts while he attended to the business of the ACC and Berry dealt with the Rumanian political leadership.

Major Robert Bishop and the "Bishop Traffic"

My duty in Italy was prolonged by the determined efforts of Major Robert Bishop (whom I was designated to replace) to extend his stay in Rumania. One of Major Bishop's incentives to remain involved a very attractive 24-year-old Rumanian woman, Elizabeth Mezey-Feher, also known as Jocky Cristea, who was reportedly a mistress of the Luftwaffe Commander in Rumania. After persistently evading OSS's orders to leave Rumania and to return to Italy and the U.S.A. for interrogation, Bishop assisted Jocky Cristea before he finally departed Bucharest in April, 1945. He arranged for Rumanian Lt. Teodore Negropontes and other employees to drive Jocky by car from Bucharest via Timisoara to Belgrade, Yugoslavia. They deposited Jocky literally on the doorstep of the OSS Mission in Belgrade. The leaders of the OSS Mission in Belgrade were horrified and surprised since they had no advance warning. Lt. Negropontes returned quickly to Rumania on the same day, so OSS Belgrade could not send her back with them. Major Frank Lindsay in Belgrade sent a cable to OSS headquarters labeling the matter an "irresponsible operation." The OSS Mission in Belgrade promptly placed Jocky on the next U.S. military plane, which arrived in Naples, Italy, on April 24, 1945, where I was still stationed. Thus, the Jocky Cristea problem was passed on to the U.S. OSS and G-2 authorities in Italy.

She was kept in "internment" as a "security threat" in a Naples OSS hotel-billet, guarded by U.S. military police. Since she had "worked" full-time for Bishop from September 16, 1944, to March 21, 1945, as a "translator and informant" in Bucharest ("without remuneration"), and had shared Bishop's accommodations, the dilemma was passed to OSS for solution. To complicate things further, she claimed to be the fiancée of a U.S. 1st Lt. William H. Spector, whom she had met in Bucharest.

I spent three hectic days in Naples, by direction of my OSS superiors, interrogating this gorgeous creature, and attempting to confirm whether she was a "security risk." To say she "had been around" was a bit of an understatement. Her former husband, Ion Cristea, had been a Rumanian "Legionnaire." Then, when the Americans and British arrived, she changed sides instantly and leaped into several arms including those of Bishop, one of our more senior OSS officers. The OSS hierarchy in the U.S. was aghast that one of its supposedly well-trained officers would succumb to the charms of this vixen, but the poor guy was hooked.

She knew that her future was at stake, and during the three days that I interrogated her in Naples she made full use of her ample and striking feminine charm to try to "win me over." However tempting she was to a 25-year-old bachelor, I was fully briefed concerning her very active past reputation as a "seductress," and I tried to maintain a balanced approach. There was no doubt, however, considering her close connection both with the Germans and Major Bishop and her intimate knowledge of the Rumanian OSS operation, that she constituted a "security risk." She wasted no time trying to seduce me. Another time, another place, and I could have wound up in her arms. This lovely vamp was a charming, scheming, sensuous, and extremely intelligent woman. My willpower stood the test, or was it the fear of being put in a compromising position by her?

While OSS and G-2, AFHQ, pondered my report and the problem of what to do about Jocky, that *very* resourceful young woman took matters into her own extremely capable hands. She approached the officer in charge of her U.S. military police guards and secured his approval to descend to the lobby area of the Naples hotel where there was a USO recreation center. She went on various evenings to the USO, ostensibly to help "entertain the boys." Within several days she found a vulnerable U.S. Army Air Corps Lt. Colonel and speedily married him, thus instantly changing her status from "internee" to "wife of a senior U.S. officer."

Life in Bucharest

My orders to proceed to Bucharest (which had been known as the "Little Paris" of Eastern Europe) came on July 18, 1945, and upon my arrival, I was attached to the U.S. Military Representation of the Allied Control Commission for Rumania (USMR/ACCR). My initial instructions were to "clean up the mess" left by Bishop, and I was then named to replace the departing Lt. Col. Walter Ross as Chief of the OSS Station.

I fully expected Rumania to be different from France but had underestimated the disparity. In Rumania the war was almost over when I arrived, but the political pot was boiling. An amazing collection of personalities contested for power and in some cases for simple survival. It was Balkan politics at its best — or worst — with all the conspiracy and intrigue, nastiness, double-dealing, dishonesty, occasional murder and assassination compounded in an atmosphere of betrayal and deceit. It was class war, a conflict waged by the aristocracy and the nobility, on the one hand, and the left-wing working class and their Communist allies, on the other. There were fascists, monarchists, anarchists, moderates, and intellectuals all thrown into the mix. Inside this political maelstrom, a small band of American and British military and diplomatic personnel struggled to sort things out and represent their nation's interests. Additionally, there was sharp discord among the ranks of the OSS. I was the officer designated to step into this situation, a role in which I was part investigator, part administrator, and part OSS operative.

The Cold War was rapidly developing, although none of us realized at the time the depth and breadth or the nature of that struggle. We were ill-prepared for the fight. In the ranks of OSS, there were moderate conservatives (which included General William Donovan back in Washington), who pushed their philosophy, and others, particularly a few at the OSS station in Bari, Italy, who described some of their colleagues as paranoid individuals who saw the Russians as sinister monsters. My sympathies were with the former rather than the latter, a position which history, I believe, proved to be correct.

Rumania in some ways was a theater of the absurd. The uneasy aristocracy embraced the Americans and the British with a sense of panic. They welcomed into their elegant homes the Western diplomatic and military missions. Many of our personnel moved right in. Some of the beautiful Rumanian women went a step further and welcomed the Americans into their arms. It was a political and social environment for which young American officers were poorly prepared. Judgment often was set aside for affairs of the flesh. A few gorgeous women, stunningly charming and astonishingly amoral, had bid good-bye to the departing Germans on one day while welcoming the Americans the next. Some of the OSS sources had worked for the Germans and now worked for us. Their reliability was at question.

The city of Bucharest was marked by war damage and some errant bombings by the Americans. Too often attacks had missed industrial and military targets and destroyed residential neighborhoods. But most of the classic buildings still graced the city. The trappings of the monarchy dazzled us. The sight of the tall cuirassiers in plumed steel helmets and their polished breast plates at public functions was impressive. The King's Royal Horse Guards cut a dramatic figure. Sometimes it seemed we were in a kind of fairyland. Dining out at exotic restaurants like The Priest Who Weeps established a life style that contributed to the corruption of some American personnel. The Americans, British, and Soviets cruised around the city in luxury vehicles temporarily "requisitioned" from the aristocracy.

The wealthy and the middle class played a role, and there were the Peasant Party leaders, social Democrats, Communists, and fascists. Among the latter were the opportunists who had done the bidding of the Nazis. There was guilt all around and a host of characters ready to carry out the will of some really dangerous people.

Rumania was still the "breadbasket of Europe," and skiing in Transylvania and swimming along the Black Sea coast continued for the wealthy Rumanians. The OSS personnel were at that time disproportionately exposed to the view of the elite with whom they lodged and socialized. Sylvia Press, one of Major Bishop's agent-handlers, recalled in her debriefing that Mitu Bragadiru (the "host" of the OSS Unit) often "tried to convince me that the Germans 'were gentlemen.' I heard this phrase repeated many times at parties and in private homes of the so-called elite." These, Miss Press continued, were "the people who entertained us and — as in the above case — ate and lived with the American officers and enlisted men" and "who quite brazenly referred to 'the next war,' meaning a war between Russia and the Anglo-Americans, which they would give their eye-teeth to help bring about."

By October, 1944, Major Bishop and the X-2 unit had the use of a number of agents and sub-agents in part thanks to Frank Stevens, an American educator and one-time correspondent for the *Christian Science Monitor,* who had resided in Bucharest since the 1920s (see photo #13). During the war Stevens had served as an agent for the OSS and had in this capacity developed ties with the Rumanian Serviciul Special de Informatii (SSI), an intelligence service controlled by the Council of Ministers, with both foreign and domestic responsibilities. Frank Stevens, using the pseudonym Crayfield, was later probably Bishop's co-author of the book *Russia Astride the Balkans.* Stevens arranged that Bishop utilize the services of Lt. Teodor Negropontes of the Rumanian Army, who was soon attached to the AMU as a liaison officer with the Rumanian intelligence services. As source number AD-201 (in the OSS agent code system AD meant Rumania, AE was Germany, and so on; for example, I was AD-1), Negropontes was the link that furnished X-2 with approximately sixty per cent of its information. Negropontes transmitted reports dealing with a variety of subjects and usually identified as the originating sub-sources SSI and Sectia 2 of the Marele Stat Major (Section 2 of the General Staff, the army's intelligence service). Much of this information was said to come from sources for these services in the Italian, Bulgarian,

Swedish, Japanese, and Turkish legations, the Iron Guard underground, and in Bucharest's foreign communities. Bishop apparently also had contacts with the Sigurantza (the political police) through his second most prolific agent, AD-120.

The OSS's X-2 unit produced approximately 800 reports. The majority dealt with individuals who were being vetted for various security purposes, such as visas. The vetting reports were based on information from the Rumanian counter-intelligence organizations. During the fall of 1944, X-2 also sent to Washington many documents of historical interest, most of which came from the personal archive of Mihai Antonescu, General Ion Antonescu's foreign minister. A third category of reports dealt with material from the captured German records, which X-2 screened while preparing them for shipment, as well as reports on the German resistance movement written by Dr. Fritz Theil, a German journalist who fled to Bucharest after the abortive *coup d'état* of July 20, 1944.

In the early stages of the crisis following the naming of Petru Groza as the Communist Prime Minister (see photo #14), AD-201 began to deluge Bishop with alarming reports about the Soviets, which he quickly accepted as accurate. Previously he had rated AD-201's reports as "C-3" and described AD-201 as "a well placed source whose reliability is not yet entirely proven." But after the Communist takeover Bishop rated nearly all the reports on the Soviets as "B-2" and began to describe AD-201 as a source "whose reliability now seems to be fairly well established." Sadly, the "Bishop Traffic" was ultimately shown to consist of largely ambitious but crude fabrications. That AD-201's stream of reports on the Soviets began shortly after the onset of the political crisis touched off by Ana Pauker's return from Moscow was probably not coincidental. It was widely believed in Bucharest that the United States was so much stronger than the Soviet Union that the Americans had only to stand up to the Soviets in order to preserve Rumania's independence and social structure. The problem, as the Rumanians saw it, was that America was blind to the Soviet danger. AD-201's (Lt. Negroponte's) reports were presumably an attempt to educate the ignorant giant. Given his connections with the Rumanian military, the effort most likely was officially inspired by anti-Communist elements in the Rumanian government.

To U.S. and British diplomats in Bucharest, some of Bishop's reports seemed a spectacular revelation of what they had come to fear on the basis of daily experience. However, in the context of the desk officers in Washington, whether in the U.S. State or War Department or in the OSS, it was but one of hundreds of reports pouring in about the Soviets from all over Europe, mostly alarming but also unverifiable. This was an example of an often observed phenomenon — the difference in perspective between desk officers in Washington and officials in Eastern Europe — the former thinking chiefly in terms of the overall relationship with the Soviet Union, the latter generally outraged by Soviet actions against locals with whom they sympathized and socialized.

An exasperated Lt. Col. Walter Ross, skeptical about the value of Bishop's reports, ordered an investigation of the operations of the departed Bishop. In requesting the permission of OSS/X-2 Washington to review Bishop's files, Ross stated that it was already apparent that many of AD-201's reports were "wholly false and others contain many inaccuracies or misstatements." With the approval of X-2, OSS officers Madison and Roberts reviewed Bishop's files and interviewed one of his agents, who admitted that he had also been working for both the Germans and the Soviets. In their final report, Madison and Roberts described Bishop's reports as a "mass of false information, half-truths, false predictions, and sinister insinuations" that had "contributed, in an irresponsible way, to the deterioration of (Soviet-American) relations."

At a number of junctures our relations with the Soviet occupying forces in Rumania (and the Soviet element of the Allied Control Commission) became particularly tense. For example, I received secret written orders from General Schuyler, dated October 23, 1945, to proceed on an intelligence gathering mission by vehicle through the area containing Constanza (on the Black Sea), Tulcea, Braila, and Buzau, accompanied by a trusted civilian employee of the Mission. The purpose of the mission was "to obtain as completely as possible the order of battle of Soviet troops in the area visited. Particular attention will be paid to movements of troops (transient and semi-permanent), unit designations, names of commanders and armament."

The Soviets apparently had been made aware of our mission, and we were followed on a large portion of our travels. In the evenings we were pointedly "invited" to the local Soviet Headquarters and units. On one particularly amusing evening a Soviet General during dinner plied us heavily with vodka. At one point when he engaged us in a series of toasts, I jokingly switched glasses with the General and found to his great embarrassment that he was drinking his toasts with water while mine were straight vodka.

University of Bucharest

During this turbulent era I decided to attempt to find time to register for study at the Faculty of Law at the University of Bucharest. I was admitted in accordance with Decree-Law 275 of 1945. My registration number was 452 bis/1942. I was fortunate to have the help and guidance of the dedicated Dean, C.V. Stoeanovici. It was not easy to squeeze into my hectic operational schedule the time for study, classes, and examinations, particularly since much of it was in the Rumanian language. However, I persevered. For the first year examinations in June, 1946, I received high grades in Roman Law, Civil Law, Constitutional Law, Theoretic Economy, and Introduction to the Study of Private Law.

My OSS activities, as Chief of Station, had increased to the point that for the second year examinations I only had time to complete Administrative Law in November, 1945. Properly authenticated documents were issued testifying to all of this by the University, which were in turn verified by the Rumanian Ministry of Foreign Affairs and then by the U.S. Vice Consul in January, 1947. I was often in the past intrigued by the possibility of returning one day to wonderful Bucharest and completing my legal studies. In retrospect this extracurricular study probably saved me from getting too involved with many temptations of the fascinating Rumanian social scene.

The OSS operated in Bucharest under severe limitations. Its uniformed personnel could hardly have been more conspicuous; few spoke Rumanian or knew Rumania. There were no preexisting sources of established reliability against which new sources could be judged. This was a serious liability, for virtually every Rumanian with whom the OSS came into contact belonged to one or another faction of a highly polarized society steeped in traditions of duplicity. Yet OSS Bucharest did produce a stream of reports on all parts of Rumania's military, political, and economic situation. Its personnel used a high degree of initiative, it had funds to pay informants, and most importantly the Rumanians largely (aside from the Communists) were so anxious about the Soviets and the prospect of Communist rule that they willingly sought to help the American and British missions. Rumania was noted for its beautiful women, many of whom were highly motivated to leave Rumania and its problems by traveling westward, hopefully with the help of an American or British officer.

On November 15, 1945, Captain Norman Armour and I were ordered to travel via military aircraft from Bucharest via Vienna, Austria, to Naples, Italy, for a period not to exceed eight days. We took the special written examination for Foreign Service Officer status in the U.S. State Department. The exam was held at the Royal Institute of Chemistry of the University of Naples. I was quite unprepared for this difficult exam and don't suppose that I did well. However, it was great to have the opportunity to travel to Naples again.

When OSS was being dissolved, I was selected to go to Vienna, Austria, to change my status from being a U.S. military officer to that of a U.S. civilian employee of the successor clandestine organization called the Strategic Services Unit (SSU) of the War Department. This was part of SSU's transition to eventually become the CIA following the end of WWII in Europe. However, I was directed to continue wearing my uniform in Rumania so most persons believed I was still a U.S. officer. I was promoted to the rank of the Lt. Col. in the Army of the U.S. Reserve (effective May 1, 1946).

Help to Jewish Community

The Jews were badly treated in Rumania by the Axis during WWII. Many were killed or transported to Axis concentration camps. As I had been raised in the Hollywood area of California, it became known among the film industry that I was serving in Rumania. Many Jewish families had relatives who had been affected by the wartime pogrom against the Jews and the Gypsies in Rumania. Hollywood filmmakers began communicating with me from the U.S.A. asking for information and help for their families, many of whom lived in the Transylvanian area of Rumania.

Though it was not "in my job description," I did my very best to be responsive to all of them. Among those appealing for assistance was the famous film producer Joseph Pasternack, who particularly sought news of his relative Samuel Pasternack of Simeul Silvania in Transylvania (which was in those days over a 13-hour trip of hard driving each way from Bucharest). It turned out that Samuel had been sent to Auschwitz concentration camp on June 7, 1944, with six family members, and none had returned. We did learn of four other Pasternack family members living in other parts of Transylvania, who had returned but needed help. I also got the International Committee of the Red Cross's Delegate in Rumania, Mr. J. A. Graf, to assist these unfortunate people. I provided similar assistance to Leslie Kardos of MGM pictures, Mr. Guttman, David Rub, the C.Z. Sakalls,

Rudy Monta, the actor Edward G. Robinson, Frank Kaftel, Nicky Nayfack, and others.

The Communist Takeover

The critical point of many Rumanians' complaints in that era was that Rumania had been abandoned to the Soviets, first by the deference of Anglo-American representatives to the Soviets during the Armistice negotiations of September, 1944, in Moscow and then by the failure of the United States to protest what the Rumanians described as a harsh and exploitative Armistice regime. These Rumanian grievances were of course not placed in full perspective, including the reality that Rumania had freely participated in the German attack on Russia and that their troops had been involved in atrocities in the foreign areas they had occupied.

When one of the principal leaders of the Rumanian Communist Party, Ana Pauker, returned from a trip to Moscow in mid-January, 1945, Bucharest was swept by rumors of an impending Communist bid for power. The Communist-led National Democratic Front (NDF) opened a drive for power on January 28, 1945, but failed at first without overt Soviet support. At this point the Soviets began to intervene and assist. The Soviet press began to attack Prime Minister Radescu, while in Bucharest the Red Army provided logistical support for a major Communist demonstration on February 24, 1945. At the rally shooting broke out, and

Radescu went on the radio to denounce Pauker and Luca as "hyenas" and "foreigners without God or country" (Pauker was Jewish, and Luca Hungarian). Andrei Vyshinsky, the Soviet Deputy Foreign Minister, arrived in Bucharest on February 27 and, in a famous meeting, gave King Michael two hours to announce Radescu's dismissal. Vyshinsky returned to the palace on March 2, 1945, to demand that Communist sympathizer Petru Groza be named prime minister. King Michael acceded, and Groza formed a government dominated by Communists, which soon began to repress the traditional political parties.

The Communist-controlled Groza government set about physically eliminating political opposition, including members of Dr. Juliu Maniu's National Peasant Party and the Liberal Party of Dinu Bratianu. A number of the leaders of the traditional parties were abducted or disappeared at night under unusual circumstances. Not strangely, some sought our help or tried to flee Rumania.

The Cold War Scare of 1946 and the Disastrous Hall-Hamilton Affair

The Strategic Services Unit (SSU) of the U.S. War Department in turn was transitioned into a temporary organization in the War Department called the Central Intelligence Group (CIG), which later became part of the independent agency today known as the CIA.

The Allies had become apprehensive over what they saw as Soviet moves against Turkey. In a note to the U.S.S.R. of August 19, 1946, the U.S. repeated its previously expressed willingness to see the Montreux Convention revised, but firmly rejected the U.S.S.R.'s call for a joint Turkish-Soviet sovereignty over the Bosphorus Strait and warned the Soviets that aggression against Turkey would fall within the purview of the U.N. Security Council. This was one of the early beginnings of the Cold War.

In WWII Allied military planning had paid considerable attention to covert operations and resistance behind enemy lines. Thus, in August, 1946, the SSU began collecting information on armed underground movements in the Soviet Bloc. In the event that the Soviets invaded European Turkey, their lines of communication would pass through Rumania so the U.S. Joint Staff asked the Office of Special Operations (OSO) of the newly formed Central Intelligence Group (CIG) to undertake a covert operation in Rumania. The Rumanian government was then firmly in the hands of the Communists, and about 500,000 Russian troops still occupied Rumania, but there was a substantial and spirited opposition, which included Maniu's National Peasant Party (NPP). The U.S. Joint Staff asked the OSO/CIG very secretly to organize an underground force in Rumania that could, if needed, be used to interdict Soviet supply lines, as in the pattern of the French resistance during WWII's Operation Overlord.

Unknown to General Schuyler, or Minister Burton Berry, or myself, this newly-formed OSO/ CIG in Washington, D.C. secretly briefed and ordered two U.S. CIG officers to begin clandestine meetings with the NPP. In September, 1946, these two Americans, Lt. Ira C. Hamilton and Major Thomas R. Hall, surreptitiously called upon the NPP leaders to organize a partisan army. It was to be clandestinely supplied and subsidized by the U.S.

Hall and Hamilton met several times with two leading members of the National Peasant Party (NPP), Grigore Niculescu-Buzesti, a former foreign minister who was the chief advisor of the party's leader (Juliu Maniu), and Victor Radelescu-Pogoneanu, a former diplomat who was the NPP's leading intellectual, along with Ion de Mocsony-Styrcea, formerly Marshal of King Michael's Court. On September 30, 1946, Hall, Hamilton, and the above Rumanians plotted a clandestine army for use in the event of war, to be directed by two committees, one in Rumania, the other abroad. Niculescu-Buzesti was smuggled out of Rumania on October 5, 1946, aboard the U.S. Mission DC3 aircraft, carrying with him a letter from Maniu designating him as the NPP representative abroad. Also Ioana Bujoiu (later Lady Joan Gordon), who had bravely been an intermediary and typed the various agreements, secretly left on the same aircraft.

My own Rumanian secret sources warned me that these supposedly clandestine meetings by Hall and Hamilton with the NPP had been penetrated and were well known to the Communists. As the SSU/CIG's station chief, it was my responsibility promptly and discretely to report this rapidly impending disaster to General Schuyler, who immediately confronted Hall and Hamilton. Schuyler could not believe their explanation that their activities had been directly and secretly ordered by the OSO/CIG in Washington and gave them 24 hours to leave Rumania. Schuyler then cabled Lt. General Lauris Norstad, the War Department's Deputy Chief of Staff for Plans and Operations, to explain these developments. General Norstad met with representatives of the OSO/CIG in Washington, D.C. on November 8, 1946. OSO/CIG then conveyed General Vandenberg's apologies to General Schuyler and confirmed that Hall and Hamilton had been operating "under instructions." Aghast and apologetic on the part of the War Department, General Vandenberg also ordered the immediate curtailment of all U.S. intelligence operations in Rumania.

The leaders of the NPP had been thoroughly and fatally compromised and were left unprotected. Many Rumanian conspirators were later brought to a highly publicized trial by the Communist government of Rumania, which took place in October, 1947. The principal charges against the NPP leaders were "participation in a conspirative organization" with Hall and Hamilton. A number of the Rumanian defendants admitted the charges, and many of them used the occasion of the trial to justify their actions as a response to tyranny. The defendants were found guilty and were subjected to very heavy prison terms. Many of them died in prison including brave Lady Joan Gordon's father (former Minister of Economy, Ion Bujoiu, who was sentenced to hard labor for life, and died in the prison hospital at Vacaresti on May 20, 1956). Among those arrested was the fine medical doctor Cornel Petrassevich, who was imprisoned because he had cooperated as a good Rumanian patriot in helping me and the OSS to keep informed on Communist activities. He was forced to work largely in a lead mine for 15 years and kept alive many of his fellow prisoners through his adept medical skills. On his release I was able to utilize my resources to help him to come to U.S.A., which took some doing. He was given employment as a medical doctor with the American Bureau of Indian Affairs. Of great importance to him was the public recognition he was given for his valuable services to the OSS by the Veterans of the OSS, through the help of its fine President, Geoffrey Jones.

The Communist Build-Up and "Hostler's List"

Toward the end of WWII America appeared invincible, and many Rumanians visualized the United States as a potential emancipator. As the Communists strengthened their hold over Rumania, the U.S. Military Mission found itself being sought out as a safe haven by pro-Western political leaders. Among those who took refuge with the U.S. Mission were high officials and persecuted Ru-

manian employees of our mission and their terri-
fied families.

We tried discretely to protect key Rumanian
leaders and our loyal employees and sources. I remember vividly receiving a phone call about 6:30
one morning from one of our Rumanian staff members, Theodore Manicatide, pleading that a Rumanian Sigurantza (secret police) team was at his
home. He and his family had been ordered to dress
and pack. Incompletely dressed in my uniform, I
leaped into my jeep and drove frantically to his
residence. Jumping out, I rushed up to the senior
Sigurantza leader waving my Allied Control Commission credentials. Being a part of the "old school"
(pre-Communist) remnant of the Secret Police, he
was taken aback by an American officer's forceful
demand for a release of this family. He hesitated
and went to the telephone to confirm his instructions. While this was happening, I quickly rounded
up the family with their meager baggage and drove
them away in a screech of tires to the U.S. Military
Mission and to safety. This family were early members of what ultimately came to be about 50 mostly
Rumanian refugees who moved in and out of our
Mission building.

This "rescue," of course, came to the attention of the newly appointed Rumanian Minister of
Interior, Emile Bodnarash, a real Communist thug
who had earlier been a Second Lt. in the Rumanian Army and was a long-time Communist and
former resident of the U.S.S.R. He took immediate
action to discipline and punish the wavering

Sigurantza team leader. Bodnarash then protested to General Schuyler about "this interference with Rumanian authority" and demanded that I be sent to the Ministry of Interior so that he, Bodnarash, could personally question me.

General Schuyler warmly congratulated me on saving these persons from being jailed by the Sigurantza. However, he hesitated to openly defy the new Minister of Interior's insistent request so, in an attempt to seek to develop a rapport with the new Groza Communist government, Schuyler told me to respond affirmatively and to go to the Ministry of Interior. None of us believed that the Rumanian Communist government would dare to lay hands on a uniformed American officer acting in what I believed was the legitimate performance of duty.

Thus, I was driven to the Ministry of Interior in a U.S. Mission car accompanied by two pistol-armed U.S. enlisted men for protection. We were ushered up a sweeping and ornate "fin de siècle" spiral staircase into Bodnarash's office. He was livid with fury and shouted at me in a rapid mixture of Rumanian, Russian, and French. I responded in French saying politely and calmly that employees of the Allied Control Commission were not subject to arrest by the Rumanian government without proper justification. At this point Bodnarash seemed almost hysterical with hatred at apparently being defied by this young American officer. He ordered his guards to take me under arrest. The click of weapons being drawn and cocked was heard throughout the room, as we expeditiously backed out and down the staircase. We promptly dived into our car and accelerated toward the massive iron gates of the Ministry courtyard. Guards were rushing to close the gate, but we made a narrow escape and drove furiously back to the U.S. Mission.

With this, as well as the Communist penetration of the Hall-Hamilton effort, our lives became much more complicated and threatened, not only by the Rumanian Communist government, but also from the Soviets. Many of the U.S. and British Mission members, including me, had shots fired at night through our vehicles by Soviet sentries or others, accidentally or otherwise.

Over time, as the number of Rumanian occupants of our U.S. Mission grew, it became a serious problem to feed and accommodate these fugitives and still carry on our duties. As a solution I recommended to General Schuyler that we resort to a potentially dangerous strategy. The U.S. Mission had a small DC-3/C-47 aircraft that was primarily used to make a once a week mail flight to the nearest U.S. military outpost, which then happened to be at Vienna, Austria. We sent official and personal mail and packages out in standard canvas U.S. mail sacks. This escape plan, which was ultimately adopted, involved our having the U.S. Mission doctor give the refugees a strong sedative inoculation. We then placed these sedated persons in individual mail sacks and carried them out past the Soviet sentries "guarding" the U.S. Mission.

The sacks were taken by truck to the Baneasa Airfield, past other Soviet guards, and were tossed unceremoniously onto the floor of the DC-3. We usually sent out about four to five persons per week, along with the other mail and packages, where they were discretely unloaded and cared for by U.S. intelligence personnel in Vienna. This was accomplished successfully on about ten flights; thus, about 50 persons (including Theodore Manicatide and family) were saved from Communist jails and mistreatment. Some of these evacuees, like former Foreign Minister, Constantine Visoianu, later formed a Rumanian "Government in Exile" and worked tirelessly with the West to seek to liberate Rumania from Communist rule.

After the release of the renowned movie "Schindler's List," which involved the saving of many from Fascist punishment during WWII, my dear friend, Ms. Chin-Yeh Rose, has always referred to the above "Evacuations" as "Hostler's List." It is true that these persons were saved from Communist retribution, and the Soviet and Rumanian Communist governments did not learn (in that era) of our success in saving these people. However, one of the successor agencies to the OSS, temporarily known as the the Central Intelligence Group (CIG) of the War Department, which ultimately became the CIA, did not look favorably on the matter. They internally referred to it and their disastrous Hall-Hamilton affair as a "war-time, cowboy operation," which they did not want to happen again as they tried to assume their new peace-time "striped-pants" image. At the end of November, 1946, as part of their attempts to clean up the Hall-Hamilton tragedy, all SSU/CIG intelligence operations were ceased in Rumania. As part of the close-down, I was ordered (then as an American civilian employee of the War Department) to report to the Assistant Secretary of War responsible for the new CIG in Washington, D.C. As the Station Chief in Rumania, I was pressured to take some responsibility for all of the CIG's unfortunate actions in Rumania. General C.V.R. Schuyler, the head of the U.S. Mission to the Allied Control Commission, completely supported me in what I had done (see letter dated Jan. 25, 1947, p. 84). As you see, General Schuyler wrote (somewhat belatedly), ". . . It was a great surprise to hear that the people in Washington have attached any blame whatever to you for the unhappy situation which occurred here. On receiving your letter, I considered the advisability of writing personally to General Vandenberg about it. I decided against it, however, first because already it was too late and, second, because I am sure that in my messages I made it quite clear that you were not at all to blame. . . ." Nevertheless, the new leadership of the CIG were embarrassed and wanted to cover up the Hall-Hamilton misadventure. I chose to resign (at the age of 27) and to return to California, after five tense years of war-related clandestine service. The fine General C.V.R. Schuyler finished his distinguished U.S. Army career as a four-star General and died in retirement in Savannah, Georgia.

25 January 1947.   CVRS-pcd

Dear Charlie:

    I was most interested in receiving your note written on the train enroute to Los Angeles. It was a great surprise to hear that the people in Washington have attached any blame whatever to you for the unhappy situation which occurred here. On receiving your letter, I considered the advisability of writing personally to General Vandenberg about it. I decided against it, however, first because already it was too late and, second, because I am sure that in my messages I made it quite clear that you were not at all to blame. As you say, somehow the thing doesn't seem to make good sense.

    As soon as we finish up here I expect to be back in Washington, on a visit if not for station, and at that time I shall certainly look into the whole thing personally. I hope to find out what statements or insinuations were made by the two young men you referred to in connection with the activities of this Representation. I am indeed sorry to hear that they thought it necessary to pass the blame on to other shoulders.

    As I told you before you left, I greatly appreciate your loyalty to me during your assignment here in Rumania. I am sorry we could not have both gone on to see this thing through. I think that working together we would have been able to dope out a good solution which would have been best for everybody's interest. As it is, you can at least feel that the situation in Rumania was a guinea pig and we can hope that some useful lessons for the future have been learned therefrom.

    Nothing of much importance has happened here since your departure. The famine in Moldavia is becoming much more severe and, as yet, the Government appears to have taken no effective steps toward securing relief. Unfortunately, I am afraid, many people in that area will die before Spring, and we can expect other parts of the country to be affected also. Politically, there is no activity, all parties apparently maintaining the status quo until after the Peace Treaty. We are keeping busy on our usual type of work, but are getting ready to pull out at short notice.

    I certainly wish you all sorts of good luck in your new assignment. I shall keep my eye open for your name among the Big Shots of the motion picture industry, where I look for you to make a name for yourself before you are through. Your many friends here join me in warmest regards.

                         Sincerely,

                         C. V. R. SCHUYLER,
                         Brigadier General, U. S. Army.

Mr. Charles W. Hostler,
8027 Willow Glen Road,
Hollywood 46, Calif.

Personal Footnote

When I arrived back in the U.S.A. in December, 1946, from WWII duty in Europe, I called on my wonderful uncle, Paul L. Sipp, a senior partner in the fine municipal bond firm of First of Michigan Corp. in New York City. He was a great gentleman and firmly advised me to begin investing in the securities market.

As a young officer, returning from overseas, I literally had the majority of my assets in my pocket in the form of government paychecks and cash, perhaps totaling about $10,000. Uncle Paul introduced me to a young, savvy, recently discharged WWII Air Force officer named Harry Jacobs, who later became the CEO of Bache & Co. We became good friends, and with his guidance and that of Uncle Paul Sipp, I began what became of life-long program of successful investment in securities (later also real-estate). I remember the consternation of their Wall Street colleagues when I paid for part of my stock purchases with cash, since Wall Street rarely dealt with real money. By 1954 this small investment had grown over ninefold.

Uncle Paul and Aunt Loreene Sipp had three fine sons, Paul, Jr. ("Bud"), Peter, and John, who were my only cousins and were life-long friends. Only my close cousin Paul ("Bud") and his lovely wife Mitzi are still alive and living happily on Amelia Island, Florida.

Chapter Four
The "Cold War" Begins in Turkey (1947 - 1950)

U.S. Reacts to Soviet Territorial Demands upon Turkey

With the end of WWII and the demobilization and the re-organization of the U.S. Armed Forces, I was offered a commission in the regular Army Air Corps in October, 1947, by then Army Chief of Staff, General Dwight Eisenhower. This organization soon became the new U.S. Air Force, which had emerged from WWII with a great victory, well-equipped, and on the threshold of the jet age.

In the years following WWII, the Soviets did not rapidly reduce their military forces and made territorial demands on Greece and Turkey. On August 7, 1946, the Soviets handed Turkey an ultimatum insisting on a "new regime" in the Turkish Straits that would have allowed the Soviets to garrison troops in the Black Sea Straits area. The U.S.S.R also wanted to regain the Kars-Ardahan districts, which are within Turkey's northeastern border. Turkey flatly refused these claims and had the support of Britain. The U.S. President Harry S. Truman in a historic speech to Congress on March 12, 1947, declared that unless the U.S. aided Turkey and Greece these countries would fall to Soviet aggression. This U.S. effort to help weaker countries who were resisting the Soviets became known as the Truman Doctrine and was a very early U.S. response to the Cold War. Congress voted to offer 400 million dollars in military and economic aid, and established U.S. military advisory missions to help Turkey and Greece retain their autonomy.

The American Mission for Aid to Turkey (AMAT) consisted of U.S. Army, Navy, and Air Force advisory groups whose task would be to advise, procure military equipment, and train Turkish servicemen. The overall Chief of Mission was Major General Horace Logan McBride, U.S.A. The mission's objective was to modernize the Turkish armed forces to enable them to resist any Soviet advances without unduly elevating the Turkish defense budget.

I was selected on February 26, 1948, from my position on the intelligence staff of Headquarters USAF to be a member of the initial U.S. Air Force Group (TUSAFG) to Turkey. We quickly departed from Washington, D.C. on March 3, 1948, on a USAF special mission aircraft (a C54E), which stopped in Bermuda, the Azores, Wiesbaden, Frankfurt, Berlin, Munich, Paris, Rome, and Athens during a fascinating ten-day liaison journey en route to Turkey. We ultimately landed at Etimesgut Airport in Ankara, Turkey, on March 13, 1948, after flying 8,027 total miles. Among those on board was our dedicated chief, Major General Earl S. Hoag, USAF, M/Sgt. William J. Mandros (who later retired as a Lt. Col.), and Major Paul E. Gardiner.

After arriving in Turkey and making a quick orientation visit to Turkish Air Force (TAF) facilities in Bandirma, Kutahya, Afyon, Eskisehir, Izmir, and Istanbul, we soon realized that the mission of updating the TAF was not going to be an easy task. The TAF had dedication and enthusiasm but was organizationally underdeveloped and lacked the industrial infrastructure necessary for repairs or to produce replacement parts for their equipment. Their minimal prior exposure to modern technology meant that in 1948 relatively few Turks had sophisticated technical experience, so that intricate training in subjects such as radar technology and photo interpretation proved challenging. The Turkish airfields were underdeveloped, and few were able to operate on a year-round basis. An early warning system and centralized control were lacking. The TAF's two air divisions then flew a complicated mixture of *18* different models of aircraft variously built in Germany, U.S., and Great Britain. TUSAFG helped the TAF transition to F84 jets. By the end of 1953 it had an all-jet fighter-bomber air force organized into several air regiments (the equivalent of the USAF group) as well as some C47 transport squadrons.

The Turkish Army then dominated the Turkish General Staff, which gave the Army's needs full first priority. Only limited translating assistance was available when we first arrived, but fortunately the Turkish military had drafted bright young graduates from the legendary, then U.S. operated Robert's College on the Bosphorus in Istanbul, as liaison officers. Among these were the very capable Altemur Kiliç (later an eminent journalist) and Dimitri "Taki" Andriadis (now a retired senior executive with the DuPont Corporation), both of whom are still my close friends. I first met Taki Andriadis in Istanbul in 1946 when I travelled on the Rumanian ship "Transylvania" from Constantza, Rumania, and cruised across the Black Sea. The famous Rumanian composer, George Enescu, was on board.

Thus, TUSAFG did not transform the TAF quickly into a modern air power. However, we began the process of modernization and standardization that made Turkey ready for introduction into NATO in 1952.

My assignment was as Chief of the Combat Information Branch of TUSAFG, which was a polite title adopted to avoid the use of the sensitive word "intelligence." In 1948 the TAF had no fully trained air intelligence personnel or photo interpreters and no courses or schools for this purpose. Therefore, I developed a plan that was adopted by the Turkish General Staff in August and September of 1948 to remedy this situation. I established the first Turkish Air Intelligence Instructors School, which began on March 1, 1949 (with a total of 24.5 weeks of full specialized training) held at Etimesgut Airport near Ankara. I was helped by the knowledgeable Captain Louis Karably, USAF. We ultimately organized a substantial Turkish air intelligence organization with a qualified staff. On June 15, 1949, I arranged for, and escorted, 20 of the new Turkish air intelligence instructor officers to visit the Headquarters of the U.S. Air Force in Europe (USAFE) at Wiesbaden, then to Furstenfeldbruck (for photo laboratories, 7498th Recon. Sq., and photo interpretation), Neubiberg, Oberamergau, and Heidelberg for orientation and to further their training. These 20 Turkish officers observed the gamut of U.S. military air intelligence techniques for seven days. All of this was very successfully accomplished, and I was commended by both the TAF and USAF for establishing this innovative program for our Turkish allies.

The Turkish-American Relationship

After the beginning of the Truman Doctrine, Turkey began to look like an American outpost. To this republic of unyielding people created 26 years before by iron-willed, Western-minded Kemal Ataturk (the "Father of the Turks"), the U.S. began sending a steady flow of moral, military, and economic help.

Istanbul's paved boulevards and narrow cobbled streets competed with aging taxis, horse-drawn carts, and blind beggars. Smoke-blackened industrial towers, dubbed "Ataturk's minarets," struggled for space between graceful, historic Ottoman spires. The muezzin still called the faithful Moslems to prayer, but in place of his natural voice, an amplified speaker relayed his call, and his flowing robes were replaced with Western business suits. Tottering wooden tenements still clogged the waterfront areas. The nearby Park Hotel was then still sleek and active with its international ambiance and a busy bar full of intelligence agents of all nations (replacing the German military intelligence officers we had encountered a few years earlier during WWII), mingling with American engineers and Balkan refugees. A well-known U.S. personality who frequented the Park Hotel was Leo Hochstetter of the Office of War Information (OWI) and later a European Chief (in Rome) of the U.S. Motion Picture Association. The Park Hotel's pianist Eddie was a memorable character. They were still drinking our wartime concoction of Turkish Vodka and readily available orange juice, called a "Screwdriver." Generally, only the Turkish oldsters drank Raki (or grape brandy), which we Westerners called "Lion's Milk."

The Turks in this era reflected a dizzying mixture of progress and backwardness with a strong anxiety over the possibility of war with the U.S.S.R. and hopes for a modern future. The Turks felt they were in a state of siege since Russian propagandists were claiming Turkey's eastern provinces. Radio Sofia talked of the happy lives of Bulgaria's Turkish minority, and Radio Azerbaijan was calling on all Kurds, including Turkey's, to revolt.

Cement pillboxes dotted the rolling plains of Thrace; piles of rock lay by the roadsides for emergency roadblocks. From the border of Bulgaria in the west to Mount Ararat in the east, Turkish riflemen stood guard. There were almost half a mil-

lion Turks in the armed forces. This was a stagger-
ing burden for a struggling country then composed
of 19 million people. Defense expenditures at that
time took 40% of Turkey's budget. Kemal Ataturk
once said to his soldiers, "Victory lies on the points
of your bayonets." The fierce Turkish national
pride, the hard discipline and courage of the Turkish soldier, the large numbers of infantry, and the
rugged terrain were Turkey's chief military assets
in those days. Between 1948 and 1952 the U.S. furnished about $1 billion of military equipment and
supplies to Turkey.

Turkish police in those days maintained day
and night surveillance of the large, drafty Soviet
Embassy in Ankara and the Soviet Consulate General in Istanbul. Russian cars were trailed relent-
lessly. Counter-espionage was an active affair.
From the time any foreigner, from private citizen
to Ambassador, entered the country his movements were known. A vast army of full-time and
part-time informers kept Turkish counter-intelligence posted.

Even our U.S. military personnel in Ankara
were watched closely for several weeks following
our first arrival. After a certain period it seemed
that Turkish intelligence tired of this or became
overwhelmed as the sheer numbers of Americans
increased. Favorite eating places like Papa
Karpich's White Russian restaurant in Ankara were
always watched, though Turks and foreigners alike
enjoyed his food, particularly, his Russian borscht.

The U.S. military were coached in 1948 to protect themselves against three diseases that were most prevalent then, in order of importance: malaria, tuberculosis, and the venereal diseases, especially syphilis and gonorrhea. In one city, Eskisehir, where a prominent air base was located, it was estimated that approximately 40 per cent of the civilian population then had tuberculosis.

Occasionally, the Turkish newspapers would note briefly and enigmatically that the body of a Turk or an Eastern European had been fished up from the dark waters of the Bosphorus. One local definition of such events was "death from over interrogation." The U.S. Consulate General in Istanbul had a local employee named Betty Carp, who was a tiny dynamo, and she knew "more about everybody than anybody else." It was informative to keep in close touch with Betty.

The Turkish Communist party was underground and outlawed and probably numbered fewer than 5,000 sympathizers. Turkey in this period was not quite a democracy, yet Ataturk's successor, President Ismet Inonu, had guided his nation into a freer political climate than it had ever known. Ismet Pasha, as he was popularly called, worked hard to be beloved by the population. At least five million portraits of him, in formal evening attire, adorned Turkish offices and parlors. The Turkish government leaned toward Statism in its economic policies and had grandiose dreams of industrialization and self-sufficiency. Unfortunately, Turkish coal mines then dug only one-tenth as efficiently as American mines, and Turkish farmers still had few steel plows. All Turks wanted improvements and modernization, and Americans did its best to help Turkey in critical activities, such as the military, road building, and oil drilling. For more than 53 years it has worked, and the Turks and Americans have become close allies and successful partners as a result of this fine relationship that started in 1948.

In August of 1948 I took official leave and went on a nine-day trip by auto with friends, Altimur Kiliç (Turkish writer), Tom Graves (a U.S. liaison), and Sally Betar. We had a delightful visit to Afyon, Isparta (rug-making), Antalya, Denizli, Ephesus, Izmir, Bergama, Edremit, Troy, Çanakkale, Gallipoli, Kesan, Tekirdag, and Istanbul.

Reconnaissance Mission along the Soviet Caucasian Frontier and Eastern Turkey, Iran, and Iraq

In July of 1948 the Intelligence Division of the U.S. Army's General Staff, sensitive to the mounting tension with the U.S.S.R., realized that it, and the Turkish Government, were not sufficiently well informed as to the topographic and militarily sensitive details of the possible invasion route the Soviet Union might take into eastern Turkey, Iran, and Iraq. The Soviets wanted to regain the Kars and Ardahan regions that formed the northeastern border of Turkey and the Soviet Union. These were the early days before the current sophisticated satellite technology and reconnaissance techniques. The U.S. Military Attaché in Ankara, Turkey, Col. Robinson, along with his able assistant, then Captain Michael Hansinger (later a Lt. Col.), and myself were selected to make an extended 28-day, 5,500-mile overland survey trip (in two jeeps and a cargo trailer) with the help of one Turkish civilian driver/mechanic. Our historic yet arduous and dangerous itinerary took us through the strategically significant and then quite primitive areas of eastern Turkey, paralleling the Soviet frontier, and along the great trade route connecting Europe with Iran and Central Asia, through Turkish Armenia, Kurdistan, and the Iranian province of Azerbaijan to Tehran, Baghdad, and Mosul.

The eastern area of Turkey is a harsh but beautiful region with roads that even today are still described as basic to primitive. The region has lonesome plains, imposing black mountains, and alpine forests. If you are an adventuresome and hardy traveler and are willing to disregard the U.S. State Department's current strong advice not to travel there, it is a unique region. Fascinating points include the ruins of the unusual Armenian Kingdom of Ani (now close to the border of the Armenian Republic), Mt. Ararat, where according to Genesis, Noah's Ark came to rest, the immense and desolate brackish Lake Van, the large, black basalt fortress at Diyarbakir, and the awe-inspiring temples on top of Mt. Nimrod (the Tumulus of Antiochus).

The population of Turkey's eastern provinces today is primarily Kurdish. There have been serious clashes in recent years between the Turkish armed forces and Kurdish separatists, who are trying to establish an independent Kurdish state out of portions of eastern Turkey, Iraq, Syria, and Iran. This has hindered the free movement of foreign visitors to this truly unusual area.

Our real survey purposes included a reconnaissance of advanced air strips and a terrain study of the airborne troop potentials in case of a Soviet invasion of the area. Our expedition set out on September 2, 1948, with the full knowledge, approval, and cooperation of the Turkish General Staff and the U.S. Military Attaché in Iran, with whom we shared the resulting intelligence and military planning data (see photo #15). The route went through then largely unpaved roads to Kayseri, Sivas, Erizincan, Erzurum, the Black Sea's Pontic town of Trabzon, Hopa, Ardahan, Kars, Dogubayazit, crossing the Iranian frontier on September 14 and into Tabriz, Zanjan, and Ramsari. We stayed three days in Teheran at the palatial old Iranian villa that was used as a mission residence for Brig. General Norman Schwarzkopf (of 1935 Lindbergh kidnapping fame while he was Chief of the New Jersey State Police). In the 1940s, he was Chief of the U.S. Mission to the Imperial Iranian Gendarmerie. Also resident in the villa at the time was the General's son, H. Norman Schwarzkopf (then about 11 years old), with whom we shared the swimming pool and house. Later when I was U.S. Ambassador to

Bahrain (1989-1993), the son, then four-star General Schwarzkopf had become CINC, U.S. Central Command, and was the successful allied commander during the Gulf War/Desert Storm conflict with Iraq. We have discussed together those interesting days we briefly shared in Iran in his youth. The General describes this villa and his days in Iran thoroughly in his book *It Doesn't Take a Hero*.

On the return trip our four-man team left Iran via Kermanshah, crossed into Iraq via Baghdad and Mosul through a corner of Syria, and re-entered Turkey at Nusaybin. We arrived back in Ankara on September 30, 1948, after a rugged and exhausting but very successful journey. Our sturdy jeeps had been repaired regularly; however, the trailer was demolished by the punishing roads and trails.

After arriving back in Ankara, I was hospitalized on November 17, 1948, with a serious case of hepatitis and jaundice. Relying as we had to on local water, apparently I had drunk infected water from a mountain stream, and it had taken several weeks to take effect. I was recovering in the American Mission Dispensary (15 beds and two doctors) in Ankara for about 17 days.

Ecumenical Patriarch

Soviet plans for expansion were not limited to Turkey, Greece, and Iran. In a sentiment that went back to the 17th century when the Czars first sought control of the Black Sea Straits, the Turks had long opposed and resisted the Russians. At the time of the Soviet's 1946 ultimatum, the Orthodox Ecumenical Patriarch of Constantinople died. In the hierarchy of all Orthodox Patriarchs, he was the "first among equals" and was roughly equivalent in rank to the Catholic Pope. The Russians, Serbs, Rumanians, and Greeks are among those who are largely of the Orthodox faith. The Soviet leaders saw this death as an opportunity to expand their influence over the worldwide Orthodox community. They began a campaign to influence the Holy Synod to elect a pro-Communist cleric as the new Ecumenical Patriarch of Constantinople.

President Truman was quickly made aware of this threat, and a pro-Western candidate was sought. The Orthodox Archbishop of North America, Athenogoras, then resident in New York City, was an obvious choice. He was Greek-born, tall, able, wise, with a long, white, saintly beard. However, a major problem was that he was very happy to continue in his North American post. Athenogoras was ultimately convinced of his "duty" to become the Western world's candidate after he received assurance of full support and assistance from the Western powers. One of his wishes was that the U.S. demonstrate its backing of him by providing a visible U.S. military aide on key occasions. As a U.S. military officer who was assigned "in-country," in Turkey, who was understanding of the Orthodox faith, fascinated with the beauty and history of icons, and was eager to help, I was chosen. After Athenogoras was elected by the Holy Synod as Ecumenical Patriarch, I was present at his side in full U.S. military uniform during the enthronement proceedings at the historic Greek Orthodox cathedral in the Phanar district of Istanbul in January, 1949. With the help of his able and trusted advisors, I was a friend and unofficial aide to His Holiness and visited him frequently in Istanbul. In later years, His Holiness kindly presented me with a 17th-century icon of Saint Marina, who had confessed her Christian faith to the Roman ruler of the region of Pisidia in Asia Minor. Saint Marina had been imprisoned, tortured, and martyred.

In future years, through these experiences, I also became close over time to the Orthodox Patriarch Benedictos of Jerusalem, the Orthodox Patriarch of Antioch, and the Orthodox Patriarch of Alexandria. As a U.S. Military Attaché in the U.S. Embassy in Beirut in the 1958-1961 period, the Ambassador, Robert McClintock, enjoyed referring to me as his "Ecclesiastical Attaché" because of my interest in and continuing relations with the many historic religious sects in the Middle East. Over time these traditional religious leaders kindly recognized my helpful assistance by awarding me with the prestigious "Order of the Holy Sepulchre" (Grand Commander) and the "Order of Saints Peter and Paul" (Grand Commander).

Prince Matei Ghica-Contacuzino

During my earlier days with the OSS in Rumania, I became a close friend of Prince Matei Ghica-Contacuzino, then a Rumanian Air Force Lt. Colonel. As the descendant of several princely Phanariot families, he was short in stature and a sophisticated, brave, and patriotic person. He fought as a Rumanian Air Force pilot in the Axis campaigns against Russia, then "borrowed" a Rumanian aircraft to fly an important secret mission to Cairo composed of key Rumanian political negotiators in June, 1944, to seek to reach a peace agreement with the Allies. After the Communists took over Rumania he "appropriated" a second aircraft and escaped permanently by flying out another group on a flight to Turkey. He was living in Istanbul during my period in Turkey, and we reunited frequently. He then worked for the CIA in Istanbul and married Virginia, an American lady. They ultimately moved to Caracas, Venezuela, where I visited him before sadly he died after a long and fascinating life.

Catherine Marshall Hostler

In April of 1949, I was able to arrange for my dear mother, Catherine Marshall Hostler, to join me in Turkey. She was a wonderful and adventurous person who had served honorably in France in WWI as a member of the British Women's Army Auxiliary Corps. In France she met my father, who was a young U.S. Army officer.

My mother enjoyed seeing Turkey and remained there until October of 1949 when she returned to California (via Rome and England, where she re-visited her family). She was a unique personality, and it was from her that I first learned the value and excitement of real estate investment and ownership, which was to provide a successful and solid foundation for my later life. Very sadly, my mother died in 1952 at the early age of 52 and is buried in Palm Springs, California.

"Turkism and the Soviets"

In Turkey at the end of December, 1949, word was received of my selection by the USAF to be sent as a full-time military student for a Master's degree at Georgetown University, Washington, D.C. While I had been in Rumania and Turkey I had developed a deep and life-long interest in the geographic origins and political objectives of ethnic Turks, particularly those in the Balkans, the Caucasus, and Central Asia. In 1945 and 1946 in Rumania and Bulgaria I began collecting notes and information on the Turks who lived along the periphery of the Black Sea. From February, 1948, until late December, 1949, while in Turkey, I continued my field research.

At Georgetown University in the year of 1950, I wrote my Master's thesis on "The Pan-Turanian (or Pan-Turkic) Appeal." Then when I was later sent by the USAF to pursue an M.A. (in Middle Eastern Studies) at the American University of Beirut (1953-55), my research vista was again enlarged by further travel throughout the region. In June, 1955, I returned to Georgetown University's graduate school (at night, thanks to the wonderful "G.I. Bill") to complete my Ph.D. in political science under the direction of the talented Dr. Stefan T. Possony. I then submitted my doctoral dissertation entitled "The Turks of the Soviet and Western Orbits, and Their Unifying Ideals." The warm interest generated by the pioneering subject of this dissertation resulted in its being published as a book entitled *Turkism and the Soviets* by Allen and Unwin in London. It was later translated into German and Turkish language editions. I updated the book later, and it was published in 1992 as *The Turks of Central Asia* by Praeger/ Greenwood Publishers. With the independence of Central Asia and the Caucasus from the U.S.S.R. in the 1990-1991 era, and the renewed exploitation of oil and gas in the Caspian Sea, Khazakhstan, Turkmenistan, and Azerbaijan, the question of Turkism has continued to be an important issue. The problem of developing oil pipelines to bring this precious commodity from Central Asia to the rest of the world was a dilemma because of international wrangling over the routing and destinations of the pipelines.

After being chosen to participate in a Master of Arts graduate program in Psychological Warfare at the legendary Georgetown University, Washington, D.C., I was instructed to report there on January 20, 1950. Thus, I departed Ankara on

Chapter Five
CIA Intrigues in Lebanon
and Syria (1951 - 1955)

After completing my U.S. Air Force-sponsored year at Georgetown University in Washington, D.C. in June, 1951, I received a Master of Arts degree in international relations. This program of training focused on psychological warfare operations, unconventional warfare, and propaganda and was designed by the U.S. Department of Defense to bring a deeper understanding of these subjects to the U.S. military leadership. This concept was very appealing to President John F. Kennedy in the early 1960s, who revived interest in unconventional warfare and in "Special Forces" and gave it his encouragement over the years. Being among those fortunate officers from each of the U.S. military services who had been selected for assignment to the Joint Subsidiary Plans Group of the Joint Chiefs of Staff, we were recognized in a formal ceremony on the portico of the West Wing of the White House. President Kennedy lauded the activities to stimulate the use of unconventional warfare as Americans were deployed to Vietnam and Laos. Kennedy's visit to Fort Bragg, N.C., along with Barry Sadler's chart-topping recording, "The Ballad of the Green Beret," brought public attention to the Army's elite Special Forces.

During the early 1950s in Washington, D.C., I met a charming lady of Belgian origin, Ruby How

Buzard. We were married in a full military wedding complete with upraised sabers at the Chapel at Bolling AFB in Washington, D.C. on December 16, 1951. We lived happily in a Georgetown apartment while I worked in the Pentagon initially as an officer in the Headquarters USAF Intelligence Directorate. Our son, Charles W. Hostler, Jr., was born on November 28, 1952, a healthy strong boy. He graduated from California State University in Long Beach and owns a home in National City, California.

In July of 1953 I was chosen from within Headquarters USAF for a special two-and-a-half year assignment on loan to the Central Intelligence Agency. My classified assignment involved a task in Syria of the greatest sensitivity.

The idea was conceived in the CIA of placing me, as a USAF Lt. Col., in an existing U.S. military graduate-student program at the American University of Beirut (AUB) in nearby Lebanon. This legitimate two-year, full-time U.S. military program had the useful objective of training American officer specialists in Middle Eastern geopolitics and the Arabic language (for which they could receive an M.A. in Middle Eastern studies). AUB, founded by American missionaries in 1866 (originally named the "Syrian Protestant College"), is a fine, private, non-sectarian institution that provides a Western-style education in the Middle East primarily using the English language, and has a distinguished record of educating Middle Eastern leaders. Arab historians have given AUB credit for having a greater influence on the Arab revival than any other institution. The strategic location of AUB in Beirut, which has long been the meeting place of Western and Near Eastern civilizations, has increased its importance over the last almost 140 years.

Beirut, Lebanon, is only about a two-hour drive from Damascus, Syria. The concept was for me to be enrolled as a full-time M.A. graduate student at AUB, where I was accessible, but not resident in Syria where I would be subject to suspicion. When messages or communications arrived from U.S. government sources that were intended to influence or inform Syrian President Shishakli, I would be quietly contacted by CIA officials stationed in the American Embassy in Beirut. The information would be passed to me in a discrete meeting in a Beirut coffee-house or elsewhere. I would judiciously make contact with an intermediary in Damascus to establish a meeting time and place convenient to the President. At the agreed time I would drive across the Lebanese and Syrian borders, usually late at night, to a safe-house in Damascus. Then, escorted by a Shishakli henchman, I would proceed usually to one of the presidential palaces, or elsewhere as arranged. One of the Syrian officials who was involved was the able Colonel Talat Abdul-Kader.

American University of Beirut

My wife, Ruby, and 10-month old son, Charles, Jr., had a most enjoyable move to Lebanon. We sailed from Jersey City on the new U.S. mail steamer belonging to the American Export Lines, the S.S. Exochorda, which departed on September 11, 1953, and arrived in Beirut on September 30.

To our delight, the 19-day voyage on this pleasant combination mail, cargo, and passenger ship stopped at Barcelona, Marseilles, Naples, Alexandria (Egypt), and then Beirut. After that the ship proceeded around the Mediterranean to Iskenderun (Turkey), Latakia (Syria), Piraeus (Greece), Leghorn and Genoa (Italy), before returning to the U.S.A. There were about 120 passengers aboard, a congenial mixture of the President of the American University of Cairo, Arabian American Oil Company (ARAMCO) officials, missionaries, teachers, a U.S. Congressman and wife (Hon. Lawrence H. Smith of Wisconsin), and U.S. embassy staff members proceeding to various assignments in the area.

On arrival in Beirut we stayed at the renowned and beautifully located St. Georges Hotel, with a room and balcony facing the sea. We dwelt at the St. Georges for about a month, as we searched for an apartment for the two-year stay. Graduation with an M.A. was scheduled for AUB's commencement day on June 28, 1955.

I registered at the historic AUB on October 5, 1953. My faculty advisors were Professors Nicolas A Ziadeh and Zeine N. Zeine. Daily courses included tutoring in Arabic, which took place in consonance with about ten other U.S. military officers who were doing graduate study at AUB. Our regular courses were supplemented by talks from Arab leaders, businessmen, and experts, along with periodic travel throughout the Middle East and elsewhere. A lifelong friend from this period is Ann Zwicker Kerr, who married my AUB classmate Malcolm Kerr. Malcolm later became the valiant president of AUB who was assassinated on campus in 1984. Ann has led a very successful life as an AUB trustee, author of two books, coordinator of the Fulbright Visiting Scholar Enrichment Program for Southern California, and mother of four children, including the famous basketball star Steven Kerr.

One fascinating orientation trip was to Iraq. Several of our U.S. military students assigned to AUB arranged an overland trip to Iraq during a school break. We traveled in a privately owned vehicle from Beirut to Damascus and across the then unpaved Syrian desert through Al-Rutbah (Rutbah Wells), which lies on a high plateau halfway between Damascus and Baghdad. From the 1920s to 1940s, Imperial Airways had a weekly air service between Cairo and Baghdad and developed an overnight rest house in an old fort at Rutbah Wells. There was a circular stone staircase to the roof where one could enjoy the breathtaking stars sparkling in the clear desert sky. Above the roof there was a radio and observation tower whose beacon was visible to aircraft 130 kilometers (80 miles) around. On this trip, we also visited historic Karbala, Baghdad, the Kurds in Kirkuk and Irbil, and of course the port of Basrah.

During my summer vacation in 1954, I traveled with my wife to Germany and Belgium. Ruby underwent medical treatment at the U.S. Military Hospital in Erding, Germany, to try to prevent a miscarriage, which tragically occurred on May 29, 1954.

Some months after the beginning of my interesting studies at AUB, I was in contact with the Commanding General of the USAF Second Air Division, which was training the Saudi Arabian Air Forces at Dhahran in eastern Saudi Arabia. About 800 USAF personnel were in Dhahran, and the unit provided various kinds of support to U.S. interests in Iraq, Iran, Pakistan, and Ethiopia. Eggs and fresh produce were flown into Dhahran from Beirut or Asmara when available. In those days there were no fences around the base. Before each aircraft's arrival and departure the airdrome officer was required to check the runways for obstacles, including transient Bedouins or loose animals. Through Brig. General Orrin L. Grover, USAF, I was able to arrange a three-day visit to Dhahran in May, 1954, for Dr. Costi K. Zurayk, Acting President of AUB, Dr. Charles J. Miller, Dean of the Faculty of Arts and Sciences, Dr. Nicolas Ziadeh, Acting Director Arab Studies Program, and other AUB officials. They traveled to Dhahran on a regularly scheduled USAF aircraft for a most useful orientation. I accompanied the group as their escort officer.

Beginning on August 16, 1954, I participated in a U.S. Near Eastern survey field course involving travel to Cairo, Cyprus, Rhodes, Turkey, and Greece for 25 days to augment my AUB studies. During this period in Beirut, I was able to upgrade my draft Ph.D. dissertation, which was completed on February 18, 1955, with the helpful guidance of Dr. and Mrs. Kerim K. Key (now deceased), the distinguished Chairman of the AUB Department of History, Dr. Zeine N. Zeine, and the invaluable help of my delightful and scholarly Polish friends, Wlodzimierz and Maria Baczkowski, who were active in the Polish Promethean League.

In the meanwhile my young son, Charles, Jr., who had the nickname "Pogo," was growing rapidly. He had his second birthday party on November 28, 1954, in Beirut with 15 of his friends attending the gala event. We were happily living near the Bain Militaire with a fine view of the Mediterranean Sea from the third floor of Immueble Alwan off Rue Chouran, close to Avenue Bliss and AUB.

On February 26, 1955, Ruby and I traveled for three weeks of vacation in Greece, Italy, Switzerland, Germany, Belgium (to visit Ruby's relatives), France, England, and Tripoli, Libya. It was a splendid trip, and while in London I called on Mr. C.A. Furth, MBE, Director of George Allen and Unwin, Ltd., and visited Macmillans Ltd., who showed interest in publishing my Ph.D. dissertation. This was a good period for us since I received word of my promotion by the USAF to the rank of full Colonel (after only 13 years of service) effective April 21, 1955 (see photo #16).

Syrian President Adib Esh–Shishakli

Syria had been rocked with internal disorders and assassinations throughout the 1950s. A new constitution was adopted on September 6, 1950, and Hashim El-Atasi became president. A crisis developed when the U.S., France, Turkey, and Great Britain submitted a scheme to the Arab League in October, 1951, for a Middle East Defense Organization called the Baghdad Pact. Hasan Hakim, who had become Prime Minister of Syria in August, 1951, wanted to accept the plan and resigned in November because of cabinet opposition to the proposal. After three weeks of turmoil, Maruf ed-Dawalibi formed a cabinet but was overthrown nine hours later by a *coup d'état* on November 29, 1951, engineered by the chief of the Syrian general staff, Col. Adib Esh-Shishakli. President Atasi resigned on December 1, and the higher military council under Shishakli appointed Col. Fawzi Silo as Chief of State and Prime Minister.

Shishakli, as deputy premier and chief of staff, controlled the government. On June 21, 1953, he announced the end of the Syrian provisional regime. A new constitution was accepted by a referendum held on July 10, 1953. On the same day Shishakli (now a Brigadier General) was elected President of the Syrian Republic with 86.6% of the vote.

Shishakli was a tough military leader. While he did not adhere to the political principles pursued by the U.S. government, he was savvy enough to recognize the value of having a covert "anchor to windward" with the U.S.A. He needed to have a means of exchanging thoughts, questions, and information with the West, but he did not want the public or his political enemies to be aware that he was doing so.

He knew very well that the American Embassy in Damascus was under very close technical, physical, and internal surveillance by various Syrian groups (both official and unofficial) so he declined the idea of having any sensitive political contacts with the U.S. Embassy or through its agents in Syria. There was such close surveillance of foreigners, particularly Americans and British, that the idea of establishing in Syria a CIA-sponsored U.S. businessman as a covert liaison with Shishakli was clearly unfeasible.

President Shishakli and I exchanged greetings and messages usually in French or my fairly basic Arabic, which I was perfecting at AUB. We got along quite well together, perhaps because we both had military backgrounds. For better or for worse, Shishakli's regime did not last long. In January, 1954, it was faced with political disturbances allegedly fomented by Iraqi army leaders. Sultan Al-Atrash, the old Druse leader (of the about 150,000 Druse resident in Syria), revolted in the Hauran area, and Syrian army dissidents joined the movement. On February 25, 1954, Shishakli resigned and left Syria. Seventy-nine-year-old former President Hashim El-Atasi was restored as President, and the Shishakli constitution was replaced by the former one of 1950. On August 18, 1955, Shukri Al-Kuwatli, who in 1949 had taken refuge in Saudi Arabia, was elected President for the third time.

These clandestine meetings in general all went smoothly, except for some excitingly close calls, which I fortunately survived without detection. One grave difficulty was my inability for security reasons to explain satisfactorily to my wife, Ruby, the true reason for my fairly frequent extended absences late at night. While this may seem humorous, it was a major problem that later contributed to our divorce.

The abrupt resignation and departure of President Shishakli from Syria marked the end of my covert liaison relationship. It had been a successful mission on behalf of the CIA.

Later when Syria began receiving Soviet arms and instructors matters did not go smoothly for the U.S.A. In August, 1957, three officials of the U.S. Embassy in Damascus were accused of plotting to overthrow the Syrian government and had to leave the country. A month later an international crisis developed when Syria and the U.S.S.R., claiming that Turkey was massing troops near the Syrian frontier, accused the U.S. of plotting a revolution in Syria with the help of Turkey and former President/General Adib Esh-Shishakli (who was sentenced "in absentia" for a life term, in trials in Damascus during February, 1958, for participation in a CIA plot).

On February 1, 1958, President Kuwatli and President Gamal Abd-El-Nasser of Egypt formally proclaimed a union of Egypt and Syria into the United Arab Republic (UAR). Only two and a half years later, on September 28, 1961, following another army coup, Syria seceded from the UAR. Syria then rejoined the United Nations on October 13, 1961.

Armenian Government in Exile

I was progressing well into the second year of my graduate studies at AUB and was enjoying life in Beirut, then called the "Switzerland or Paris" of the Middle East, with my wife and young son Charles, Jr. The CIA next assigned me the task of liaison with the Armenian "government in exile," which was then headquartered in Beirut. The talented Armenian people, who made their first appearance in history as Indo-Europeans toward the end of the 7th century B.C.E., had historical geographic boundaries that formerly included the northeastern part of Turkey and today's independent Armenian Republic in the Caucasus. After various periods as independent kingdoms over the centuries, many Armenians, traditionally Monophysite Christians, largely belonging to the Armenian Apostolic (Orthodox) Church, emigrated abroad and became successful leaders and businessmen. After the Russian Revolution of 1917, the Georgians, Armenians, and Azerbaijanis had formed a Transcaucasian Federal Republic on September 20, 1917. On May 26, 1918, this entity was broken into three independent republics. On August 10, 1920, the Allies provided *de jure* recognition to the Armenian Republic by admitting its representatives to sign the Peace Treaty of Sevres with Turkey.

At the end of September, 1920, the Turks attacked the Armenian Republic, while at the same time the Russians advanced from Azerbaijan. On December 2, 1920, a peace treaty between Armenia and Turkey was signed at Alexandropol (Leninakan), which not only annulled the provisions of the treaty of Sevres concerning Armenia but also stripped the Kars district away from Armenia. Kars is now still part of Turkey.

On the same day that the Alexandropol treaty was signed by the Armenian council of ministers at Yerevan, the capital, authority was ceded to General Dro Kanayan, the commander in chief. The next day, December 3, 1920, a new government composed of Communists and Dashnakists (the Dashnaks were an ultra- nationalist party founded in 1890) proclaimed Armenia a Soviet Republic. Shortly afterwards the Dashnakists were eliminated from the government, and one of them, Simon Vratzian, led an armed anti-Communist uprising in February, 1921. Since no help came from abroad, this uprising failed.

On March 12, 1922, Armenia, Georgia, and Azerbaijan were again combined to form the Transcaucasian Soviet Federated Socialist Republic (TSFSR), which became a part of the U.S.S.R.

On December 5, 1936, the TSFSR was dissolved, and Armenia became a constituent republic of the U.S.S.R.

After this, over the years, the Armenian Dashnak party, under the brave guidance of General Dro Kanayan and its former President Simon Vratzian, continued its work largely with help from the prosperous Armenian world-wide overseas community. The Dashnaks were not the only Armenian political grouping (which also included the Hunchak and Ramgavar parties), but they were the strongest and best organized and sought to coordinate all Armenian revolutionary groups. Operating largely outside of the Soviet Union's Armenian Republic, the Dashnaks and related parties established an Armenian "government in exile" located in Beirut, Lebanon.

Beirut was a quite logical choice because Lebanon had a sizable Armenian community (which has three Armenian representatives in the Lebanese Parliament). Lebanon was quietly approving of the concept of an ultimate Armenian independence from the U.S.S.R. Simon Vratzian, the "President in Exile," and General Dro were dynamic in keeping in touch with Armenian communities around the world. The capable Armenians abroad were supportive with funds and useful information, which flowed discretely in and out of their headquarters in exile in Beirut.

Outside of Beirut in the Lebanese community of Antelias was the head of the Armenian Apostolic Church Abroad (the Catholicate of

Cilicia) and an Armenian Theological Seminary. These existed in religious opposition to the Soviet dominated Armenian Apostolic Church, which was located in Etchmiadzin, then Soviet Armenia. My task was to be the covert liaison for the CIA and the U.S. government in maintaining discrete contact with this important world-wide community. The Lebanese government was undoubtedly aware of the existence of this "Armenian Government in Exile," but preferred (because of the power of the U.S.S.R.) to contend it did not exist on Lebanese soil so all U.S. (and presumably other countries') relationships were carried out in a thoroughly clandestine fashion. As happened in my contacts with President Shishakli of Syria, I would respond to discrete messages from personalities in the American Embassy of Beirut to receive incoming information. Then utilizing various safe houses in Beirut, I would carefully meet with General Dro, President Vratzian, or their representatives, to exchange data or points of view.

The Armenian personalities were all very experienced, capable, and discrete. They knew what information, much of which come from the U.S.S.R., was of interest to U.S. authorities. This useful relationship continued undetected. It was passed to other capable hands when on June 27, 1955, I happily graduated from AUB with a Master's degree in Middle Eastern Studies. It was a delightful ceremony in a wonderful setting on the AUB campus. On July 11, 1955, Ruby, Charles, Jr., and I sailed from Beirut on the American Export Lines S.S. Excalibur for a delightful trip back around the Mediterranean and arrived in New York on August 1. I was to be assigned to intelligence duties in Headquarters USAF in the Pentagon, Washington, D.C.

The CIA was most pleased with the results I was able to achieve on this assignment and kindly wrote a glowing effectiveness report to the USAF. They said in part ". . . He was required to plan, organize, and direct highly complex and sensitive foreign intelligence, psychological, and political warfare operations . . . They were aimed at implementing U.S. government policy objectives established by the National Security Council. Col. Hostler was called upon to conduct personally discussions with one Chief of State in connection with his operations. He was also required to assure that commitments between the U.S. government and an important political group were fulfilled . . . The assignment may be classified as unusual in the extreme, of the very highest significance, complexity, and importance." Additionally, the Deputy Director of Central Intelligence, Lt. General C.P. Cabell, USAF, took the unusual step of sending the attached Commendation to the Chief of Staff, U.S. Air Force.

CENTRAL INTELLIGENCE AGENCY

WASHINGTON 25, D. C.

OFFICE OF DEPUTY DIRECTOR OF CENTRAL INTELLIGENCE

17 NOV 1955

MEMORANDUM FOR: CHIEF OF STAFF, U. S. AIR FORCE

SUBJECT: Commendation - Colonel Charles W. Hostler, 8567A

    1. I wish to commend Colonel Charles W. Hostler, USAF, 8567A, for the outstanding services performed by him while assigned to the Central Intelligence Agency.

    2. During the period March 1953 to September 1955, Colonel Hostler distinguished himself by exceptionally meritorious conduct in the performance of outstanding service to the United States. While on duty in a highly important field assignment in a strategic Near Eastern area, this officer was required to plan, organize and direct highly complex and sensitive foreign intelligence, psychological and political warfare operations. These vital operations were conducted with the greatest effectiveness and discretion. They successfully implemented high-level U. S. Government policy objectives established by the National Security Council.

    3. This assignment has given additional proof of Colonel Hostler's outstanding abilities and his exceptional growth potential. His fitness is evidenced by his effectiveness, skill in leadership, superior judgment, and the significance of assignments he has been called upon to perform. Typical of his ability and initiative is the fact that he has, on his own time, just completed an important book in the field of political science, which will be published this year.

    4. Colonel Hostler's service has reflected the highest credit on the U. S. Air Force, this Agency, and himself.

C. P. CABELL
Lieutenant General, USAF
Deputy Director

Chapter Six
Military Attaché
in Lebanon, Jordan, and Cyprus
(1955 - 1961)

The Pentagon and Life in Washington, D.C. (1955 - 1958)

Upon our return to Washington, D.C. from Lebanon, I was assigned to very interesting duty in the Subsidiary Plans Division, dealing with unconventional warfare, special operations, and psychological warfare, in the Directorate of Plans, Headquarters USAF in the Pentagon. With the help of a VA loan we purchased a new home, still under construction by M.T. Broyhill and Sons at 5622 N. 33rd St., Arlington 7, Virginia, and moved in about September 15, 1955.

From October 26 to 29, 1955, I was ordered to Stead Air Force Base, Reno, Nevada, to coordinate USAF prisoner-of-war (POW) and survival training programs and supporting research activities. In January, 1956, I attended class 56-5 of the Air Weapons Orientation course at the Air Command and Staff College at Maxwell AFB, Alabama.

In this period I resumed contact with my good friend from my days in Turkey, Mr. Altemur Kiliç, who was then Turkish Press Attaché for the U.S.A. in Washington, D.C. He was helpful and interested in my book on Turkism and has been an eminent journalist in Istanbul.

In January, 1956, I initiated action through Dr. William H. Shehadi to form a Washington Chapter of the AUB Alumni Association of North America with an inaugural dinner on March 22, 1956, attended by about 50 alumni. I was supported by Mrs. Angela Khouri, Mr. Ned Makdisi, Mr. Francis Boardman, Dr. Majid Khoury, and other friends and alumni of AUB. I was president of this Chapter in 1957 and 1958, which is still very active and helpful to AUB today.

On May 17, 1956, I was inducted into the Gold Key Society of Georgetown University, which represents the highest scholastic honor that may be attained by a student of that university "in recognition of high attainments in liberal scholarship." On June 11, 1956, I officially received my degree of Doctor of Philosophy in political science from Georgetown University.

On June 4, 1956, I was moved upward from the Directorate of Plans in Headquarters USAF to the Directorate of Plans in the Office of the Joint Chiefs of Staff (JCS), also in the Pentagon. Admiral Arthur Radford, the Chairman of the JCS, sent me a note saying ". . . the work in which you will participate will form the basis for implementation of our national military policy and strategy. It deserves and requires the best efforts of the finest officers of our armed forces. . . ." I was assigned to the Joint Strategic Plans Group where I was actively involved with psychological and unconventional warfare and policy and frequently briefed the Chairman of the JCS on these matters.

In March, 1957, I was assigned to highly classified duties as a member of the Joint Subsidiary Activities Group of the Joint Staff. Also part of this elite team was the justly famous John "P.T." Bulkeley, who was awarded the Congressional Medal of Honor (later Vice Admiral USN), and Colonel English (later Major General USMC). Our leader was Lt. General Victor ("The Brute") Krulak, USMC, now retired and living in nearby La Jolla, California. His son was later Commandant of the USMC. Col. William "Barry" Taylor, USAF, was a great friend.

During my years in the Pentagon, I had the good fortune to be selected to be the U.S. Escort Officer for a number of groups of foreign dignitaries who made extended official visits around the country as guests of the U.S. Department of Defense. These tasks were great fun and took me, and them, to all corners of the U.S.A. and gave me the opportunity to meet many interesting personalities. Among these foreign visiting officials were:

1. Major General Florent Van Rolleghem, Commander, Belgian Air Defense Command (in mid-1956) and a party of four other officers

2. In my 1953-1955 days in Lebanon, I and my family became very friendly with Colonel (later General) Simon Zouain, the Commander of the Lebanese Gendarmerie (a form of militarized national police). Col. (and Mrs. Renée) Zouain were charming people and members of a prominent Maronite family whom I visited often in their family village of Yahchouch in the Lebanese moun-

tains. In 1956 I was able to assist in arranging an official USAF-sponsored trip around the U.S.A. for Col. Zouain, Under Secretary of the Lebanese Ministry of Defense Mounir Takieddine, and Col. Emil Boustany. In 2001 I was happy to visit again Mme. Renée Zouain and her two children (Georges was the son) in their home in Jounieh, Lebanon.

3. Lt. General Pierre L. Bodet of the French Air Force and party (where we had a private meeting in 1953 in the White House with President Dwight Eisenhower).

4. Major General Antonius Baretta, Vice Chief of Staff, Royal Netherlands Air Force, and party (April 15-May 2, 1951).

5. Major General Ihsan Orgun, Chief of Staff, Turkish Air Force (April, 1952) and colleagues.

6. General Octave L'Heritier, General Viguier, General Jean L.N. Nicot, and others of the French Air Force (June, 1957). General Nicot was a descendant of a prominent French family of whom then French Ambassador Jean Nicot won royal favor in 1561 in Lisbon by bring into Europe an American weed named tobacco (which was nationalized into a golden harvest for the French treasury by Napoleon). It was from their family name that the word "nicotine" originated.

During this interesting period of my duty in the Pentagon, I was asked in 1956 as an extra-curricular activity, to be a Lecturer in Middle Eastern international relations for the School of Social Sciences and Public Affairs at the American University in Washington, D.C. Over the years as I continued this happy relationship at American University, I was promoted by them to be a Professorial Lecturer, Assistant Professor, Associate Professor, and ultimately to Adjunct Professor. I also lectured to CIA's Area Training Programs on the Middle East in 1957, various Air Intelligence Reserve Groups, the Georgetown TV Forum, and others.

In 1956 I did extended official travel to various parts of the world in connection with my work with the Joint Strategic Plans Group, including Japan, Korea, the Philippines, France, England, and others. Additionally, I was a co-author (with Col. Don Decker, USMC), of a portion of a book entitled *The Challenge to Science Education* (N.Y., Philosophical Library, 1958) and wrote an article for the September, 1958, issue of the *Middle East Journal.* In October, 1957, I was a participant in the televised "Georgetown University Forum," which was a series of four presentations on the Soviet Union (along with Dr. Lev E. Dobriansky). Ruby, Charles, Jr., and I traveled to Cuba, Puerto Rico, and the Panama Canal Zone by ship for a vacation over Christmas, 1956.

U.S. Air Attaché to Lebanon, Jordan, and Cyprus

In February of 1958, I received word that I had been selected for an overseas assignment as U.S. Air Attaché to Lebanon and was also to be accredited as U.S. Air Attaché to Jordan and Cyprus. Preparatory to this, I attended the U.S.

Army's Strategic Intelligence School and received further Arabic language training. The various orientations and training were completed by October, 1958, including 61 days of Arabic language training at the Sanz School of Language in Washington, D.C. On our departure for Beirut we sold our house in Arlington, Virginia, in September, 1958. We made advance arrangements for our son, then six years old, to be enrolled in the first grade of the American Community School in Beirut. My family and I were delighted to be able to travel again through the Mediterranean on the American Export Lines, this time on the SS Excambion. We departed on October 23 from New York City and arrived in Beirut on November 11, 1958, to begin an extended tour of duty of almost three years.

The delicate balance among Lebanon's 16 different religious communities and sects, as was provided for in the Lebanese National Pact, was precariously maintained, and undercurrents of hostility were evident in this era. The Moslem community criticized the governing regime in which Christians, alleging their numerical superiority, occupied the highest offices in the state and filled a disproportionate number of civil service positions. Thus, the Moslems asked for a census, which they were confident would prove their numerical pre-eminence. The Christians refused unless the census were to include Lebanese emigrants abroad (who were mainly Christians), and they argued that Christians contributed 80% of the tax revenue.

This tension came to a boil when on July 14, 1958, a revolution in Iraq overthrew the monarchy, and the entire royal family was killed. In Lebanon jubilation prevailed in those areas where sentiment against President Chamoun (a Christian) predominated. Radio stations in Lebanon were announcing that the Chamoun regime would be next to go.

Chamoun requested immediate assistance from the U.S.A., France, and Britain and invoked the terms of the Eisenhower Doctrine, which Lebanon had signed the year before. According to its terms, the U.S. would "use armed forced to assist any [Middle East] nation . . . requesting assistance against armed aggression from any country controlled by international communism." Arguing that Lebanese Moslems were being helped by Syria, which had received arms from the U.S.S.R., Chamoun appealed for U.S. military intervention. The U.S. responded principally because of concern over the situation in Iraq and the wish to reassure its allies, such as Iran and Turkey, that the U.S. could act. U.S. forces began arriving in Lebanon from the 6th U.S. Fleet by mid-afternoon of July 15, 1958. Five thousand U.S. Marines were landed on the beaches near Beirut and waded ashore with bayonets fixed among surprised and relaxed sunbathers and swimmers in a situation some regarded as a comic opera. The U.S. forces played a symbolic rather than an active role; however, one U.S. soldier of the 24th U.S. Airborne Brigade was killed by Moslem snipers on August 2, 1958. In the course of the 1958 Civil War, in which U.S. forces were not directly involved, between 2,000 and 4,000 Lebanese casualties occurred, primarily in the Moslem areas of Beirut and Tripoli. At the end of the crisis, the Lebanese Chamber of Deputies elected General Fuad Shihab, then Commander-in-Chief of the Lebanese Army, to serve as President.

President Shihab cultivated nonpartisanship and strengthened the role of the executive at the expense of the traditional family tribal leaders (or zaim). He concentrated on improving Lebanon's infrastructure and asked the U.S. to withdraw its troops from Lebanon by the end of October, 1958. Shihab pictured himself as a military statesman like Charles de Gaulle and relied heavily on the military intelligence branch of the Lebanese Army as his power base with whom I cooperated in the U.S. interest. President Shihab surrendered command of the Lebanese Army and did not rule as a military dictator.

Life In Lebanon

With the advice and guidance of the esteemed Col. and Mrs. William A. Eddy (USMC retired), who was with the OSS in WWII and was U.S. Minister in Saudi Arabia and the Arabic language interpreter in the important discussions between President F.D. Roosevelt and King Ibn Saud of Saudi Arabia, I was able to sub-lease a fine apartment from Mobil Oil Lebanon. It was on the second floor of the Elias Salamoun building on Rue du Mexique and had a magnificent view of the Mediterranean Sea.

The U.S. Ambassador in Lebanon was an experienced career Foreign Service Officer named Robert McClintock. His wife Elenaita was a beautiful lady of Chilean origin. They had a beloved poodle named "Golly" whose leap into the parade reviewing stand in Beirut caused the Lebanese press to howl with disapproval. The Deputy Chief Mission (DCM) was a foreign service career officer named Robert C. Creel.

Among the fine Assistant Air Attachés that worked for me in Beirut were Captain (later a Lt. Col.) Albert and Mrs. Barbara Restum, who transferred to Beirut from Rhine Main Air Base in Germany in early 1959, as well as Captain and Mrs. Martin L. Kammerer, USAF (who arrived in Beirut in May, 1959). The able enlisted men assigned to the OAIRA Beirut included T/Sgt. Donald K. Fleming and T/Sgt. Clyde H. Skinner, who were very helpful to our mission.

I was fortunate to have two great Lebanese drivers at the Embassy. One was Jamil Boghos. The other was my long-time friend, Jamil Sema'an, whom with his lovely wife Laurice and children I was able to help immigrate to the U.S.A. in 1961. Sadly, he died in 1997 in nearby Torrance, California, where his wife and family still live.

In December of 1958, I traveled to Headquarters USAFE (U.S. Air Forces in Europe) in Wiesbaden, Germany, for coordination purposes.

Because of my prior duty in Lebanon, my acceptance into the local community in Lebanon was quickly re-established. However, I was surprised to be soon awarded the high Lebanese decoration "The National Order of the Cedars" in the grade of Officer.

My arrival back in Lebanon was noted promptly and viciously by the U.S.S.R. in the Soviet-sponsored "Our Radio" broadcast (via Leipzig) on December 24, 1958, in the Turkish language directed to Turkey. This 15-minute broadcast was monitored by the U.S. Listening Station in Cyprus and by the similar French Station located elsewhere. It said, in part:

> . . . Colonel Hostler is one of the deadly enemies of our people. He is the American Air Attaché in Lebanon. The Colonel performs special duties for the Pentagon and for the Near East section of the State Department. He works for the secret service.
>
> He is one of the CIC, that is, the American Military Espionage Service, and is specially trained for the Middle East. The Colonel attended Georgetown University, Washington, D.C. . . . . He entered the American University of Beirut, toured Turkey and the Arab countries, and followed the path of Lawrence of Arabia. He learned the methods of the German espionage services which worked in the Near and Middle East during WWI and WWII. . . . Now that he is the Air

Attaché in Lebanon, he is still closely interested in the atomic bases and missile sites in Anatolia. Colonel Hostler is a cold-blooded murderer.

In Lebanon, he had many patriots killed. Every day he creates a new provocation along the borders of Turkey, Syria, and Iraq. During the past two months, 120 Turks were killed on the southern frontier of Turkey as a result of provocation fabricated by this American spy Colonel . . . He wrote a book entitled *Turkism and the Soviets,* which shows how to reach the "Red Apple," which is the dream of Turanists, the people who want to establish a homeland comprising all people of the Turkish race including those of U.S.S.R. . . . The book you wrote and put on the market is nothing but a provocation. You want to create enmity between the peoples of Turkey and those of the Soviet Union. American Colonel! You are a spy! A deadly enemy of our people!

It was interesting to me that the Soviets had reacted so vehemently to my book *Turkism and the Soviets.* It showed that the U.S.S.R. was concerned about the question of Turkism and its potential impact on the Turks living in Central Asia. The breakup of the U.S.S.R. in 1991 resulted in the independence of Kakhistan, Uzbekistan, Kirghigistan, Turkmenistan, and Azerbaijan, all countries with a strong Turkic heritage.

Very unfortunately, in early April, 1959, Ruby had to enter the AUB Hospital for a hysterectomy operation. She and I enjoyed our lovely five-bedroom apartment and entertained often, sometimes for up to 400 persons for cocktails or thirty persons for dinner. My work normally required 12 or more hours of effort per day, followed by social engagements for Ruby and me almost every evening. We had frequent official visitors from all U.S. services and many countries and from adjoining posts and U.S. Naval ships coming from Europe, Turkey, or further distances. We were fortunate to have a wonderful home staff consisting of Emil Daccash, the cook, and Maria Hanna, our loyal maid, who was a faithful Assyrian Christian who came from a mountain village in Syria. Maria later on joined Charles, Jr. and myself in the U.S.A. and France and worked for us until she died of cancer in Newport Beach, California, in the 1980s.

In June of 1959 an old acquaintance, Major General James "Doc" C. McGehee (and his wife Nettie), USAF, was named as Chief of the U.S. Military Training Mission in Saudi Arabia. This U.S. Mission in Dhahran was our support base and had a USAF C54 aircraft, which traveled at least once a week to Beirut to purchase fresh vegetables, eggs, and other supplies for the U.S. military and diplomatic contingent in Dhahran. This unit did great work in training the fledgling Saudi Air Force. One of the fine young Saudi pilot officers I met there was the talented Prince Bandar Al-Saud, who is now the long-serving Saudi Ambassador to the U.S.A. (and is Dean of the Ambassadorial Corps in Washington, D.C.).

In January of 1959 I was advised that the Frankfurt publishing house of Alfred Metzner had arranged to translate my book *Turkism and the Soviets* from English into German. The translation was capably done by Dr. Tilemann Stelzenmuller and Miss Gisela Alles, who were later married. On business trips to Frankfurt on Main, I had the opportunity to meet this talented couple and to clarify questions occurring during the translation. I later learned indirectly that the costs of translation and publishing had been underwritten by one of the branches of the German Intelligence Service because they found the subject of Turkism to be of continuing German national interest in their relations with the U.S.S.R. and Turkey.

New Soviet Radar in Syria

In addition to Lebanon, I was also accredited as U.S. Air Attaché to Jordan and Cyprus. To reach Jordan from Beirut for duty each month, we normally drove to and from Jordan by car. The closest overland route took us through Damascus, Syria. The Syrians in this period were receiving extensive Soviet military assistance and were quite unfriendly to the U.S.A. because of U.S. support of the Israelis. It came to the attention of U.S. military intelligence that the Syrians had received from the Soviets a particularly interesting new type of radar facility. This had been erected on a hill near the center of Damascus in a busy part of town. Headquarters USAF was most eager to have close-up, ground-level photos of this new equipment.

My office was not accredited to Syria, and there was no U.S. Air Attaché in Syria so Headquarters USAF could not instruct us to take the pictures. They made it clear that they eagerly wanted these important photos so it was decided to try to take these pictures on a trip driving through Damascus, with the help of my assistant, Captain Martin Kammerer. We drove to the crowded market area and as inconspicuously as possible, we quickly made a series of photos and estimates of dimensions of the radar from within the car. Unfortunately, in the crowded bazaar, we were detected by on-lookers, and they began an outcry and blocked the car. We could not proceed forward or backward. We promptly locked ourselves in the car. The crowd angrily began rocking the vehicle from side to side.

Within about 20 minutes, Syrian Secret Military Intelligence officials arrived on the scene and took us to their military headquarters for interrogation. It was no use trying to claim diplomatic immunity because we were not "accredited" to the U.S. Embassy in Syria. We tried to tough it out, by being polite but denying any intention to photograph their sensitive equipment. This interrogation process went on for four to five hours. The Syrian officers were very frustrated and angry but did not want to resort to the physical abuse of two U.S. officers, in order to avoid a diplomatic incident with the U.S.A. The Syrians wanted us to turn over to them the film in our camera for development.

During our interrogation, the U.S. Embassy in Damascus was informed, however, they were denied the right to visit us in confinement. The U.S. Embassy officials in Damascus were angry because we had taken our actions without their knowledge or approval.

After many hours of confrontation and discussion, in a fit of desperation (or brilliance), Captain Kammerer and I exchanged eye glances at the camera. Simultaneously, we grabbed the camera on the table and wrestled it from the Syrians. Quickly, we unloaded the film and pulled it out of the cassettes so that the film was exposed and thus useless in proving their charge against us. "You wanted the film; here it is!" we proclaimed.

Our interrogators were absolutely furious. However, after a few hours more we were released, and we drove back to Beirut. The U.S. Embassy in Damascus was upset with us, but we stressed the importance of the information to the U.S. Washington denied having asked us to proceed. In the end, the matter was forgotten, and we were credited for bravely trying, and for bringing back some information, such as the visual descriptions and estimates of this new Soviet radar facility which we did acquire.

On July 7, 1959, I was fortunate to be sent on what was called a U.S. official "area orientation" for 23 days to Moscow, Ordjonikidze, Tbilisi, Sukhumi, and back to Moscow. This trip was arranged for and by U.S. Air Force Intelligence for me to carefully photograph and survey priority targets in the area. The voyage permitted me to travel through parts of Russia and the Caucasus, which were important to my Turkic research. I flew via Aeroflot from Sofia, with brief stops at Bucharest, Odessa, and Kiev to Moscow, where I stayed at the Hotel Metropole. The Soviet government was aware of my trip since all internal travel in the U.S.S.R. in those days was necessarily arranged through official Intourist channels. From Moscow I went in a crowded train to Ordzhonikidze (in the northern Caucasus) via Tula, Orel, Kharkov, Artevovsk, and Rostov, and it took a burdensome 40 hours (two nights and a day). My tour by train was constantly under Soviet government surveillance, including an attempted seduction of me by an attractive Intourist guide in a Russian railway car en route to the Caucasus. Common sense prevailed, and I resisted temptation. I had been carefully briefed concerning Soviet regulations on photography, including being forbidden to photograph or make drawings in the 25-kilometer frontier zone or from airplanes in flight over Soviet territory. However, my mission was successfully accomplished. I traveled back from Moscow to Prague, Czechoslovakia, in a Czech TU 104 transport (and made a visit to my good friend Colonel George Weinbrenner, the U.S. Air Attaché in Prague).

In August, 1959, our attaché office in Beirut underwent an official inspection visit that was very thorough. When the team was finished, they classified my intelligence work as "outstanding." Ambassador Robert McClintock added a letter to General Thomas White, Chief of USAF, saying he heartily agreed, adding: "Hostler is in fact one of the best intelligence officers I have served with in almost 30 years in the Foreign Service."

In October of 1959, Ruby and I flew to Ankara and Istanbul (staying at the pleasant Hotel Istanbul Hilton) and then back through Ankara to Beirut on an interesting ten-day trip. In Istanbul we visited with the great Mr. and Mrs. Otton Andriadis (father of Dmitri "Taki" Andriadis). We also made a warm courtesy call on His Holiness Patriarch Athenogoras.

The British ran a fine training course for their diplomats and officers who specialized in the Middle East. It was called the Middle East Centre for Arab Studies (MECAS) in the Lebanese mountains at Shemlan. The locals called it "The British Spy School." The British kindly offered selected U.S. officials a background course, run by Donald Maitland, which I was happy to have a chance to attend.

The periodic U.S. Air Attaché Conferences in Wiesbaden, Germany, were always interesting, and as they involved about 12 days per conference, I had opportunities to explore that beautiful part of Germany, including Rudesheim and Garmisch. Additionally, they gave me the chance to meet again with wonderful friends like Col. George (and wife Billie) Weinbrenner, U.S. Air Attaché in

Prague, and Col. Walter "Steve" Hammond, U.S. Air Attaché in Hungary, who were also attending. Through these conferences I became friends with the other U.S. Air Attachés in the Middle East area including those accredited to Iran, Ethiopia, Pakistan, and Afghanistan. Since they had aircraft at their posts, when I was on official leave they were able on occasion to take Ruby and me along on a space-available basis to visit their interesting posts. On April 9, 1959, I was fortunate to take a fascinating trip to Saudi Arabia, Iran, Pakistan, and Afghanistan. This involved flying to the alluring town of Peshewar in Pakistan, then traveling overland through the famous Khyber Pass, visiting the renowned military unit of the Khyber Rifles, and finally to Khandahar and the Afghani capital of Kabul (later the focus of the "War on Terrorism" in 2001 and 2002). In November of 1959 I flew with the U.S. Air Attaché to Ethiopia on a captivating trip to Asmara (where the U.S. had a communications listening post), Addis Abbaba, Zanzibar, Rhodesia, Beiro, Mozambique, and back to Dhahran.

In early 1959, work was begun to build the elaborate new Casino du Liban on the Lebanese coast at Maameltein. It was completed in November, 1959, included elaborate space for gambling, and had a theater with fabulous shows coming from the Lido in Paris. It helped to enhance the image of Lebanon as the "Paris of the Middle East," and people traveled from all over the area to enjoy themselves, to vacation, and to do their banking. Among the cosmopolitan types we saw frequently in Beirut were Adnan M. Khashoggi, and his beautiful 19-year-old British friend, Sandra Daly. Khashoggi transformed his connections with the Saudi royal family into a colossal personal fortune. He operated as the Saudi Arabian agent representing Rolls Royce, Northrop, Lockheed, Raytheon, and other prominent companies.

In my days in this part of the world, I became fascinated with the approximately one million Druze people who live principally in parts of Lebanon, Syria, Israel, and Jordan. There had been no serious study of these people since Phillip Hitti's 1928 monograph. I began gathering material for a book on the Druze. After many months and much fact-gathering, I was discretely but firmly told by high and authoritative Lebanese sources that I should "cease and desist" since the Druze hierarchy would not welcome any outsider publicizing their beliefs.

Among my friends in Beirut were: 1) First Secretary Dr. Leslie C. Tihany (and his wife Maria), who later became U.S. Consul General in Antwerp and died in Kentucky; (2) Mr. and Mrs. Miles Copeland, Jr., senior CIA official who lived nine years in Beirut and whose young sons Miles, Jr. and Stuart used to play with my son Charles. Stuart later became a noted music composer and rock star who joined Sting in 1977. They formed the band "The Police"; 3) David S. Dodge, then with Tapline and later Interim President of AUB, now an eminent philanthropist in New York; 4) Madame Violette Mirza worked part-time for the U.S. Embassy in 1960 as an Arabic Language Instructor. Her father, Dr. Bahjat Mirza, had been a well-known Shiite physician in Nabatieh, southern Lebanon. In that year she married Mohamad Hammoud, the head of the Hammoud family clan of some 35,000 Shia from South Lebanon. He became a successful entrepreneur and died after being publicized as a prominent BCCI shareholder; (5) Jose "Pepe" Abed is a delightful restaurateur who has operated successful and unique eating places in Beirut, Paris, and now the fine Byblos Fishing Club in Byblos (where the word "bible" originated). His love of diving off the Phoenician coast resulted in his finding many antiquities which he recovered from the Mediterranean.

In early September, 1968, we were honored with a "Good Will Mission" of Chinese Nationalist military leaders headed by General Peng Meng Chi and Lt. General Lai Ming-Tang, Chinese Air Force; Vice Chief of the General Staff, Ministry of National Defense from Taiwan. I assisted them in Lebanon and Jordan where they were well-received in both countries, with the help of our local Chinese (Taiwanese) Ambassador, Dr. Kiding Wang.

My delightful aunt Loreene (sister of my father) and uncle Paul L. Sipp, Sr. visited us in Beirut for an extended visit to Lebanon, Jordan, and Jerusalem. They arrived on the S.S. Excalibur on October 21, 1960.

The well-known U.S. congressman L. Mendel Rivers spent four interesting days in early

October, 1960, in Beirut during the much-publi-
cized crash of a Syrian MIG-17F in Jordan. The
Syrian pilot committed suicide because of the intelligence sensitivity of the new Soviet-built MIG-
17F, which the U.S. was delighted to have a chance
to examine.

In November, 1959, I was invited to fly as a
passenger on the DC-3 aircraft assigned to the U.S.
Air Attaché in Addis Ababa, Ethiopia. I took a leave
of absence and flew with him to Saudi Arabia, Zanzibar, Asmara (now Eritrea), and Addis Ababa,
Ethiopia, South Africa, Tanganyika, Uganda,
Kenya, Mozambique, and Rhodesia (now Zimbabwe). It was a fascinating trip. Particularly exciting was the ability to fly very low over interesting
areas like Lake Victoria, the Serengeti plain in Tan-
zania, and watch the animals, especially the vast
numbers of migrating wildebeest, antelopes, and
elephants.

In February of 1960, I was happy to be invited to attend the Lebanese Army Ski and Mountain Combat School located in the famous Cedars
of Lebanon. Ruby, Charles, Jr., and I had great fun
taking ski lessons and romping in the snow for
seven days in a historic setting. We stayed at the
lovely Hotel Mon Repos in the Cedars. Charles, Jr.
and I later returned again in March, 1961, to the
ski school. Among my close friends in Lebanon
were General (retired) and Mrs. Jamil Lahoud, the
Parliamentary Deputy for the Metn area. His son
was named Emile Lahoud, then a young Lebanese
naval officer. He rose to become the Commander

of all Lebanese Armed Forces and a strong political figure. He became President of Lebanon in late 1998 (and presented me with the Lebanese Order of Cedars in the higher rank of Commander on February 26, 2001).

In March of 1960, I went back to Washington, D.C. for a Mid-Tour Orientation Briefing at Air Force Intelligence, State Department, and the CIA. Major General James H. Walsh, USAF, Assistant of Chief Staff, Intelligence was my helpful boss.

From April 14 to 23, 1960, Ruby, our son, and I flew to Cairo and then went by train to Aswan and Luxor and back to Cairo. We stayed at the famous Cataract Hotel in Aswan and the Winter Palace Hotel in Luxor.

My wonderful and always helpful father Sidney Marvin Hostler had retired to live in Colonia Chapalita in Guadalajara, Mexico. He had married a lady named Elizabeth "Betty" Christina Dederick, a former "stand-in" of the prominent movie actress Alexis Smith. Dad had been wounded during his service as a U.S. Army officer in France from May, 1917, to August, 1919, and had developed arterial hypertension. His health began to deteriorate in early 1959. On February 26 I received a sad telegram in Beirut from the State Department that Dad had died of atherosclerosis in Guadalajara on February 24, 1959, at the age of 68. The telegram said, ". . . in view of reported condition of your step-mother, Consulate requires immediate instructions . . ."

I arranged at once to travel from Beirut to Guadalajara on three-week emergency leave departing February 27. Arrangements were made to bury Dad on March 12, 1959, with full military honors, in Arlington Military Cemetery, as he was entitled due to his honorable service in WWI. The ceremony was attended by friends including Amy Cranton (wife of Warren Cranton, WWI companions of my father and mother and source of my middle name Warren), Johnny Sipp, George Weinbrenner, and myself. Reservations were also made for me to be ultimately buried in the adjacent Arlington Cemetery grave site (Section 46, Grave 631).

Betty, my step-mother, was an uncomplicated and lovable person. However, she had become mildly addicted to prescription drugs and alcohol. I had to try to sort things out in Guadalajara as Executor of my father's small estate, which was essentially a note worth $13,000 on his former house and a small pension. Because of Betty's condition it was the formal recommendation of her physician, the American Consul, and other friends (as well as Betty's wish) that she continue living in Guadalajara, and arrangements were made to assist her there. She died on March 14, 1960, and was buried in Guadalajara. It took until August 30, 1963, to legally sort out the two probates on this small estate.

From August 28 to 30, 1960, we had a visit in Beirut from Lt. General and Mrs. Elmer J. Rogers, Jr. USAF, Chief of the U.S. Element of CENTO in

Baghdad. He and his staff stayed at the Excelsior Hotel, used our "Guadalajara" cabin at Beirut's Acapulco Beach, visited Baalbeck and Damascus, and, of course, went to the grand Casino du Liban in Maameltein with its magnificent Lido floorshow from Paris.

In January of 1961, we were delighted to receive a visit in Beirut from the famous aviator (Brigadier General) Charles A. Lindbergh, who lived in Darien, Connecticut, but who was then advising Pan American Airways. He was kind enough to send me autographed copies of his wife's books *North to the Orient* for my son Charles and *Listen the Wind* for myself. Lindbergh asked me to write my son's name on my calling card. I hurriedly wrote under my printed name the word: "same – Jr." since my son's name is Charles W. Hostler, Jr. When the two books arrived one of them contained a pleasant inscription addressed to "Sam" Hostler, Jr.

In February of 1961, I was able to travel to Iraq for eight days. It was a delight to explore historic Baghdad, Mosul, the archeological sites of Ctesiphon, Babylon, Karbala, Samarra, and Nippur, for which special permission then had to be obtained from the Iraqi Director of Military Intelligence

My responsibilities as U.S. Air Attaché included not only Lebanon but also Jordan and Cyprus. These were posts that from a USAF standpoint were not prominent or significant enough in those days to justify a separate U.S. Air Attaché, so we handled them from Beirut. I normally traveled with a car and driver via Damascus, Syria, to Jordan for about four or five days each month. My trips to Cyprus increased after its independence on February 19, 1960.

Republic of Cyprus

Cyprus was just emerging from being a British colony (the British occupation began in 1878) and was moving toward independence in 1958 and 1959. As part of my duties in maintaining USAF liaison in Cyprus, it was important to be in close touch with our British allies who maintained significant military forces there. Group Captain R.F.H. Clerke, DFC, under the command of Air Marshal MacDonald, was our contact in the British Headquarters of the Middle East Air Force in Episkopi, Cyprus. On August 10, 1959, Ruby, Charles, Jr. (then seven years old), and I (as well as briefly my assistant Captain Martin Kammerer) went for several pleasant weeks in Episkopi, Platres, Trodos, Prodomos, and Nicosia. Ruby, Charles, Jr., and I enjoyed visiting in Cyprus, and particularly enjoyed Kyrenia with its 12th-century castle and harbor along with the Trodos mountains and the British Black Watch Battalion.

One day we were driving in a rented Fiat car through the picturesque Trodos mountains (Mount Olympus is 6,403 feet in height) when we were stopped by pro-Greek Enosis guerrillas. They probably initially thought we were British and were at first quite hostile since under their leader, Col. Georgios Grivas, they had bombed several British installations on Cyprus. When I satisfactorily identified myself as a U.S. Military Attaché their attitude changed, and we were taken further into the mountains to meet with Col. Grivas. He was quite an old mustached, former Greek officer-patriot type. He was very careful and kind in making Ruby and Charles, Jr., feel at ease and assuring them they were in no danger. We spent one or two days engaged in intense discussions, which, with Grivas' knowledge, I reported in detail to the U.S. and British, in the interests of peace in Cyprus. An American lady journalist also intervened in the matter since Grivas was being sought for arrest by the British. Ultimately, the British retained sovereignty over two of their military bases (involving an area of 99 square miles). After a later election the Republic of Cyprus officially came into being on August 16, 1960.

I was accredited to be U.S. Air Attaché to the new republic and was present in Nicosia from February 16 to 21, 1960, for various historic inaugural ceremonies. At the Investiture Ceremony at the Council of Ministers building in Nicosia, the Greek and Turkish members of the House elected a President and Vice President of the House. Then the first President and the Vice President of the Republic of Cyprus arrived for their Investiture heralded by trumpets. They made their affirmations of office and then left the Council of Ministers building. Music was provided by the Police Band.

After the ceremony the new flag of the Republic of Cyprus was raised outside the building in the presence of the Cypriot President (Greek Cypriot Archbishop Makarios) and Vice President (Turkish Cypriot Fazil Kutchuk).

On the Independence Day of the Republic of Cyprus, August 16, 1960, through the help of General Menelaos Pantelides, Commander of the Tripartite Headquarters, Ministry of Defense, Republic of Cyprus, I was able also to be a close official U.S. observer of the debarkation of the Greek and Turkish national military contingents, and the arrival welcome of the EOKA fighters. The U.S. had not yet appointed an Ambassador and was then operating out of the old U.S. Consulate General building. These were all memorable and historic events.

Hashemite Kingdom of Jordan: Political-Military Background

King Abdullah of Jordan had been assassinated on July 20, 1951, as he entered the revered Al-Aqsa Mosque in Jerusalem with his grandson, 15-year-old Prince Hussein, at his side. Hussein attended Harrow and Sandhurst in Britain, and when he was 18 years old, in May, 1953, he took the constitutional oath as King of Jordan (where he reigned for 46 years until his death from cancer in 1999).

Israel attacked Egyptian forces in the Sinai Peninsula on October 29, 1956, and British and

French forces landed at Port Said, Egypt, on November 5. British participation in the attack on Egypt made it politically necessary that Jordan end its special relationship with Britain. The Anglo-Jordanian Agreement of March, 1957, abrogated the basic Anglo-Jordanian Treaty of 1948, terminated the British subsidy, and initiated the turnover of British installations in Jordan and the withdrawal of all British troops still in beleaguered Jordan. The pro-Nasserities were arrayed against the King, the British subsidy was gone, and the rift was wider than ever between the East Bank Bedouins and the West Bank Palestinians.

The U.S. replaced Britain as Jordan's principal source of foreign aid. In April, 1957, President Eisenhower regarded "the independence and integrity of Jordan as vital." Jordan received an emergency financial grant of $10 million, and Washington expanded existing development aid and initiated military aid.

On July 14, 1958, the Hashemite monarchy in Iraq was overthrown in a swift pre-dawn military coup. King Faisal and other members of the Iraqi royal family were murdered. Brigadier Qasim became President of Iraq.

Jordan was isolated, and King Hussein appealed to the U.S. and Britain for help. The U.S. instituted an airlift of petroleum, while Britain flew in troops to Amman. These events in Iraq and Jordan coincided with the landing of U.S. troops in Lebanon to bolster the regime there.

For some weeks, the political atmosphere in Jordan was explosive, but the government kept order through limited martial law. The army continued its unquestioning loyalty to King Hussein, and the Israeli frontier remained quiet. The ensuing two-year period of relative tranquillity was broken in August, 1960, when the pro-Western Prime Minister Hazza Al-Majali was killed by a time bomb in his desk. The plot was traced to Syria and further identified with Cairo.

Thus, during my period as U.S. Air Attaché to Jordan (1958-1961) the U.S. became the principal source of military equipment to Jordan following the termination of the British subsidy. The British influence continued to be strong, however, and the U.S., British, and Jordanians generally worked together well in this era. From 1950 through 1988, the U.S. furnished Jordan a total of about $1.5 billion in military aid and training.

I often traveled from Beirut to the capitol Amman and then to Jerusalem where a portion of that city was still in Jordanian hands. Through my long-standing relationship with His Holiness Athenogoras, the Ecumenical Patriarch of the Orthodox Church in Istanbul, I was introduced to His Beatitude, Benedictos I, the 96th Orthodox Patriarch of Jerusalem. This gave me an opportunity to have a deeper understanding of the complex religious inter-relationships in the Holy City of Jerusalem. Patriarch Benedictos in February, 1960, awarded me the ancient and distinguished ecclesiastical Orthodox "Order of the Holy Sepulchre" in the grade of Grand Commander. This order dates originally from the Byzantine Emperor Constantine (4th century C.E.). Later, on October 6, 1961, I arranged a luncheon at the Pentagon's General Officers' dining room for the Patriarch and two of his Archbishops while they were on a visit to Washington, D.C. Present at the luncheon were the Chiefs of Chaplains for the U.S. Army, Navy, and Air Force and myself.

My closest daily contacts in Jordan were with the capable Col. Ibrahim Othman, the Commander of the Royal Jordanian Air Force, and Col. Emile Jumea'an, Public Relations Officer for the Jordan Arab Army. I frequently had the opportunity to relate with King Hussein, and upon my departure he personally presented me with an inscribed autographed photo of himself (see photo #18).

Ruby's Illness

On May 3, 1960, I was notified that Ambassador McClintock wished to see me. He greeted me with a cordial but serious mien and handed me a typed "Personnel Report on Representatives of Other Departments Abroad." It said, in part:

> As in my previous report on our Air Attaché, I believe that Col. Hostler is a truly outstanding officer in the field of military intelligence. He is keen, resourceful, diligent, and has a flair for this type of work. I should think that the Department of the Air Force

would be well advised to continue him in this specialty.

I have noted with regret that Mrs. Hostler has not enjoyed good health during this year under review and that, in fact, she did undergo surgery. This may explain the fact that Mrs. Hostler seems to be a young lady of considerable excitability, whose incursions, although well intended, into the life of the American and diplomatic community may at times have proved a certain hindrance to her husband's top-flight efficiency. I trust, however, that this is a passing phase in Mrs. Hostler's medical history, and that her apparent nervous instability will be only temporary in character . . .

Needless to say, this was a devastating shock to me and to Ruby. While her nervous state had become more acute and obvious over the last year, it was very disturbing to both of us that this matter had now become an official problem.

Ruby ultimately, but reluctantly, agreed to seek professional help with the leading Lebanese authority in these matters, Dr. A.S. Manugian, Clinical Professor of Psychiatry at AUB, and Physician Superintendent at the Lebanon Hospital for Mental and Nervous Disorders (at Asfuriyeh, near Beirut). On May 17, 1960, he wrote the following evaluation:

To Whom It May Concern:

   This is to certify that Mrs. Ruby Hostler has been under my care since March 26, 1960. She suffers from an acute emotional disorder. She previously had been under psychiatric care by Dr. F.S. Caprio, 1835 I St., NW, Washington, D.C. At present this disorder is of an intensity to threaten her health. In view of a combination of social and medical factors, it is my opinion it would serve the best interests of Mrs. Hostler to continue psychiatric treatment with a specialist in the U.S.A. . . . Mrs. Hostler agrees.

A.S. Manugian, M.D., D.P.M.

   In early June, 1960, the USAF arranged for a medical evacuation aircraft to take Ruby (and me and a medical nurse) from Beirut to the USAFE Hospital in Wiesbaden, Germany. At first Ruby refused to go after the plane arrived in Beirut, and it waited for several days before she concurred. We ultimately traveled together to Wiesbaden, where she was admitted for medical evaluation and treatment. Later she was placed on "out-patient" treatment status and lived at the American Arms Hotel in Wiesbaden.
   In this era in Beirut (June, 1960), there was a rash of bombings and shootings related to the Lebanese elections. However, I traveled to Germany frequently to see Ruby. In August of 1960, I bought

a Volkswagen in Germany and drove back from Germany through Yugoslavia and Greece with my son (then seven and a half years old). Our trip included a visit to the world-famous Passion Play given every ten years in July by the village of Oberamergau in Bavaria.

On November 14, 1960, following a careful exchange of reports between the USAF medical experts in Wiesbaden and Dr. A.S. Manugian in Beirut, Manugian sent me the following evaluation:

> Dear Col. Hostler:
>
> I have studied carefully the reports and the letters you submitted to me concerning Mrs. Hostler. I myself have received letters from Mrs. Hostler in Europe. . . . There is full agreement between the specialists concerning the diagnosis. Mrs. Hostler suffers from a constitutional behavioral disturbance which is at times called Psychopathic constitution. What is not clear in the Military Report is the fact that this disturbance at times takes temporary forms of severe social disturbances with psychotic intensity. I have myself witnessed several of those episodes. It is these phases which finally made me decide that for the best interests of Mrs. Hostler, her son, as well as the professional interests which Col. Hostler represented, it would be highly desirable for Mrs. Hostler to receive care away from Lebanon. This was my hope when I recommended her leaving Lebanon for treatment abroad.

Judging from the documents I have studied, I do not feel her medical condition has improved sufficiently to justify her return to Lebanon. . . .

Thus, it was eventually arranged, by mutual agreement with Ruby and all concerned, that she would remain in Wiesbaden where she had been given a secretarial job with the USAF. Charles, Jr., and I made periodic visits whenever possible, but over time it was obvious to all that our marriage relationship was unsustainable.

Ruby ultimately returned to the U.S.A. and transferred her employment to Washington, D.C. In June of 1961, my duty in Lebanon was finished, and I returned to my new assignments in the Pentagon, Washington, D.C., accompanied by Charles, Jr.

Ruby and I realized our marriage was finished but initially could not agree as to custody of Charles, Jr., which we both wanted. Ultimately, Ruby conceded that I could provide the better long-term conditions and stability for our son, and a mutual visitation agreement was arranged for him. We signed a Legal Separation and Property Settlement Agreement in March, 1961.

"Note in the Bottle" at Antiparos Island, Greece

While on leave from Beirut in July, 1960, Charles, Jr. and I took a cruise ship voyage around the Mediterranean Sea. To amuse my eight-year-old son on board, I proposed that we place a note in an empty wine bottle. Charles, Jr. wrote, "My name is Charles Hostler, Jr. Please write me in care of U.S. Embassy, Beirut." The bottle was tossed overboard, and the matter was forgotten. On August 24, 1960, a charming letter was received by mail from an 11-year-old boy, Stephanos Kalargyros, who had found the bottle. He lived on the tiny island of Antiparos (in the Cyclades island group in the Aegean Sea). The Greek boy did not speak English, so he took the note to his school teacher who kindly became the intermediary. This boy was one of 13 children, the son of a poor Greek fisherman, and they lived largely on a diet of fish and dark bread. My son responded on August 31 and corresponded a number of times with this boy, whose letters had some very pleasant things to say about the islanders' friendship and respect for the American people.

I learned that the island of Antiparos was almost directly below the air route between Beirut and Athens. The USAF had relatively frequent transport flights that passed close to this island. This situation had obvious human interest. On October 10, 1960, with the warm approval of Ambassador Robert McClintock, and in accordance with the "Military Suggestion Program," I proposed to Headquarters USAF that authorization be granted to utilize available space on an otherwise regularly scheduled USAF aircraft to parachute Christmas gifts to the island. This official authorization was approved, and voluntary gifts flowed in from the American community in Beirut, the U.S. Sixth Fleet, and the U.S. Air Force in Dhahran (particularly organized by Major General and Mrs. James C. McGehee). Foreign journalists took warm interest in this appealing "note in the bottle" story, and it spread to many newspapers and magazines. The contributions grew quickly and spontaneously to about 1,000 pounds in weight, as a personal expression of Christmas feeling largely from private Americans to a representative Greek island community.

With the close cooperation and support of the American Embassy in Athens (particularly the USAIRA, Colonel Frank Scofield, the U.S. Naval Attaché), and the Greek Embassy in Beirut (Ambassador A. Antonopoulos and Colonel C. Lianis), proper advance arrangements were made. Plans to parachute the gifts were amended because the Greek government did not want the world to think that Antiparos Island was in distress..

On December 12 the USAIRA in Cairo (Colonel Howard Bechtel), in connection with other authorized duties, transported the cargo of gifts to Athens. My son, Charles, Jr., proceeded to Athens via Olympic Airways. On December 13 the gifts were delivered to Antiparos Island in the amphibious aircraft (a SA-16) of the U.S. Naval Attaché in Athens.

The reception accorded us by the people of Antiparos Island was spontaneous and magnificent. Though the island then had a population of 606 persons, I would estimate that 500 of them were lining the shores to welcome us with banners and American and Greek flags. As was recorded in hundreds of photographs and videos by foreign reporters, we were received by flowers, speeches, and sincere greetings. It was touching and warm. After a token distribution to the Kalargyros family, the balance of the gifts were presented to the President of the Island Council for equitable distribution to the population (see photo #17).

The reaction of the news media was warm and universally favorable. The story was carried widely by Associated Press, Agence France Presse, Stars and Stripes, Greek, Arabic, Italian, English, and other newspapers. The activities were filmed by NBC-TV (for television use on the "Today" program) and by the USAF and publicized by USIS. Editorials naming the project "Operation Heart-to-Heart" lauded it as "the most heart warming story since Bobby Hills' mercy mission to Dr. Schweitzer." Friendly cards and letters came from all parts of the world. In June,1962, I was asked to write an article for *Airman Magazine* describing how a note in a bottle brought about our pleasant adventures in Antiparos.

After our successful visit to Antiparos and the presentation of the mail sacks filled with gifts, the Communal Council of Antiparos (under President/Mayor Nicolas Roussos) voted unanimously to proclaim Charles, Jr. and myself as "Honorary Citizens." This proclamation was later confirmed and approved by the Prefect of the Cyclades Island (located in Hermoupolis) on April 11, 1961.

Because of the island's beauty and the friendship of the people of Antiparos, I began a search there for a beach property as a site for a part-time vacation home. A vacant waterfront parcel was ultimately purchased, though the home was never built (largely because of my ever-changing assignments). I still own this lovely site on Antiparos.

On June 2, 1961, King Paul of Greece awarded me the "Royal Order of the Phoenix" in the grade of Grand Commander. The Order was presented in a formal ceremony by the Greek Ambassador for Greece in Lebanon in recognition of my "People to People" Christmas Mission to Antiparos Island and my cooperation with and assistance to the Greek Orthodox community in the Middle East.

As my wonderful period as U.S. Air Attaché in Beirut came to a close, we had a pleasant series of farewell parties. Charles, Jr. and I sailed from Beirut on the SS Excalibur on June 26, 1961, via Naples and Marseilles and disembarked in Genoa on July 4. We took the train from Genoa to Wiesbaden and arrived on July 6 to begin six days of debriefing at USAFE. Using my diplomatic discount, I bought a Mercedes Benz 220S in Stuttgart, Germany, and drove it to Bremerhaven for shipment to the U.S.A. We sailed from there on the USNS Patch on July 25 and arrived in New York on August 2. We drove to Washington, D.C. and stayed at the Visiting Officers Quarters at Bolling AFB. I took 20 days' leave before reporting for duty again in the Pentagon on September 8, 1961.

Chapter Seven
Washington, Geneva, Paris, Beirut,
(mid-1961 - 1966)

My new assignment in Washington was as Assistant to the Director of Disarmament in the Office of the Secretary of Defense. My superior was John T. McNaughton, Deputy Assistant Secretary for International Security Affairs.

I located a nice apartment at 4814 Kenmore Drive, Seminary Hills, Arlington, Virginia, and installed my household goods when they arrived from Beirut. The U.S. Embassy in Beirut kindly helped arrange a U.S. Immigration Visa for our loyal maid, Maria Hanna, to immigrate from Lebanon to the U.S.A. She arrived via Pan Am on September 21, 1961, and was helpful in making a home to care for young Charles during the illness of his mother, Ruby. Charles, Jr. entered the Minnie Howard Grade School in Alexandria, Virginia, and I became active as an officer of the school's Parent Teacher Association while Jr. was in fifth grade.

In November, 1961, I was fortunate to be named to be a member of the "U.S. Delegation to the Conference on Nuclear Weapons Tests" being held in Geneva, Switzerland. As the conference representative for the U.S. Department of Defense, I departed November 25, 1961, on an indefinite assignment to Geneva. I stayed at the Hotel d'Alleves at Square Kleberg in Geneva and reported to the Chief of the U.S. Delegation, Ambassador Arthur

H. Dean. The Chief of the Soviet Delegation was Semyon Tsarapkin, and the British Chief was Minister of State Joseph Godber.

Our first official meeting with the British and the Soviets took place at the UN Headquarters in Geneva on November 28, 1961. The Soviet Delegation settled in for a long stay, and we had plenary meetings about twice per week. The West (U.S. and Brits) was pushing hard for international controls on nuclear testing, but the Soviets were stalling. The main political decisions apparently were to be made in the UN General Assembly debates and in the Zorin/Adlai Stevenson talks, wherein our and their discussions would ultimately be merged.

With the slow pace of the talks, I and my colleagues, Dr. Carl Walske, Vince Baker, and others settled in to a pleasant routine of touring the area. We became "Geneva Gastronauts" and carefully sampled the fine local cuisine. Our expanding waistlines were matched by our deflating pocketbooks.

As Christmas approached the talks were at an impasse when the Soviet Delegate Tsarapkin flatly refused even to discuss international verification and control of nuclear tests. I and my U.S. colleagues flew home for Christmas in Washington, D.C. The talks were not reconvened in Geneva, and we went back to our normal duties in Washington, D.C. with fine memories of Switzerland.

For many years I had been a Member of Board of Governors of the esteemed Middle East Institute (MEI) located in Washington, D.C. and where I am now a Governor Emeritus after more than 20 years on the Board. The MEI was founded in 1946. In September of 1962, I was one of the organizers of the 16th Annual MEI Conference on the "Moslems of the U.S.S.R.," which was held at the Statler-Hilton Hotel in Washington, D.C. This was one of the first such conferences ever held on this subject. On September 29, 1962, I was the Conference's Chairman of a discussion on "National Reactions to Soviet Policies," which was presented by a panel of prominent Tatars, Azerbaijanis, Uzbeks, Tajiks, and North Caucasians. An interesting and intense scholar named Gare Le Compte was a co-director of the conference and was very intrigued with Pan-Turkism, as was the recognized British scholar Col. Geoffrey Wheeler of the *Central Asian Review*. The conference was very successful.

During 1962 and 1963, I continued my part-time duties as an Adjunct Professor in The School of International Service, American University, Washington, D.C. I taught courses entitled "The Soviet Union in the Middle East" and related subjects.

From September 4 to October 5, 1962, I participated in a U.S. Department of State Foreign Service Institute (FSI) course in counter-insurgency. In January, 1963, I taught at FSI's Interdepartmental Seminar on "Problems of Development and Internal Defense."

In July of 1962, I was transferred to the very interesting Special Operations Division of the

Policy Planning Staff of the Office of the Assistant Secretary of Defense for International Security Affairs. Our sensitive task was to develop plans and policy in relation to special operations, counter-insurgency, and cold-war action.

On July 17, 1962, I was awarded the Haitian National Order of "Honor and Merit" in the grade of Commander by the Haitian Ambassador in Washington, D.C. This was presented in recognition for my solving certain problems that arose in the Middle East and came upon the warm recommendation of His Excellency Joseph Sarkis, Haitian Minister Plenipotentiary in Lebanon.

On June 15, 1962, Charles, Jr. and I traveled together to the Panama Canal Zone on the USN's M/S "Geiger," which departed from Brooklyn. We stayed at the visiting officers quarters in Albrook AFB, Panama, and returned to the U.S.A. in July. During this period I pursued my security investments with Bache & Co. in New York City, with the continuing kind help and guidance of friend, Harry Jacobs, Jr., who was then a senior executive and ultimately CEO. His firm's research department provided a careful annual review of my account. In this era I began to explore the concept of investing in income-producing real estate such as apartment buildings and offices, which later proved to be a fortunate path.

Planning for the Future

Following my return to duty in the Pentagon, I again had the opportunity to talk and socialize with fellow USAF officers. It was clear that, unfortunately, at that period of time, the statistical record of past USAF promotions to Brig. General for non-rated (not pilots) officers was dismal, particularly for those Colonels assigned to other than Major USAF commands and who were not Academy graduates.

The thought of becoming a super-annuated Colonel with little possibility for advancement to General and endlessly trotting down Pentagon hallways became distressing. The prospects were dim even though my official Effectiveness Reports prepared by superiors consistently attested to my "outstanding" performance and stressed (a) considered judgment and initiative; (b) being an "idea man" in planning, research, and in developing better methods; and (c) my success in quickly and tactfully "getting the job done" whatever the obstacles.

I became restive at the lack of opportunity to use personal initiative in meeting official needs. In Beirut I had a considerable measure of independence and free movement, and my initiatives had been welcomed and rewarded. In the Pentagon one faced a mammoth hierarchy that demanded conformity. "Idea men" were not comfortable in this atmosphere.

At this point in time, I had accumulated over 18 years of service and was eligible to retire from the USAF in early 1963 with 20 years duty with health benefits and a 52.5% compensation rate. I would then be 44 years old. It was appealing to think of beginning a new, rewarding, and challenging life outside of the service.

Rightly or wrongly, over the period of my 20 years of active service as an OSS/CIA/USAF intelligence officer, I had come to think, and still believe, that such duty as an intelligence/"special operations" officer is not fully appreciated or recognized. Intelligence operatives in the field, perhaps because of the closed, covert nature of human intelligence, do not get the recognition, decorations, or understanding that persons in comparable fields do. Even today when I am asked by young people who are intrigued by the thought of entering this field (the CIA is even advertising in full-page ads now in the *Economist* for candidates under 35 years of age to enter the "Clandestine Services"), I recommend them against it. Enter the State Department as a FSO (Foreign Service Officer), or go into international business if you want to be more fully appreciated and compensated for your international achievements.

The U.S. intelligence agencies unfortunately have not yet learned that the optimum way to cope with terrorist groups is to penetrate the organizations involved. The obvious method to do this is to carefully insert our agents in their midst. Americans are not sympathetic to spies, but we have used them successfully in the OSS and elsewhere in the past. If we are to succeed in the war against terror, we need to again and not to be bound by a "case-file mentality."

I began to consider the possibilities of changing my life after nearly 20 interesting years in military and intelligence service. I focused on the possibility of working for the U.S. defense industry, hopefully abroad, where my background could be best utilized. Inquiries were begun discretely with appropriate U.S. defense companies so that the matter could be happily resolved by mid-March, 1963, when I could retire after 20 years service.

A New Career with Douglas Aircraft Company, Paris

On November 16, 1962, I made contact with the esteemed Donald W. Douglas, Sr., Chairman of the Board and founder of the Douglas Aircraft Company. I had been employed in 1941 at Douglas' Santa Monica plant (while working my way through UCLA on Douglas' DC3 production lines' "graveyard shift"). A reply was received from Charles Warren Hutton, then Assistant to the Vice President, General Manager. Through him I was introduced to Jack Shaver, International Sales Manager for the Douglas Missile and Space Systems Division, and Croy Hartley, Director of International Military Sales, whom I met in the Douglas Corporate office in Santa Monica, California, on February 8, 1963. Through the years Charles Warren Hutton and I have remained close friends. Because our names were quite similar, he was known within Douglas as "Charlie Hu," while I was "Charlie Ho."

Though I had offers from other large defense corporations, the one from Douglas Aircraft was by far the most interesting to me personally. My initial assignment was to Paris to represent them in Europe and the Middle East in the international marketing of their military aircraft and equipment. Thus, I applied to the USAF for voluntary retirement effective April 30, 1963, and was credited with 21 years of service for retirement purposes. A fine retirement party was held on April 23 with a reception at the Army & Navy Country Club in Arlington, Virginia, attended by about 150 friends and associates. It was arranged for me to travel first to Santa Monica, California, to undertake briefings and orientations in the various Douglas plants and offices before settling into residence in Paris about the first week in September, 1963.

My work for Douglas was specifically to promote the international sales of the A4D-5 and A4E Navy Skyhawk aircraft, the application of the Thor-Delta satellite launch system to the European Space Research Organization (ESRO), the non-nuclear version of the GENIE rocket, as well as other accessory equipment. I worked in Paris with Michael E. Oliveau, Jr. His father, in Geneva, Michael Oliveau, Sr., was the European V.P. for Douglas. Our tasks included maintaining liaison, market analyses, and sales negotiation with foreign defense ministries, scientific and research agencies, universities, and related industries throughout Europe, the Middle East, and Africa. It also involved professional and social responsibilities in Paris, which meant entertaining important clients who visited the City of Lights. This was fun and gave me the opportunity to experience all of the great restaurants and night-clubs in Paris, at company expense. During the Paris Air Show (every two years) the entertaining became truly hectic, and then on alternate years the Farnborough Air Show took us to London for similar activities.

One of my superiors in Douglas was B.F. "Sandy" Coggan (and his wife, Bonnie), V.P. for Operations, with whom I made a number of long international trips to Africa and the Middle East. We also became life-long friends and investment associates. The Coggans lived in retirement in nearby La Jolla, California, until Sandy's death in 1999.

The Crosthwaite Family

My mother's sister, Mahoney, was married to Major Cecil Crosthwaite, MBE, the son of Sir William Crosthwaite, who had bravely and tenaciously assembled a monopoly of tugs and salvage ships on the Tees River in North Yorkshire, England. Sir William was knighted by the Queen for being Lord Mayor of Middlesborough and for faithfully guiding the Conservative Party in Northern England. Sir William was a bluff and independent Northerner but was kind to me. When I was living in Paris, Sir William (at the age of 84) took me to meet his French friend Jean Valby, the Grand Chancellor of the world renowned "Confrerie de la Chaine des Rotisseurs," arguably the world's leading organization of gourmets and chefs. Mr. Valby brought this organization (originating in the year 1248) back to vibrant life in 1950 as a much-sought honor for gourmets and chefs worldwide. Through Mr. Valby I was invested as an Officer of the Confrerie in 1965 at a ceremony in Switzerland and was later active again in the Chaine des Rotisseurs chapter in Bahrain.

As a youth for two years I had attended Sir William Turner's Coatham School located on the North Sea in Redcar, England. This was a typical British boys boarding school, with tough discipline (which included paddling with boards and canes) and requiring attendance at sessions in two different Anglican churches each Sunday. At 12 or 13 years old the boys were reasonably tolerant to the only Yank in their midst, though when I suggested that we save money by buying in bulk our "tuck" of goodies, cookies and candy, I was told scornfully that they were "not in trade," and the idea was rejected.

The Crosthwaites lived fairly nearby in their spacious and beautiful Langbaraugh Hall estate. I was made welcome there on week-ends and holidays. The close-by village of Great Ayton had been the home of the famous 18th-century sailor Captain James Cook. In later years when my son went to a similar boarding school (Branksome-Hilders in Haslemere, Surrey), he was also made equally welcome at Langbaraugh Hall by the Crosthwaites. Cecil used to arrange for me to also be a guest on the fine seagoing vessels of the Tees Towing Company, and I frequently enjoyed traveling out to sea on the working tugs. Coming on board, one was always given a huge mug of steaming British tea containing about 50% milk, which has since always been my "cup of tea."

During WWII when I was in England receiving OSS, training with MI-6, the British Intelligence Service, Cecil was stationed in London as a major in the Royal Signal Corps. He and Mahoney had a pleasant London apartment located at Campden Hills Court. When the German bombings became seriously destructive, followed by the terrible V1s and V2s, Mahoney and her children were sent to the relative safety of North Yorkshire.

Cecil kindly took me under his wing as his young American cousin in wartime London. He introduced me to a number of his friends (like the fine Jeremy Pemberton living in Albany, Picadilly, whom I still see in London), associates, and clubs (like the Conservative Club on Saint James Street). On various occasions he kindly made his apartment available to me. In one horrible period Cecil's building was hit by a German aerial bomb while he was standing near the building's entry, and he was blown to the rear and injured, fortunately not gravely.

After the war, the Crosthwaites returned to their influential life in North Yorkshire. In the 1970s a new County called Cleveland was created within North Yorkshire. Cecil was given the great honor of being Her Majesty's Lord Lieutenant and "Custos Rotulorum" for Cleveland County. This meant that Cecil was the Queen's representative for official and ceremonial matters in that county.

On the occasion of Queen Elizabeth's Silver Jubilee tour around England, she traveled on board her royal yacht Britannia to Cleveland County (see photo #22). It was exciting for me to receive an engraved invitation from the Master of the Household of Queen Elizabeth the Second, to a reception to be given by the Queen and the Duke of Edinburgh on board H.M. Yacht Britannia at Tees Dock, Grangetown, Middlesbrough, on Thursday, July 14, 1977, at 10 p.m. I was instructed to reply to the Master of the Household, Buckingham Palace. Guests were asked to arrive between 9:40 p.m. and 10 p.m. The dress code was "black tie or lounge suit."

When I arrived on board the Britannia there were perhaps 200 guests, largely local dignitaries (mayors, industrialists, and so on). Upon the emergence of Her Majesty and Duke Philip into the entertainment area, they wisely split forces (that is, they proceeded in opposite directions) to greet the many guests on deck.

Circling around the deck Prince Philip (then called the Duke of Edinburgh) engaged me in conversation, as I was one of the few foreigners on board. He asked me what I was doing in Yorkshire. I tried to give him a straightforward reply. Prince Philip has had a long-time reputation of being an impatient and outspoken bully-type with a forceful personality. I encountered this plain-spoken tendency of his when, apparently dissatisfied with my answer, he said brashly, "It sounds like some kind of a fiddle to me," implying an untruth, and moved on through the guests.

The Queen, however, was quite different. When I encountered Her Majesty she was very pleasant, engaging, and interested. We had a conversation of about five minutes that involved eye contact and enjoyable substance, largely about U.S.-British relationships during WWII. In 1977 Cecil kindly sent me a massive official certificate saying, ". . . By Virtue of the Power and Authority vested in me and with the approbation of Her Majesty Queen Elizabeth the Second, I do hereby constitute and appoint you to be Deputy Lieutenant of and for the County of Cleveland in an Honorary Capacity."

After Cecil's death, his son Richard Crosthwaite was appointed High Sheriff of Cleveland in the 1980s and, of course, inherited the lovely Langbaraugh Hall in Great Ayton. He and his wife Judy were equally hospitable until Richard's untimely death in the crash of his motor-powered aerial glider (from which he had taken of beautiful photos, later published in books, of Cleveland's historical areas) (see photo #23).

As plans with Douglas Aircraft firmed for my extended residence in Paris, I began seeking the best solution for preparatory schooling in Europe for Charles, Jr. (he was then 11 years old). Correspondence was begun with well-known schools like Gordonstown School in Moray, Scotland (which then 14-year-old Prince Charles was attending, and his father Prince Philip had earlier attended), Aiglon College in Switzerland, and finally focused on Branksome-Hilders School in Haslemere, Surrey, England. After a visit with Charles, Jr. to Branksome-Hilders, arrangements were made for him to begin preparatory school there on September 24, 1963. Also, he was registered for a future start at the Senior School at Gordonstown in Scotland beginning in September, 1965. We went together in August to the well-known school outfitter Frederick Gorringe, Ltd. on Buckingham Palace Road in London to outfit Charles, Jr. with the proper blazers, soccer and cricket uniforms, and equipment he would need at Branksome-Hilders.

He settled into school well. I visited him on October 9-10, 1963. At the end of the term he traveled to Paris, and I eagerly met him at Le Bourget Airport on December 20 for Christmas holidays. On December 27 Charles, Jr. and I went for a grand skiing vacation at the Val D'Isere (Savoie) until January 5, 1964.

In the interim I had located a nice new apartment (after much searching) directly on the Seine River at 11 Quai Paul Doumer, Courbevoie (Seine) across the river from Pont Neuilly in Paris. It had a lovely view of the Seine, two bedrooms, and a den/study. Maria, our Lebanese maid, arrived in Paris at the end of September from the U.S.A.

During this period a divorce was proceeding by mutual agreement with Ruby. On June 27, 1963, the divorce was granted by the Corporation Court of the City of Alexandria, Virginia, on the grounds of "having lived separate and apart for three years." Sole care, custody, and control of Charles, Jr. was granted to me, with the exception of one month per year with his mother during vacation. A lump sum was paid to Ruby at her request in lieu of alimony.

I attended the Prize-Giving and Concert at Branksome-Hilders School on March 1, 1964, and was pleased that Charles, Jr. had moved up to #2 position in his class and had earned a "red mark" for improvement. I sent him to the Centre Linguistique de Niege at Tende (Alpes Maritime) in order to improve his French and skiing from March 26 to April 9. From June 5 to 9 he spent vacation time with the Crosthwaites at Langbaraugh Hall in Great Ayton. Early August, 1964, he spent vacationing with me at Sveti Stefan and Dubrovnik in Croatia exploring and doing underwater speargun fishing. He went on vacation via Pan Am to see his mother in Virginia from August 20 to September 7. Charles, Jr. had an interesting and exciting year.

International Activities for Douglas Aircraft

In May of 1963 I departed on my first extended trip for Douglas by traveling to Lebanon, Saudi Arabia, and Kuwait with Russ Denzer and others. I arranged for them to call on President Chehab in Lebanon, HRH the Prince Sultan, Saudi Minister of Defense and Aviation in Jidda, and our agent Morad Behbehani (and his four brothers) in Kuwait concerning the sale of Skyhawk military aircraft. In October, 1963, I returned again to these countries to orient and introduce Croy Hartley, Director of International Military Sales for Douglas.

In October, 1963, I was accepted as a candidate for a "Doctor of the University" degree at the University of Paris in the Faculty of Letters and Human Sciences. My dissertation was to be on "Research of the Contemporary Druze People." The Druze are a unique Muslim sect located mostly in Lebanon, Syria, Israel, and Jordan. On November 29 there was a large strike and manifestation by students and others against the University of Paris. The almost incessant traveling and entertaining that I had to do for Douglas Aircraft made it almost impossible to make any progress on my dissertation. Ultimately, I sadly had to abandon the Sorbonne project when we moved to Beirut.

Confrerie des Chevaliers du Tastevin

On June 11 and 12, 1965, Mr. Donald M. Douglas, Jr. and his lovely wife, Jean, along with their

174

friends Robert S. Bell (President of Packard-Bell Electronics), his wife Carolyn, and a chauffeur drove us to Burgundy to attend the Chapitre d'Ete of the Confrerie des Chevaliers du Tastevin at the Chateau du Clos de Vougeot. We stayed at the Hotel de la Cloche in Dijon. Don was promoted to "Commander du Tastevin." Mr. and Mrs. Douglas were attending the Paris Air Show, and we arranged for the wonderful Jacques and Eleanor Chevignard (he was the esteemed Grand Chamberlain of the world renowned Confrerie des Chevaliers du Tastevin) to visit the Douglas Chalet at the Air Show at Le Bourget Airfield on June 18, 1965. I have now been a loyal member of the Chevaliers du Tastevin since 1964 and enjoy visiting the Chateau du Clos de Vougeot now as a "Grand Officer."

Before the drive back from Burgundy to Paris on Sunday, June 13, we had a marvelous wine-tasting at the caves of Marc Missery at Nuit-St-Georges and a superb lunch at the "three starred" (per Guide Michelin) Coq d'Or restaurant at Saulieu. The car was loaded with cases of fine Burgundy wine. During our time in Burgundy, we were entertained by Bernard N. Grivelet, who feted us at his beautiful Chateau de Chambolle-Musigny in the Cote d'Or, not far from the Chateau du Clos de Vougeot. He later visited Beirut and the U.S.A. and explored the idea of selling his chateau (now called the Chateau Ziltener) and wine business in the Cote d'Or.

In 1992 I was asked to "preside," giving a speech in French at the Chateau (see photo #36). On June 4, 1994, the Chevaliers du Tastevin commemorated the 50th anniversary of D-Day (see photo #37) in the presence of Grand Chamberlain Jacques Chevignard and his wonderful American wife Eleanor and son Louis-Marc. We have been close friends now for almost 40 years.

Because of the social responsibilities (and pleasures as a wine-taster and gourmet) of my tasks in Paris, I also joined the American Club of Paris, the TNT Club, the U.S. Aerospace Industry Club, the Confrerie de la Chaine de Rotisseurs, and other pleasant organizations. While I loved my exciting life in Paris, it was crowded, expensive, and hectic, particularly since I was traveling a great deal and frequently to the Middle East.

Madame Suzanne Bonnier was a cultured pleasant French divorcee whom I was fortunate to have as a friend in Paris, and she later visited me in Greece and Lebanon. She was very helpful in expanding my understanding of French art, culture, and mores.

Back to Beirut

By November of 1964, Douglas Aircraft realized that the tempo of their business potential, and the volume of my travel to the Middle East made it wise for them to establish a regional headquarters in Beirut, Lebanon.. In March of 1965 this was accomplished, and I opened an office for Douglas Aircraft in suite #N809 of the well-known Starco Building in downtown Beirut. My role was as Regional Manager for the Middle East and Africa. Thus, I was responsible for activities in the area from Greece through India as well as Africa. To assume my new post I moved from Paris to Venice by train in February, 1965, and then went by ship, the SS Esperia, from Venice to Beirut. Both the office in the Starco Building and my apartment (in the new Malas Building, Talaat Americaine St., Mamara, Ras Beirut) had lovely views of the Eastern Mediterranean Sea.

My duties took me frequently to India and especially Bangalore, New Delhi, Bombay, and Agra. I remember that in those days in order to drink alcohol foreigners had to apply for a Liquor Permit, which authorized one to "buy, possess, and consume bottled liquor" in India. One objective of Douglas Aircraft at the time was to negotiate a licensing agreement with Hindustan Aeronautics, Ltd. in Bangalore to co-produce in India the new DC-9 jetliner and the A4E military Skyhawk for the Indian Navy, along with ejection seats and bomb-racks. I dealt principally with Air Vice Marshal Ranjon Dutt, Managing Director of Hindustan Aeronautics, Ltd.

Charles, Jr. wanted to return to Beirut and to attend the American Community School in September, 1965, so he did not re-enroll in his British school. Maria, our maid, returned to Lebanon to help us, but she missed her life in the U.S.A. It was very pleasant tolive in Lebanon. However, I was traveling almost constantly to Saudi Arabia, Kuwait, Greece, Turkey, Egypt, Africa, Pakistan, India, and elsewhere. In May, 1965, I was elected as President of the Association of U.S. Aerospace Industry Representatives in the Middle East (AUSAIRME), which met monthly in Beirut.

On November 29, 1965, I went to Washington, D.C. to be a guest-participant in the White House Conference on International Cooperation (on the Aviation Panel). While there. I had the opportunity to renew my friendship with G. Griffith Johnson, Executive V/P of the Motion Picture Export Association of America, and the delightful Leo Hochstetter, then their representative in Rome, one of the world's most amusing fellows and a long-time friend dating from WWII activities in the Balkans.

After two previous tours of duty in beautiful Lebanon, my return for the third period in February of 1965 was most satisfying. There were so many good friends in Lebanon. We had a grand "office inauguration" on June 2 with the Coggans and Mike Oliveau, Sr. present.

One of our biggest competitive battles on behalf of Douglas Aircraft involved the potential sales of five new commercial DC-8 jets to Middle East Airlines (MEA). The purchase decision was to be made in part by Sheikh Najib Alamuddin, CEO of the airline. This crucial decision would probably determine whether British aircraft would retain their, until then, dominant position among the airlines of the Middle East or whether the rapidly growing airlines of Saudi Arabia, Egypt, Jordan, and the Arabian Gulf, would shift to American manufacturers (Boeing or Douglas). The competition was fierce, and the British government pushed hard for the VC-10 aircraft. Entrepreneur Yusuf Beidas, head of Intra Bank, was the Chairman of Middle East Airlines and was also key in the decision, which ultimately involved MEA buying three of our stretched Super DC-8 jets (with an option for two more) in February, 1966. It was then called "the hardest fought battle in the history of commercial aviation."

In those days Beirut was "where the action was." Beirut's Phoenician traders had been busy making money for the past 3,500 years, but in the 1965-66 era Gulf oil money made Lebanon the general store and financial factotum for the entire Arab Middle East. Beirut was then the Midle East's supermarket, bank, middleman, and touristic Fun City.

In April of 1966, Douglas Aircraft began having corporate financial difficulties, and later merger discussions began with the McDonnell Aircraft Corporation, which ultimately created the McDonnell-Douglas Corporation, with its headquarters in St. Louis, Missouri.

The Chairman, John S. McDonnell, was an able and canny Scotsman who was adverse to spending money on overseas international offices. He quickly made it clear that most of the costly offices abroad would be closed as part of a tighter financial regime for McDonnell-Douglas. As a result, the Beirut office and most other Douglas offices abroad were closed in June, 1966, and I was transferred to a position with the Missiles and Space Systems Division in Huntington Beach, California.

On June 17, 1966, Charles, Jr. and I left Beirut for the return trip to California via an interesting two-week journey through the Far East. We stopped in Bombay (Taj Mahal Hotel), Bangkok (Erawan Hotel), Hong Kong (Hong Kong Hilton), Taipei (Grand Hotel), Tokyo (Okura Hotel), and Honolulu (Surfrider Hotel). In Tokyo we both were entertained by Mitsubishi Heavy Industries at a delightful Geisha restaurant.

My new work at Douglas MSSD in Huntington Beach, California, was in the field of aerospace systems analysis, which involved international studies and threat analysis. I provided studies and briefings and worked closely with the U.S. Department of Defense, the U.S. Arms Control and Disarmament Agency, and the U.S. State Department.

It was a pleasure to lease a sunny house on the Grand Canal of Balboa Island, part of Newport Beach, California, and about a 20-minute drive to Huntington Beach. My household goods were shipped back from Beirut and with the faithful help of Maria, we finally were installed in our new home. Charles, Jr. was then eligible to begin high school, and he enrolled in Corona Del Mar High School. It was a new life—back again in California.

Chapter Eight
Business Endeavors and Public Service
(1966 - 1989)

Life in California beginning in 1966 was enjoyable, and my work at McDonnell Douglas Missile and Space Systems Division (MSSD) was interesting but did not involve the earlier high level of business travel. Therefore, I had time for social, political, business, and yachting activities in the nearby lovely town of Newport Beach.

Through my fellow Colonel USAF-retired, Ted Erb, I met his vivacious and delightful neighbor, Patricia Consuelo Spielman, recently widowed. Patty was lively and eager for life. She told Ted and others in semi-jest that for the person who introduced her to a man whom she would marry, she would arrange for that person's entire house to be re-carpeted, since she had inherited the substantial RHS Carpet Mill from her late husband.

Later at a barbeque party at Ted Erb's home in Newport Beach, I met Patty. About a year later, we were married in Las Vegas, Nevada. We purchased a bayfront home at 120 Via Lido Nord on Lido Isle in Newport Beach. We moved in with a full household composed of Patty, her two daughters, Debbie and Suzie, myself, Charles, Jr., and Maria, our faithful maid. The five-bedroom house was on Newport Bay, almost opposite the Balboa Bay Club. We bought a new 25-foot power boat for jaunts around the local area, including Catalina Island on occasions.

After several years in our Lido Isle house, Charles, Jr., Debbie, and Suzie went off to college, marriage, and other pursuits. Patty, I, and Maria were left alone in this quite large house. Patty, who enjoyed daily socializing and card-playing with her lady friends, felt it would be appropriate for us to sell the large house and to move into the nearby Balboa Bay Club, which we did.

I became active in various personal business ventures in real estate and in the founding of the Irvine National Bank in 1973. I was the Chairman of the Board of this interesting venture for which we obtained a national charter from the Federal Government (see photo #19). Irvine, California, immediately adjacent to Newport Beach, was just emerging as an active business center, and the timing was right. The bank was successful, and after several years we sold out profitably to a larger financial entity.

In this period, I purchased my first apartment building (44 units) as an investment in Anaheim, California, with the advice and guidance of astute Mr. M. Douglas, who was in partnership with equally capable Jerrold Glass and David Stone. They organized Income Properties Service (IPS), which became a great success later known as Western National Property Management, Inc., and with whom I am still actively involvedas a client. It has always been a sound and trusting relationship, and they now manage or own approximately 34,000 apartment units.

I became involved in political fund-raising on the Orange County Committee to Re-elect President Nixon in 1972. As Chairman for Special Events under County Chairman Vic Andrews, I organized 150 privately owned yachts to parade in a "Salute to the President" in Newport Bay on September 17, 1972. The parade was enormously successful and was followed by a private reception for participants at the Balboa Bay Club. More than 1,300 persons (at $100 or more each) attended, along with movie personalities including John Wayne, Buddy Ebsen, Desi Arnaz, George Burns, Eva Gabor, and others. It was a big and time-consuming project but was fun-filled, particularly since Orange County was enthusiastically a Republican area. I was an active member of Orange County's Lincoln Club and enjoyed the relationships. We raised about $150,000 for the President in the Boat Parade alone. During the Boat Parade I rode on the yacht *Toh-Be-Kin* belonging to Senator Barry Goldwater, who had an apartment at the Balboa Bay Club. The Senator arrived late from Arizona, and when he rushed on board he incorrectly had been given the impression that this was to be a fund-raiser for the Boy Scouts. He looked at all the liquor and wryly commented, "Things have certainly changed since I was a Boy Scout." As the tempo and success of my private investments increased, my interest and commitment to McDonnell-Douglas naturally diminished until I finally resigned and devoted full attention to my personal financial matters.

I was asked in 1973 to coordinate the enthusiastic group from Orange County attending the Nixon Presidential Inaugural in Washington, D.C.

from January 17 to 21. Receptions, balls, concerts, and parties galore in Washington, D.C. provided Patty and me an exciting opportunity to meet prominent personalities and have fun. In December, 1973, I made a delightful trip to Mexico on board the M/V Nesco, the pleasant yacht owned by Bob and Betty Simley.

In 1973, after five years of marriage, my relationship with Patty unfortunately began to disintegrate. We had traveled together to Europe, the Burgundy Tastevin (in June, 1970), Italy, Greece, and elsewhere and in general had very pleasant times. Our basic interests, however, were quite different. Patty enjoyed daily socializing and her Rolls-Royce and many colored fur coats. I was probably too serious, studious, and reserved to match her interests. We were amicably divorced in Santa Ana, California. Patty is now retired in Palm Desert, California, and recently celebrated her 84th birthday. She never re-married.

Deputy Assistant Secretary for International Commerce

In early 1974, I was asked by Nixon's White House Office of Personnel if I would be interested in a presidential appointment. In July of 1974, I joined the Bureau of International Commerce in the U.S. Department of Commerce. Effective on August 11, 1974, I was appointed as Deputy Assistant Secretary for International Commerce and as U.S. National Export Expansion Coordinator. This also entailed being Director of the Bureau of International Commerce (BIC), which had some 600 employees in the U.S.A. and abroad. The job was challenging and involved a great deal of international travel promoting U.S. export expansion and providing assistance to U.S. business with trade missions, trade centers abroad, and importantly, with international economic and commercial data.

I was fortunate to be able to lease an apartment in Prospect House (1200 Nash St.) in Arlington, Virginia, which overlooked the Potomac River and the Lincoln Memorial. On July 4, 1976, I gave a large "Apartment Warming and View of the Fireworks Party" to inaugurate the place. Quite often I was invited to the White House for black-tie functions by President Nixon, and later President Gerald Ford, such as upon the visit of the Emperor and Empress of Japan (October 2, 1975), HM King Hussein and Queen Alia of Jordan (March 30, 1976), and on board the Presidential yacht "The Sequoia" and at literally hundreds of foreign embassy functions.

The BIC operated the U.S. Trade Centers abroad (including those in London, Paris, Mexico City, Tokyo, and Rome). We handled the U.S. participation in the Paris Air Show, the Farnborough Air Show, and U.S. International Trade Shows throughout the world. I was also the Department of Commerce's representative on the U.S.-Iranian Commission, the U.S.-Saudi Commission on Economic Cooperation, and the U.S.-Tunisian Joint Commission (see photo #20). The Bureau of International Commerce participated in the Ghana International Trade Fair in Accra, February of 1976. I was kindly invited to stay three days at the residence of Ambassador Shirley Temple Black (the talented grown-up actress Shirley Temple) and her husband, Charles, a pleasant marine biologist (see photo #21). On this visit to Ghana I had quite frequent interaction with the then Ghanaian Minister of Tourism, Kofi Annan, who later became the two-term Secretary General of the United Nations. As my superiors, I was honored to work with the Hon. Elliot Richardson, Hon. James Baker III (whom I later had as my chief when he was the Secretary of State), Hon. Fred Dent, Hon. John K. Tabor, and many others.

E Systems and Cairo

It became obvious that Jimmy Carter was going to be elected as our new President, and I chose to resign my commerce position in August, 1976. I had been offered an interesting job in the Middle East, resident in Cairo as Regional Vice President for Middle East and Africa for E Systems, Inc., which was headquartered in Dallas, Texas. I covered the 64 countries of Africa and the Middle East promoting E-Systems' high technology electronic and aircraft equipment and service. E-Systems also operated the sensitive, high technology, border-alert system to keep the peace in the Sinai peninsula between Egypt and Israel.

Cairo was an interesting place to live. I joined the famous Gezira Sporting Club and enjoyed life in Cairo between frequent business travel. I resided in a lovely high-rise apartment on the Nile River in Giza, which by chance was delicately located immediately next door to one of the palaces (a large, two-story garden mansion) of President Anwar Sadat. President Nixon had presented Sadat with a U.S. helicopter, which Sadat used to swoop into landings at his Nile palace. It could be heard approaching from a great distance, and I and my guests often rushed to my apartment windows, cameras in hand, to photograph Sadat and his guests as they arrived. This was annoying to President Sadat's alert Secret Police guards, who complained to the U.S. Ambassador (Herman Eilts) that an American was taking potentially sensitive photos. I was called into the Embassy by the Ambassador, who interrogated me closely as to whether I still represented CIA. I told him firmly and truthfully that I did not and that I would try to prevent guests from photographing. This did not satisfy the Egyptian Secret Service or the U.S. Ambassador. They began pressuring me to move to another residence. Since Cairo was terribly crowded and some of the population of the city was poverty-stricken, with people sleeping in the streets, the prospect of moving was not appealing. In the meanwhile, my business interests in California were thriving and demanding more of my time than I could allocate from Cairo. Therefore, in June, 1977, I resigned from E Systems and returned to

California. I located myself in beautiful San Diego, where certain of my commercial-industrial properties were situated that required attention.

San Diego and Public Service in California

In February of 1978 after my move from Cairo to San Diego, California, I purchased a 48-foot Grand Banks diesel trawler pleasure cruiser. At the time a very popular TV series, recently revived, called "Charlie's Angels," with three lovely ladies in the cast, was in great public favor so I chose "Charlie's Angel" as the official name of the yacht. It was a roomy boat with three cabins, and for a while I lived on board at a slip at Frasier's Dock on Shelter Island in San Diego.

In early April, 1978, I transported a scientific group from the valuable Hubbs-Sea World Research Institute studying nocturnal sea birds and pelicans to Mexico's Coronado Islands. Many trips were made to Catalina Island and along the Californian and Mexican coast. From April 21 to June, 1978, I took a long cruise from San Diego to Isla Cedros, Cabo San Lucas, La Paz, Mazatlan, and Acapulco in Mexico with a group of friends. The fun of the boat lasted about three years. As it gradually turned into a burden of maintenance and paperwork, it was finally sold.

In December, 1979, I took an enjoyable vacation flight to Portugal including Lisbon, the Algarve, Madeira Island, Funchal, and elsewhere. In the same era I purchased a condominium in Pacific Beach, California, at the top of the 12-story Capri-By-The-Sea building directly on a popular beach on the fringes of La Jolla.

I was appointed by the Governor of the State of California to be a Public Member of the California Contractors State License Board. I served from 1973 to 1979, and in 1982 and 1983 was re-appointed by a Republican and then by a Democratic (Jerry Brown) Governor. This was an interesting board that met for about two days per month usually in different parts of the State. It involved close liaison with the various building contractor associations and regulated the activities of all of the about 300,000 contractors licensed in California. I was elected as chairman for a year. This was my initial contact with interesting friends who included Reed Sprinkel, Sam Abdulaziz, Al Conahan, Armand Fontaine, and Dan Larsen.

After completing eight years on the State Contractors License Board, I was selected by Governor Deukmejian for a four-year term as a member of the prestigious California State Parks and Recreation Commission in 1983. This was a pleasant and engaging duty, which involved visits to most of the over 280 unique California Parks and Beaches under the control of the Commission (including over one million acres of California's most beautiful and irreplaceable ocean, beaches, forests, lakes, deserts, missions, and museums). In 1987 I was re-appointed by Governor Deukmejian to a second four-year term but necessarily resigned in 1989 when I was appointed as a U.S. ambassador.

On September 15, 1989, the Commission passed a Resolution that said, in part, "Charles W. Hostler has served with great dedication, commitment, and leadership on this Commission since September, 1983 . . . and as Chairman for the year 1985-86 term, and because of his effective leadership, his keen perception, and sense of fairness, he skillfully guided the Commission through many sensitive decisions . . . and took the initiative to participate in Basic Visitor Services Training (Ranger Training) at the Mott Training Center, the only Commissioner to receive training at this facility . . . Therefore the Commission and Director commend Charles W. Hostler for his outstanding dedication and service to the Commission and present to him the *Golden Bear Award*, the highest honor given by the Commission and the Department."

In 1979 I was also appointed as the Public Commissioner of the Local Agency Formation Commission (LAFCO) for San Diego County. While being on the above State Commissions I also simultaneously served for ten years on LAFCO for San Diego County (1979-1989) and was twice elected as Chairman of the LAFCO Commission. I also left this commission upon being appointed as U.S. Ambassador in 1989. A plaque was presented to me by the Hon. Susan Golding, Chairman of the County Board of Supervisors, for "A Decade of Service as a Commissioner." This LAFCO commission is composed of two elected County Supervisors, two Mayors of cities within San Diego County, two heads of County local agency or utility boards, and one public member (myself) elected by the other members. The function of the Commission was to meet once a month to settle questions relating to the boundaries, functions, and jurisdictions of the various cities, towns, and local agencies.

In this period, at the suggestion of my fine UCLA fraternity brother, Milton Shedd (and his lovely former UCLA Homecoming Queen wife, Peggy), I became a long-time supporter of the Hubbs-Sea World Research Institute. The Institute has done great work in the field of marine mammals and marine-ecology research and has established a fish hatchery facility in Carlsbad, California. Milt had been a founder and CEO of Sea World and was honored in 1998 by UCLA for his professional achievements before his death in 2002.

I continued to focus on a successful commercial industrial real-estate investment program as part of the Hostler Investment Company and the Hostler Leasing Company. In conjunction with B.F. "Sandy" Coggan, we formed the Pacific Southwest Capital Corporation. In order properly to prepare myself for the increasingly more complex intricacies of the real estate field, I realized that more formal training and a California State Real Estate Brokers License were needed so in 1976 I entered evening classes at Mesa College, a part of the San Diego Evening College system, to take classes in the field of real estate. On June 9, 1978, I received the degree of Associate in Arts in Real Estate and their Certificate of Proficiency in Real Estate. This qualified me to take the examination for a California State Real Estate Brokers License, which I acquired on February 14, 1979. Every four years, I have taken the required Continuing Education Courses, and my license was renewed until February, 2007, when I would be 87 years old. Though I did not practice as a real estate broker, I found it useful and challenging to maintain an active and valid license in the expanding world of real estate investment which I was pursuing successfully.

People to People International (PTPI)

I was introduced to the productive People to People International organization by a long-time friend, Ambassador Julian (with his lovely wife Peg) Niemcyzk. Jay and I were fellow WWII OSS veterans, USAF colonels, and U.S. ambassadors. Jay was U.S. ambassador to Czechoslovakia from 1986 to 1989. I was fortunate to be a guest at the magnificent Ambassadorial Residence in Prague during their tenure there.

Jay also had been the Chief Executive Officer of PTPI from 1983 to 1986 where I visited him at their headquarters in Kansas City, Missouri. PTPI had been founded by President Dwight Eisenhower in 1956 as a new citizen initiative by the U.S. Information Agency (USIA). Its purpose is to advance international understanding, tolerance, and world peace through direct people-to-people contacts and travel. Through the help of Joyce Hall (of Hallmark Cards) and others it is today a thriving private, not-for-profit organization headquartered in Kansas City. Its current CEO is Mary Jean Eisenhower, the very talented and dedicated granddaughter of President Eisenhower.

I was impressed with PTPI and first became an active member and Trustee about 1985. I was on the Board of Directors from 1993 to 2001 and served as Vice Chairman and Chairman of the Board. On completion of my term as Chairman of the Board in 2001 in Aalborg, Denmark, Mary Eisenhower as CEO of PTPI presented me with the Eisenhower Distinguished Service Award (see photo #76) and PTPI's Outstanding Leadership Award. I have enjoyed interacting with fine persons like Mayor Richard Berkeley, Ruth Heinz Carpenter, William Dawson, William Jarvis, Ambassador Ted Britton, Jr., Shirley Brooks-Jones, William Tucker, and Peter Tage of Denmark. It has been my pleasure to lead about 12 PTPI "Missions in Understanding" (MIUs) to countries such as Egypt, Morocco, Yemen, Bahrain, Saudi Arabia, Kuwait, Cuba, the Galapagos Islands, Vietnam, and Cambodia. These have been skillfully scheduled and arranged by Marc and Sandy Bright and Peter and John Ueberroth of Ambassador Programs located in Spokane, Washington (which is licensed by PTPI).

International Executive Service Corps (IESC)

One great and very satisfying way I found to fulfill my love of foreign travel and adventure, while simultaneously accomplishing useful international public services, was through an extremely valuable and worthwhile organization called the International Executive Service Corps (IESC). Based in Stamford, Connecticut, IESC receives U.S. Aid government grants, as well as funding from foundations and private sources, to provide developing foreign countries with technical assistance. Likening it to the Peace Corps, some have jokingly called it the Paunch Corps, since the majority of their volunteers are retired persons. Their services, normally involving one to three months on each assignment, are purely voluntary. The dedicated President of IESC is Hobart "Hobe" Gardiner, a retired Mobil Oil Vice President.

The men and women selected by IESC not only serve as advisors on short-term assignments overseas but help to implement business improvements abroad. They provide required assistance and develop guidelines that the foreign client can follow in the future. A former U.S. Under-Secretary of State has remarked, "The volunteers of IESC are playing a role in the gravest long-range problem we face today: the challenge of bridging the gap between the industrialized world and the developing countries."

The many different projects I successfully completed were located in 17 different countries. I also located and signed clients for 178 other foreign projects for IESC to undertake in the following countries: Singapore, Portugal, Tunisia, Senegal, Ivory Coast, Sierra Leone, Cameroon, Liberia, Zimbabwe, Kenya, Somalia, Morocco,

Gaza, Yemen, Nepal, Bahrain, and Russia. I also served as IESC Field Associate for San Diego/Imperial Counties. In 1995 IESC presented me with the David Rockefeller (who was the founder and first Chairman of IESC) "Spirit of Service Award." This was primarily in recognition of my initiating successful activity as the very first IESC representative in difficult, underdeveloped and needy areas like Yemen, Zimbabwe, Nepal, West Bank, and Gaza.

I had the good fortune to be a guest at five of the yearly summer get-togethers at the unique Bohemian Grove and stayed at the pleasant Owlers Camp, which is located among the towering redwood trees of Northern California. On July 28, 1993, I was asked to give a speech on "Desert Storm's Aftermath" at a Lakeside Talk at the Bohemian Grove Encampment. I encountered the renowned philanthropist and financier David Rockefeller several times among the many distinguished guests at the Bohemian Grove and had an opportunity to discuss with him the fine work of IESC. He remarked, "Of all the many things in my life, I am proudest of having founded and nourished the IESC." When I told him of my having received the David Rockefeller award, he said, "Send me the document and I will be pleased to write a personal message on it." I did. He inscribed, "Congratulations, Charles, on your outstanding service. David Rockefeller."

Prince Henri Paleologo

In the summer of 1983 I met Prince Henri Constantine III Paleologue and his charming wife, Princess Françoise of Cannes, France. Prince Henri is a descendant of the Imperial House of the Emperors of Byzantium. This led to my becoming a member of the Grand Sovereign Dynastic Hospitaller Order of Saint John, Knights of Malta (an ecumenical Order of the Holy Eastern Roman Empire). Then I became a Grand Officer on May 10, 1984, of the Sovereign Military Order of Knights of Constantinople, of which Prince Henri was the Prince Grand Master. In 1994 Chin-Yeh became a Dame of the Order of St. John, Knights of Malta (see photo #40). On May 27, 1995, Prince Henri conferred on me the title of "Count of Paros". The island of Paros is in the Cyclades Islands of Greece, next to Antiparos — the island where the "Message in the Bottle" episode occurred in 1960.

One wonderful aspect of these relationships was the pleasant opportunity to know and relate closely to international personalities such as Count Oswald Voorbraeck and Brigitte Gruyters of Antwerp, Belgium, Count George and Mary Ann Wentworth of Corona del Mar, California, Sir Wim Pichal of Belgium, Sir Salvador Mendez of Benalmadena, Spain, Lady Hermé de Wyman Miro of Palm Beach, Florida, and Lady Arlene Kieta of New York. This led to many delightful social events and investitures in different parts of the world, including Malta, Spain, Moscow, Palm Springs, Las Vegas, and Palm Beach.

Chapter Nine
U.S. Ambassador to Bahrain
during the Gulf War (1989 - 1993)

Ambassadorial Preparation

Following my ventures into the world of real estate and then very rewarding experiences with the IESC, I was ready for new challenges. Campaigning for the 1988 Presidential elections was in full swing, and I provided support for George Bush, Sr., the Republican candidate who had successfully served eight years as President Reagan's Vice-President. I was delighted when he was elected to be the nation's next President.

In recognition of my over 20 years of working and studying in the Middle East, I was contacted by the White House's Presidential Personnel Office inquiring as to my interest in being the U.S. Ambassador to Bahrain. Excited at the prospect at representing the U.S. abroad, particularly in the Middle East, I sought advice from my friends in the State Department. They immediately responded, "Take it, Charles. Bahrain is a fine post and enjoys excellent relations with the U.S." I accepted their advice, advised the White House accordingly, and the complex confirmation process began. I did not realize at that time that I was destined to be U.S. Ambassador to Bahrain throughout one of the most turbulent periods in that region since the end of World War II.

After extensive background investigation, the White House declared themselves well-satisfied with both my credibility and my potential ambassadorial credentials. In April of 1989, President Bush formally "announced his intention" to nominate me as U.S. Ambassador to Bahrain. This was followed by the enormously time-consuming and often frustrating process of re-investigation by the FBI and the IRS. There were long questionnaires, Financial Disclosure Reports, Questionnaires for Sensitive Positions, and fingerprint cards. Of the nominations to bilateral ambassadorial posts, about 75% of Bush's appointees were career foreign service officers, while 25% were non-career appointees like myself.

In the two months in Washington, D.C., prior to my Senate confirmation hearings, I spent each day in the State Department Office of the Director of Arabian Peninsula Affairs (ARP) under the capable David Ransom, later U.S. Ambassador to Bahrain, in the Bureau of Near Eastern Affairs. It involved extensive orientation, background reading of the daily cable traffic, and security briefings. This was followed by the renowned three-week Ambassadorial Seminar or "Charm School" in June, 1989, for ambassador-designates and their spouses. Under the guidance of the Foreign Service Institute this included visits to the Central Intelligence Agency (CIA), United States Information Agency (USIA), other U.S. departments, and a trip to the U.S. Government's Federal Law Enforcement Training Center at Glynco, near Brunswick, Georgia, for four days of practical security and anti-terrorism training. The Seminar orientation was an extremely beneficial experience.

During this two-month period the State Department submitted to the Bahrain Government a request for "Agreement" to my appointment as the next U.S. Ambassador. Obviously, for the State Department to try to make successful ambassadors out of "mere mortal material" in three weeks was a considerable challenge. We had much to assimilate in a short time. One important concept was that diplomacy's goal is to "bend the other person to your will and to the policies of the U.S.A." We also learned the "Canary Theory:" if you have 1,000 pounds of canaries in a 500-pound capacity truck, you must bang on the side of the truck and keep half of the birds in the air. We were also cautioned against developing "clientitis" or excessive loyalty to the host country. We were warned not to confuse the personal attention and compliments given to us with our true personal qualities. "When you depart, you won't leave a ripple." The aim of protocol is to "create an atmosphere of friendliness in which business can be transacted."

The Ambassadorial Seminar taught us to be very careful if friends or highly-placed locals were to ask us to intervene in visa matters. We were advised to say, "I have an excellent consular officer who must legally make the decision on visa applicants. I will advise that officer about your personal interest, and I will make sure that person takes your recommendation into consideration." In addition, we were warned, "Measure your words. You will be constantly observed. You do as business what others do for pleasure. Giving working luncheons is cheaper and more effective than dinners—and remember to include guests who are transiting your locale." They also offered advice on personal security. "Do not carryout extended conversations standing outside of your vehicle because you could be vulnerable to a potential assassin's bullet." Historically it is said in semi-jest that "Ambassadors are sent abroad to lie for their countries." Permanent ambassadors (as opposed to temporary envoys) became customary at the end of the fifteenth century.

On July 21, 1989, I was flown from Andrews Air Force Base in a C21A (Learjet 35) military aircraft to Headquarters U.S. Central Command (USCENTCOM) at McDill Air Force Base, near Tampa, Florida. I had a valuable briefing on their military capabilities and responsibilities for the Persian Gulf/Horn of Africa/Southwest Asia area. Meetings were held with General H. Norman Schwarzkopf, Commander in Chief, Lt. General Craven C. Rogers, Jr., USAF, Deputy Commander and Major General Joseph P. Hoar, USMC, Chief of Staff (who later succeeded General Schwarzkopf after Desert Storm). These useful executive briefings included intelligence assessments, strategy briefings, and detailed discussions of key issues such as military operations in the Persian Gulf and Gulf of Oman, the Administrative Support Unit (ASU) in Bahrain, joint military exercises, logistics

planning, pre-positioning, full storage, and security assistance to our friends and allies. As a retired Colonel USAF, I found the briefings beneficial, and later they would turn out to be very useful background during the Gulf War.

After receipt of the "Agreement" from
Bahrain, President Bush officially nominated me
on July 2, 1989. I was then 69 years old. On October 2, 1989, I had my confirmation hearing before
the Senate Committee on Foreign Relations. President Mubarak of Egypt visited the Capitol that afternoon so the hearing schedule had to be com-
pressed. Senator Daniel P. Moynihan (D), Chairman of the Committee, presided, and Senator Jesse
Helms (R) was present. The Senatorial staffs has
already carefully checked my background and had
indicated their concurrence. Senator Pete Wilson
(later Governor of California) attended the hearing and introduced me to the Committee in a very
laudatory manner. My presentation was well received. Senator Moynihan asked a few pertinent
questions, which I answered to the Committee's
satisfaction. My presentation included a plea for
settlement of the Stinger missile "buy-back" which
was then facing Bahrain. This hearing also included
the nominations of Chas. W. Freeman, Jr. (to Saudi
Arabia), Michael Ussery (to Morocco), and Marion
Creekmore, Jr. (to Sri Lanka). My confirmation was
referred to the full Senate and received uncontested
approval. Unfortunately, some of those we had
come to know during the training program were
eliminated by the Senate, including the pleasant

designee to Barbados, Mrs. Joy Silverman. She did not respond satisfactorily under questioning at her confirmation hearing and, in addition, had made the cardinal error of visiting her prospective post in advance to make housing arrangements on the presumption of confirmation.

On October 18, 1989, Secretary of State, James Baker, III, officiated at my Swearing-In Ceremony held in the Treaty Room on the 7th floor of the State Department (see phto #24). There were about 30 invited guests including the Bahraini Ambassador Ghazi Gosaibi, and my friends, Ambassador and Mrs. Julian Niemcyzk, Ambassador Lucius Battle, and Archie Roosevelt. The Bible was held by the competent David Ransom, who later succeeded me as U.S. Ambassador to Bahrain. Secretary Baker made the following generous remarks at the ceremony.

It is a particular pleasure for me to officiate at this swearing-in ceremony for Charles W. Hostler as the new Ambassador to the State of Bahrain. Charles and I "go way back" to our days together in the Ford Administration when I was Under Secretary of Commerce and Charles was the Deputy Assistant Secretary for International Commerce. He did a superb job in managing the Bureau of International Commerce and in coordinating the U.S. export promotion programs. These were the happy years when the U.S. achieved a surplus in its balance of trade.

Charles has an outstanding background educationally, as a military officer, in U.S. government service, and as a very successful businessman with extensive international experience, particularly in the Middle East.

This combination of education, government, and military experience, as well as his knowledge of business, banking, and finance, brings a background which should serve very well in Bahrain.

Bahrain is extremely significant for U.S. concerns in the Gulf. We have been close friends with Bahrain for over 40 years. Time and again the Bahrainis have demonstrated their loyal support. The government of Bahrain, by courageously and steadfastly standing up to Iranian threats, provided critical support for the U.S. Navy during the Iran-Iraq war; Bahrain continues to offer this friendship and hospitality today.

I know that Charles will wish to build on this closeness. He will wish to sense opportunities and challenges to develop further a broad-based relationship which extends beyond military cooperation to include a wide range of concerns, such as commercial and banking ties, people contacts, diplomacy, and cultural exchanges.

My best wishes to you and our good friends in Bahrain.

After my Swearing-in Ceremony in Washington, D.C., I traveled to San Diego for last-minute preparations before taking up my appointment. I left for Bahrain via Washington, D.C. to receive three days of final instruction and then had a further two-day orientation en route at the American Embassy in London.

A complex aspect of my assignment in Bahrain was diplomatically to succeed my predecessor, the personable but controversial U.S. Ambassador Sam H. Zakhem, who had returned to the U.S.A. around March of 1989. The report of the State Department's Inspector General in that month indicated that the post's objectivity and credibility had suffered and that the post lacked rapport with Washington's Bureau of Near Eastern and South Asian Affairs. The new Chancery construction project was behind schedule, and project waste and improper accounting required closer management by the Foreign Building Office (FBO) and the Embassy. The report stated the post "had a recent history of poor morale attributable in part to the Chief of Mission's style and personality." Ambassador Donald Leidel, formerly Ambassador to Bahrain, was brought in as interim Charge d'Affaires to fill the gap until my arrival in late October, 1989.

Background on Bahrain

The State of Bahrain consists of a group of 33 islands, with a total land area of about 260 square miles, connected by a fine 15-mile causeway to the east coast of Saudi Arabia. The causeway, which opened in 1986, had been built and paid for by the Saudi government to facilitate movement between the two countries and to enhance development of Bahrain's economy. The largest of the islands is Bahrain, approximately 30 miles long and eight to ten miles wide, where the capital city of Manama is located. Bahrain has a notably humid summer climate in one of the world's hottest areas, but is generally mild and pleasant from November through early April. The average rainfall is less than four inches.

Bahrain was the site of the ancient civilization of Dilmun, which flourished as a trading center in the period 2000-1800 B.C.E. Since the late 18th century, Bahrain has been governed by the Al-Khalifa family, who had moved to Bahrain from what is now the state of Qatar. In 1805, the ruler of Bahrain entered into relations with the United Kingdom, and later the first treaty between the two parties was signed in 1820. A binding treaty of protection was concluded in 1861 and further revised in 1892 and 1951. This treaty specified that the Ruler could not dispose of any of his territory except to the U.K. and could not enter into relationships with any foreign government other than the U.K. without prior British consent. The British promised to protect Bahrain and the ruling family from all aggression by sea and to lend its good offices in case of land attack. The treaty relationship ended in 1971. Bahrain became fully independent entity on August 15, 1971, as the State of Bahrain, and joined the United Nations and the Arab League.

With a total land area roughly equal to that of New York City, Bahrain has a population of almost 700,000, about one third of whom are expatriate workers and their families. The indigenous population is about 70% Shia Muslim and 30% Sunni Muslim. During my time in Bahrain the Sunni ruling family, the Al-Khalifa, governed through a cabinet headed by the Prime Minister, Shaikh Khalifa al-Khalifa, a brother of the late Amir, Shaikh Isa. There had been no elected legislature since in 1976, the Amir having suspended the Parliament, and no elections had taken place since that time. The Amir (now King) Shaikh Hamad reopened the door to elected representation in the year 2002.

Under the Al-Khalifa rule, Bahrain has been a force for moderation in the Gulf region. Its leadership and its society are very tolerant of expatriate cultures and religious practices. For example, expatriate women are not required to wear purdah, they can drive, and they are free to work in all areas of the economy. Bahrain, perhaps alone among the GCC states, has a thriving, albeit small, Jewish community and a small Jewish synagogue. Bahrain's Amir, at that time, Shaikh Isa, believed that the expatriates were guests in his country and were contributing to the development of the nation's economy. While they were in Bahrain they needed spiritual support and should be free to practice their own religion. Consequently, they had freedom of religion in their own places of worship, something not permitted in nearby Saudi Arabia and some other Gulf states.

Bahrain is a composite of peoples, with most of the population concentrated in the two principal cities, Manama and Al Muharraq. Indigenous Bahrainis are composed of two major ethnic groups, those with origins in Arabia and those with origins in Iran; almost all are Muslims. Of the non-Bahraini group, the most numerous are Omanis, followed in decreasing order by Indians, Pakistanis, Iranians, Filipinos, British, Americans, and a number of other small groups. Arabic is the official language, but English, Farsi, and Urdu are also commonly heard.

Bahrainis wear traditional Arab dress, the white thobe and head covering, or they wear Western clothing. The choice is not a matter of generation. It is common to see older Bahrainis in Western clothes and the young men and women in traditional Arab dress. The Bahrainis are a very gentle, courteous, hospitable people. They rarely raise their voice, personal violence is rare, and, in fact, in the 30 years prior to my arrival there had been only two murders in Bahrain. There was very little crime, and that was mostly of a petty nature, usually by foreign workers. A very sociable, community-conscious people, Bahrainis have a deep love of music and art and are great story-tellers, with a wonderful sense of humor. The many senior military U.S. Navy personnel whom I met during my years in Bahrain often said that Bahrain was "the best kept secret in the U.S. Navy." They were very happy with their time spent in the country and admired the many Bahrainis whom they met during their assignments. They were often sorry to leave for their next posting.

In 1932 Standard Oil Company of California, now Chevron, discovered oil in Bahrain, and became the first oil producer on the Arabian side of the Persian Gulf. The Bahrain Petroleum Company (BAPCO) was formed in 1936 as a SoCal and Texaco joint venture to produce and refine oil for export to the existing Texaco markets east of the Suez Canal. For over half a century BAPCO had educated, trained, and developed Bahrain nationals to operate and manage a modern economy. The talented and hard-working Donald Hepburn was BAPCO's Chief Executive for 16 years until his retirement to the U.S.A. in 1996.

However, by Persian Gulf standards Bahrain's crude oil reserves were very small, and production began to decline in the 1980s. Bahrain therefore sought to diversify its economy in order to become less dependent on oil revenues. A major achievement in Bahrain's industrial diversification program was the establishment in 1968 of a large aluminum smelter. Aluminum Bahrain (ALBA), with a current annual production capacity of about 513,000 tons, utilizes Bahrain's abundant supply of low-cost natural gas to generate the smelter's electrical power requirements. The bulk of ALBA's production was exported to international markets, but it also provided the raw material for the development of a substantial and increasingly important indigenous downstream aluminum product manufacturing industry. (ALBA's capacity was subsequently raised and under current plans will be 750,000 tons per annum over the next few years, making it one of the largest aluminum smelters in the world.)

In the early 1970s, due to its civil war, Lebanon declined as a commercial center and Bahrain, with its freely convertible currency, sound banking regulations, and pleasant life style for expatriates, replaced Lebanon as the banking and financial hub for the Gulf region. It is interesting to note that Bahrain has subsequently been ranked by the Heritage Foundation and the *Wall Street Journal* as the third freest economy in the world, after Hong Kong and Singapore, based on 50 criteria such as trade policy, and taxation.

The drop in oil prices in the early 1980s, combined with the turmoil related to the Iran-Iraq war and later the wars to liberate Kuwait, Iraq, and Afghanistan, had a somewhat debilitating affect on the banking industry. This also caused a reduction in direct foreign investment in the region and a drop in domestic private investment for both existing and new industries. Nonetheless, the Bahrain government remained committed to economic development to provide job opportunities for Bahrain's high school and university graduates. The government was keenly interested in working closely with U.S. companies to further stimulate the economy, and during my tenure the embassy made every effort to facilitate commercial contacts between U.S. and Bahrain business leaders.

After my arrival in Bahrain, my first official task was to present my credentials to the Amir. Arrangements to do so were made, and I attended a presentation ceremony at Janabiyah Palace, Manama, with several other Ambassadors who had arrived in Bahrain at about the same time as myself. The Palace, built in traditional Arab style, was comfortably and functionally furnished, but with none of the lavishness often portrayed by the international media. Yousif Al-Dossary, then Head of the Amiri Court, and Nabiil Qamber, Director of Protocol, also attended the ceremony. They welcomed me and escorted me through the Bahrain Defense Force Guard of Honor, accompanied by the military band, to the Reception Hall. I was warmly greeted by the Minister of Foreign Affairs, Sheik Mohammad bin Mubark Al-Khalifa. The Amir was dressed in his traditional regal flowing thobe and gold embroidered bisht, wearing a curved jambiah (dagger) in a golden scabbard. He graciously accepted my credentials and cordially welcomed me to Bahrain, saying, "Please make this your home, Mr. Ambassador." It was an auspicious beginning to what was to become a close and friendly relationship. The Amir had a very gracious style and a humorous twinkle in his eye. He was a man of short stature, but on meeting him his outgoing personality and regal bearing gave the impression of him being much taller. Little did I know as I shook his hand in that brief yet impressive ceremony that Bahrain was to become such an important part of my life.

Later that day I attended my first meeting with the Prime Minister, Sheikh Khalifa Al-Khalifa, at Government House in Manama. Government House had been built by the Bahrain government in 1960 to accommodate the Prime Minister and his staff. The outside appearance of the building was rather austere, but inside it was handsomely appointed. Like the Palace, it was functionally conservative. As the head of the Cabinet and responsible for the administrative arm of the government, the long-serving Prime Minister was pleasant but somewhat more formal than the Amir. Indeed, this was to characterize our relationship throughout my stay in Bahrain. Under the leadership of the Prime Minister, Bahrain had a well managed economy. Education for kindergarten through twelfth grade and medical services were free to all citizens. There was no personal or corporate income tax. Low-cost housing and low-cost power were available for low-income families, together with subsidized staple foods. The commercial laws and legal system were well developed, and direct foreign investment was welcomed. The literacy rate was around 90%, the highest of the Gulf countries.

During my entire tenure as U.S. Ambassador, the Ruler was His Highness, the Amir, Shaikh Isa bin Sulman Al-Khalifa (who, to the great sorrow of his people, died on March 6, 1999, at the age of 65). Shaikh Isa was born on July 3, 1933, and ruled for 38 years. He was a popular Amir, who, though an absolute ruler, was most generous towards his subjects. A religious man, the Amir arose for prayers at about 5:30 a.m. every day. He was also politically astute, with a politically pragmatic attitude in the skillful handling of his complex role as head of state and father-figure for his people. It was truly a pleasure to deal with him, and I treasure the 20 or so letters which he personally sent to me during my stay in Bahrain. He was ably assisted by his gracious and devoted British long-time private secretary and equerry, Major (now General) Gerald Green, CBE, now about 88 years old, and who has enjoyed life in Bahrain since 1956. I invited Shaikh Isa to my Residence for a small private dinner where, with his approval, I welcomed about 20 American friends. It was a tribute that His Highness accepted my dinner invitation and came alone without any of his usual retinue. As always, he put everyone at ease with his fine sense of humor and his delightful and relaxed style. The Amir seemed eager to establish a direct channel of personal liaison. During the evening he quietly encouraged me to contact him through Major Green if there were appropriately sensitive or urgent issues where he could be of assistance. I assured him that I welcomed this and would use the privilege only when absolutely essential and with the utmost discretion. As we conversed about items of interest to him, he would periodically make brief notes which he tucked into the deep pocket of his thobe. The dinner party was an auspicious beginning of a more personal relationship which subsequently proved extremely valuable when steering my way through sensitive issues, such as the annual report by the Embassy on Bahrain's human rights activities as mandated by Congress, and our complex military and security relations during Desert Storm. As always, except for most unusual matters, I continued my normal approach to the Government of Bahrain on all substantive questions through the Foreign Ministry.

In one respect the timing of my arrival in Bahrain was particularly fortuitous. It gave me about nine months to build strong working relationships with the leaders of Bahrain before Iraq's invasion of Kuwait and the onset of the turmoil of Operation Desert Shield and Operation Desert Storm. I made a number of personal visits to the Amir, the Prime Minister, the Crown Prince, to all Ministries of the Government, all the principal merchant families, members of the diplomatic Corps, members of every group within the American community, most of the foreign business community, and had met many visiting American business leaders and U.S. government officials. Hosting luncheons and dinner parties for visiting international industrial and financial leaders assisted me in the important process of getting to know the senior members of the local community on a one-on-one basis over the dinner table. For example, on November 4, 1989, there was a three-day visit to Bahrain by the Chairman of Chase Manhattan Bank, Wayne C. Butcher, accompanied by my old friend, Archie B. Roosevelt, Jr. (married to Selwa "Lucky" Showker Roosevelt). It was an ideal opportunity for me to entertain the Minister of Finance and leaders of the country's financial circle. Archie presented me with a copy of his book *For Lust of Knowing: Memoirs of an Intelligence Officer* inscribed to me as ". . . a long-time traveler on the Road to Samarkand – whose path has crossed with mine from time to time – with warmest regards." Sadly, Archie died the following May. Archie and his cousin, Kermit "Kim" Roosevelt, Jr., served in the same era with me in various Middle Eastern OSS and CIA intelligence assignments.

When I arrived, Bahrain had a vibrant American community of about 1,500 U.S. civilians along with then about 300 in the U.S. military contingent, business people and their families, some U.S. employees of the Bahrain Government, like the delightful Jim, and wife Jose Madigan, who was Civil Service Adviser to the Bahraini Government from 1982 to 1991. There were also a number of community service groups, such as the highly respected American Mission Hospital. That fine hospital had been established in 1893 by missionaries who were sent from the Dutch Reformed Church in America. The missionaries quickly realized that a medical dispensary was greatly needed in Bahrain and Saudi Arabia which, at that time, had very limited medical facilities. The missionaries' heroic medical journeys to Saudi Arabia have been recently written about by the talented Dr. Paul Armerding, Director of the American Mission Hospital. This dedication had a major influence on the high esteem in which the hospital was held by Bahrain's ruling family. The clinic, with its mail address of

P.O. Box #1, Manama), was later expanded into a well-equipped 50-bed hospital of which the Gynecology Department was particularly respected in the community. In the early 1980s, as Chairman of the Hospital Board of Management, Don Hepburn, CEO of the Bahrain Petroleum Company (BAPCO), successfully steered the hospital out of near bankruptcy, instituted new fiscal controls, and put it back on a sound financial footing. Out of his great respect for the American Mission Hospital, His Highness the Amir Shaikh Isa, although the Muslim ruler of a Muslim country, provided financial assistance, and further emphasized his public support by agreeing to become Patron of the hospital. This was in sharp contrast to the closing of similar missionary medical facilities by other governments elsewhere in the region.

Other very enjoyable local Bahraini personalities, in addition to the ruling families of Al-Khalifa, included the families of Dawani, Kanoo, Beseisu, Yateem, Shirawi, Fakhro, Al-Aujan, Al-Alawi, Al-Sho'ala, Al-Hasan, Al-Moayyed, Al-Mutawa, Al-Moyaed, Al-Manna, Al-Zayani, Bu-Hindi, Buzizi, Jalal, Juma, Kamal, Kirdar, Mamdani, Marhoon, Nass, Qamber, Rajab, and westerners like the Wannebo, Barnes, Hollyer, and Kachadurian. It was a privilege to interact with many fine diplomats in Bahrain, such as the Saudi Ambassador (and poet) Ghazi Al-Gosaibi, French Ambassador Pierre Boillot, British Ambassador Shepheard, and Muhammad Abdul-Ghaffar (now Bahraini Minister of State for Foreign Affairs).

I was an active supporter of the American Association of Bahrain, a focal point for the business men and women of the American community, and encouraged their many worthwhile initiatives. One of their programs, which I particularly admired, was the annual "Washington Door-Knock." A group of the members went each year to Washington, D.C. to meet with various U.S. Congressmen to present issues which were of importance to U.S. businessmen abroad.

The Bahrain Garden Club and the American Women's Club were two of my favorites. I often made available the Residence and its garden to the ladies' various functions. On more than one occasion they made improvised landing-pads for Santa Claus and his reindeer, and eager children shattered the peace and quiet of the Embassy Residence in celebration of the festive season.

Another favorite was the much admired Bahrain School and the Bahrain International School Association (BISA), also under the able chairmanship of Don Hepburn. This school, supported in part by the U.S. Department of Defense Dependents School system, was founded in 1968 by local community leaders and has the full approval of the Bahrain government. The Bahrain school makes available kindergarten through high school education in Bahrain for the children of resident expatriates, for U.S. military dependents, other U.S. government agencies on the Island, and for Bahraini nationals. It was initially located at the BAPCO Company compound in Awali. After the

British military left in 1971, the school was relocated to the vacated British military compound at Juffair near the U.S. Navy's Administrative Support Unit (ASU). Before I arrived enrollment had peaked at 1050 students, but during my time it was around 800 students of 50 different nationalities. The school had gained a fine reputation in Bahrain because of its capable U.S. teachers and modern curriculum, resulting in the admission of the majority of its graduates into leading U.S. universities. Many foreign residents and prominent Bahrainis, including Cabinet members and leading merchants, chose to pay substantial annual fees to send their children to this U.S. administered school in order to prepare them for further education in the U.S. In 1992 a dormitory was built adjacent to the school for the children of expatriates living in Saudi Arabia. At that time Saudi Arabia would not allow expatriate teenagers to reside in the Kingdom, and families were therefore compelled to send their children to boarding schools in Europe and the U.S. The new dormitory facility at the Bahrain School provided accommodation for 120 students, grades 9-12, with male and female students housed in two separate wings. Dormitory students came mostly from the Eastern Province of Saudi Arabia and, using the Saudi-Bahrain causeway, many were able to go home on the weekends.

In late 1989, the U.S. Department of Defense and its regional school headquarters, then located in Madrid, Spain, was attempting financial belt-tightening, and it was tentatively proposed to close the school. When word reached the Bahraini Government that this school closing was being considered, the Foreign Minister called me to his office. The highly respected and probably the world's longest continuously serving Foreign Minister, Shaikh Mohammed bin Mubarak Al-Khalifa, made it very clear to me that the Government of Bahrain did *not* want this excellent school to close. He suggested that I promptly make this unambiguous to the U.S. Government, which I did successfully. The Government of Bahrain and I recognized the great value and many contributions of this unique school to the U.S.'s political, cultural, and military presence during its many years in Bahrain.

Although I was familiar with Arab traditions there was much to be learned that was unique to Bahrain. An important means of communications between the Ruler and his subjects was the Tuesday weekly 7:00 a.m. public Majlis (meeting) at the Amir's palace in Rifaa. This was a completely "open-house" style of gathering of male foreign visitors, and his male subjects, regardless of their religious, financial, or social status. Each week approximately 250 people, from Cabinet Members to laborers, would line up outside the Palace's large reception room and be greeted individually by the Amir as they entered. After they were all seated on cushions around the sides of the large hall, in traditional Arab style, Arab servants went around the room serving coffee in small cups, the cups being re-used repeatedly as the servants worked their way around the visitors. It was the unspoken protocol that senior people in the community sat nearest the Amir, and the remainder in some unobtrusive way in descending order of political and social importance.

After the initial round of coffee had been served, people with appeals or requests would line up in front of the Amir. Then, one by one, they would go forward and kneel close to the Amir, who would lean forward, listening intently as they explained their problem. It might relate to a family member who needed funds for a surgery abroad, or a release for someone from jail, or that they required a larger house due to additional children, or some other similar problem. The Amir would listen patiently, and at the end of the conversation the petitioner would pass him a paper giving the details of the request. The Amir would usually say, "Come back next week, my son, and you will receive an answer." The petitioner would then return to his seat along the wall. When all petitioners had presented their requests, the servants passed around the room with trays of burning incense and rose water to inhale. That was the signal that the meeting was over. The Amir would then stand at the entrance to the Majlis and shake hands with each of the visitors as they departed.

The following week the petitioners went to the Amiri Court, adjacent to the Majlis and met with the Amir's secretaries, who would have checked out the facts of each petition. Generally, the Amir took a sympathetic and generous approach to resolving their problems. Typically, they would be handed an envelop containing cash for a relative's medical treatment, or a pardon for a misdemeanor, or some other assistance. I attended and observed the Majlis many times in the three and half years during my period in Bahrain, and each time I admired the Amir's patience and benevolence towards the seemingly endless flow of petitioners who came before him. How rare it is in the world when a commoner can approach a ruler or senior government official and receive such quick attention and generally positive response to his pleas. I understand that at that time other Gulf rulers performed a somewhat similar Majlis, but I believe that none responded as personally and generously as Shaikh Isa.

Local and foreign women were able to visit the Ladies' Majlis, which was held weekly by the Amir's only wife, Shaikha Hassa. This was essentially by invitation and was more of an elite social event.

Shaikh's Beach and Yacht "AWAL"

One of the most pleasant locations in Bahrain was Shaikh Isa's favorite five-acre walled beach compound at Zallaq on the west coast of the main island, known informally as "The Shaikh's Beach." The Amir enjoyed going there in the afternoons whenever his duties permitted. The compound contained one of his favorite houses together with separate living quarters for his expatriate (largely

Indian) servants. He only allowed resident foreigners, not Bahrainis, to use the beach, and all visitors were screened at the entrance of the compound by uniformed guards. Visitors were not allowed to bring cameras and recorders onto the compound, and these items were hung on the "camera tree" to be retrieved on the way out.

The Amir often would sit in an open area in the beach compound under a large umbrella. When friends or attractive ladies passed by, Shaikh Isa would frequently invite them to join him for tea and pastries served by attentive Indian servants. There was another quite large house in the compound that reportedly, in the past, been occupied by a British lady.

When I had urgent matters to discuss privately with His Highness, I would drive by myself to the "Shaikh's Beach." Shaikh Isa was always kind enough to note my arrival, excused his guests, and received me at his table. We would sit looking out over the beautiful blue-green water of the Gulf as we quietly discussed the matter at hand. The Amir was always open, honest, perceptive, constructive, and matter-of-fact in his approach to matters. During Desert Shield/Desert Storm, I called on him periodically to diminish the roadblocks on important military, political, and related issues encountered from time to time.

A useful point in my developing relationship with the Amir came in late December, 1989, barely three months after my arrival in Bahrain. I received a phone call at the Embassy Residence from Major

Gerald Green, who, on behalf of the Amir, invited me, my son, and a friend who was visiting for the holidays to accompany the Amir for lunch on his yacht. The Major personally drove us to the Al Jasrah region of Bahrain where the Amir had another newish, large, green, pagoda-style house set in about ten acres of planted gardens surrounded by a high wall. The main interior road of the compound led to a large, paved dock and an adjacent parking area.

The Amir was invariably punctual, and as we approached at exactly 10 a.m. he was standing on the dock at the foot of the vessel's gangway. During our entire visit there were no guards or servants present, only the yacht's crew of approximately 12 Greek seamen. The Amir, as always, was exceedingly friendly, courteous, and hospitable. He absolutely insisted, in spite of my protestations, that I, as his guest, precede him up the gangway and through all entrances on board.

The Amir's yacht, the "AWAL" (meaning "The First"), was built in 1980 by C.R.N. in Ancona, Italy. The AWAL was painted brilliant white with varnished teak railings and a large covered fantail. The wheel house was equipped with all the latest piloting and navigational equipment, much of it made in the U.S.A.

The vessel was very well maintained, and carpeted throughout with beige, wall-to-wall carpeting, not ostentatious but quietly luxurious in conservative good taste. The Amir escorted us below to the master salon, which extended the width of the vessel and included two elegantly equipped bathrooms. There were also four staterooms as well as the crew's quarters. The salon contained, among other things, a large color photo of HRH Prince Philip driving a four-in-hand horse carriage containing Queen Elizabeth and the Amir. Also there was a color photo of President Reagan and the Amir standing in the Rose Garden of the White House and a color photo of Queen Elizabeth and the Amir in full ceremonial regalia.

Tea and champagne were served with finger-food before the vessel departed from the dock. Following a hand signal from the Amir, the vessel got underway. We cruised for 45 minutes due south in the Gulf of Bahrain, perhaps 500 yards offshore. Then the vessel slowly turned, headed north, and anchored in the deeper water off Umm Na'San Island near the Saudi-Bahraini causeway. This quite large island, owned by the Amir, was uninhabited except for some 600 small Bahraini gazelles. There were two other islands fairly nearby that are privately owned by the Amir's two brothers: Jiddah Island owned by the Prime Minister, Shaikh Khalifa Al-Khalifa, and Mohammedia Island owned by Shaikh Mohamed Bin Sulman Al-Khalifa, the youngest brother of the Amir. Sheikh Mohamed was not a member of the Bahrain government, but was reputedly the country's largest private landowner.

After anchoring, a motor boat was launched over the side of the yacht, and the crew took provisions about 200 yards northward from the AWAL to a raft covered with green outdoor carpeting, anchored about 100 yards south of Umm Na'San Island. The raft was in very shallow water (one could have walked in waist-high water to the island).

After the raft was provisioned, the launch returned for the Amir and guests. The Amir was dressed in modest Western-style swimming shorts and a light jacket. He graciously sat on the top of the engine cowling so that his guests could take seats in the launch's cockpit. There were folding chairs and towels spread on the raft, and the Amir motioned for the guests to take places. He seated himself on a large towel and asked my guest and me to join him. We talked freely and openly for about 30 minutes. I then relinquished my position to the Amir's other guests, Mr. and Mrs. Marcus Wright. The youthful looking Mr. Wright was the Dow-Jones' representative in the Gulf, resident in Bahrain, and the son of the Permanent Secretary of the British Foreign Office. Champagne and soft drinks were offered continuously by the Greek crew, but the Amir drank only tea or soft drinks. He was constantly attentive to his guests and appeared very interested in the discussions. After about one and a half hours on the raft, we returned to the AWAL for a fine buffet lunch served on the fantail by the crew.

The majority of the crew had been with this vessel since it was commissioned in 1980. The Captain, Nicklas Karamitsos, was married and spoke English well. The Chief Engineer, Themis

Kamakaris, whose English is limited, was married with two sons. I took the occasion to invite these two officers and their families to a USO show, "The Dallas Cowboy Cheerleaders," on January 4, 1990, at the U.S. Navy's ASU, which they eagerly accepted and enjoyed.

The Amir told me that, due to his concerns about terrorists hijacking, the farthest he had traveled away from Bahrain in the AWAL was to the United Arab Emirates (UAE). I smilingly suggested a U.S. destroyer escort might be useful, to which he laughingly agreed. It is my understanding that the yacht was used only two or three times a month. The atmosphere throughout the visit was most informal, and it was a very pleasant experience. We returned to the dock at about 3 p.m., after a delightful five-hour trip. This trip further enhanced my growing personal relationship with His Highness

Embassy Duties

My Embassy specialists and I were required to handle a number of important tasks in representing U.S. interests both in Bahrain and in the region as a whole. The economic and political roles tend to be locally focused, whereas the military role was regional and beyond. I had broad responsibility for ensuring that U.S. military policy was implemented in accordance with U.S. State Department and Department of Defense policy guidelines and that the military mission meshed smoothly with

U.S. political and economic objectives. During my tenure in Bahrain the broad Department of Defense strategic interests were defined as:

(1) Assured access to Persian Gulf oil

(2) A durable Arab-Israel peace

(3) The security of key regional partners

(4) The protection of U.S. citizens and property in the region

(5) Freedom of navigation in international waters

(6) Human rights and democratic development

(7) Access of U.S. goods to regional markets

We worked together with other U.S. Embassies in the area to achieve these aims. I was fortunate to have outstanding colleagues in the Persian Gulf, including Chas. W. Freeman (Saudi Arabia), Mark (and Patricia) Hambley in Qatar (who kindly attended my 80th birthday party in California), and Edward "Skip" (and Peggy) Gnehm, Jr. (Kuwait).

Within the State and Defense Department guidelines, my efforts to promote greater respect for human rights and increase democratization were one of my thorniest dilemmas. However, after many lengthy discussions, Bahrain ultimately moved forward in a graceful and positive way to address the human rights issues.

In the 1990s Bahrain became the frequent target of international demands for the investigation of human rights abuses. The Bahraini Ambassador in Geneva at the time had responded to inquiries from the U.N. Human Rights Commission by blandly saying, in effect, "We are a sovereign nation and don't have to respond to such allegations." I discussed these matters over time with the fine Minister of Interior, Shaikh Mohammed Al-Khalifa, and he came to agree that Bahrain's interests would be better served by being more responsive to and cooperative with international inquiries. Subsequently an international organization was permitted to visit Bahrain to review the country's human rights. Although their report was critical, this and other later visits were positive steps towards what is now a much more open society.

For many years following the end of the British presence in 1971, the Bahraini Security and Intelligence Service, a separate entity from the regular police force, composed largely of mercenaries from Pakistan and India, continued to be directed by former British officers. This was especially significant since Bahrain's ruling family, as well as a relatively wealthy privileged minority, were Sunni Muslims, and they controlled a nation that was approximately 70% Shia Muslim. One such British officer was the capable Major-General Ian Henderson, who had served as Director General of Security for many years. Henderson was born in Kenya and spoke the Kikuyu language fluently. He was a key SAS Officer in Kenya during the Mau Mau period and was an expert in covert police action. His actions resulted in the capture of the two most important Mau Mau military leaders, General China in 1954 and Dedan Kimathi in 1956. His wife, Marie, was his able assistant, and they lived and worked together inside the walled police fort in Manama. There were persistent reports of brutality in the handling of political prisoners. I would occasionally see General Henderson at social gatherings of the quite large British community, and I tried genially to discuss solutions to the ongoing question of human rights. I remember one occasion when Ian lost his "cool" and exploded at me, saying, in effect, "Why the hell don't you and the CIA take over this problem and see if you can handle it better?" I tried to calm him by assuring him that the U.S. was not trying to interfere but was merely attempting to be helpful in coping with appeals by international human rights organizations. Over time Henderson and the Minister of Interior, Shaikh Mohammed, began to work closely with me on this issue, and the situation steadily improved.

The New Embassy Chancery

Despite some difficulties between the Embassy and the Bahrain government over human rights issues, relations remained very sound, and the level of activity at the Embassy continued to grow. It became apparent in the mid-1980s, prior to my arrival, that a larger and more secure Chancery would be required to fulfill effectively the Embassy's increasingly important mission in Bahrain. After utilizing for many years a villa in Adliya that was rented from the Prime Minister, Shaikh Khalifa, construction of a new U.S. Embassy

Chancery facing Tubli Bay in Manama was commenced in 1987 and completed in 1990 at a cost of about $19 million. The design was modified during construction to conform to the upgraded security standards recommended by the U.S. Admiral Inman Committee on Security in response to the many hostile incidents which had occurred against U.S. Embassies around the world. When completed, the new building proved to have several shortcomings. It did not completely meet the Embassy's requirements for office space, did not have an Ambassadorial Residence within the secure compound, and had very limited parking within the area. No nearby or on-street parking was available in the immediate region, which was a major problem because of the lack of both convenience and security.

After considerable discussion with Washington (and a pleasant meeting with President Bush at the White House on Mar. 28, 1990) (see photo #25), I was given approval to proceed promptly with negotiations for a long-term lease-purchase agreement with the Bahraini government for a large lot across the street. With my considerable real estate background, I conducted professionally tough negotiations with the government. The Bahraini Minister for Finance and National Economy, Ebraim Abdul Karim, telephoned me seeking a better price offer. When I politely declined in late August, 1990 (after Saddam's invasion of nearby Kuwait), he laughed and accepted our proposal, saying, "Well, you are now protecting

Bahrain from Saddam, so I guess we owe you this small favor."

On July 4, 1990, the new U.S. Embassy Chancery was officially opened by His Highness, the Amir (see photo #26). As a special favor to me, the Amir agreed to cut the ribbon at the entrance and unveil a permanent metal plaque bearing both our names. Several Cabinet Ministers had urged Shaikh Isa against the ribbon-cutting ceremony for fear that this would set a pattern and require him to inaugurate all new foreign embassies. Nonetheless, despite this advice, the Amir kept his promise. The opening ceremony was attended by Government Ministers, foreign ambassadors, prominent Bahrainis, American businessmen, and many Americans resident in Bahrain. A fanfare of trumpeters from the Bahrain Public Security Band marked the Amir's arrival. He was greeted by myself and Rear Admiral William Fogarty, Commander of the U.S. Joint Task Force in the Middle East (who met and married his wife Carol in Bahrain and now lives happily with two children in Minneapolis).

The 60,000-square-foot building is set on 2.8 acres of land. The principal contractor was Harbert International, Inc. of Birmingham, Alabama, and Jalal Costain was the main sub-contractor in Bahrain. The embassy staff of over 140 persons was scheduled to start moving out of the old building in Adliya in September. We had the opening ceremony just in time because on August 2, 1990, less than one month later, Saddam Hussein moved his

Iraqi troops into Kuwait, and the Gulf War began, just 200 miles away.

The new building was surrounded with 104 beautiful four-meter-high, fully grown date-palm trees imported from Saudi Arabia and re-planted in the compound. The trees soon began producing a full crop of high quality dates. One day, during a private meeting with the Amir, he said to me in a pleasant voice, "You know, Charles, I drive frequently on the highway passing by the U.S. Embassy. I have noticed that your Embassy is not properly trimming and caring for those lovely date palms. Dates are a very important delicacy in this part of the world, and we are very sensitive to their care." With this high-level caution, I quickly got together with the Embassy's Administrative Officer and his assistants and queried them closely about the care being given to the trees. They responded that the trees were bearing a heavy crop of dates and that they were perplexed as to what to do with all those raw dates. No U.S. government funds were available to properly treat and box a date harvest.

After researching this question, I inquired about date-processing plants in Bahrain and paid a visit to the largest. We worked out a mutually satisfactory arrangement wherein that firm would process and carefully pack our dates, and in return the packing plant could keep half the crop. Every season we gave many boxes of dates labeled "With the Compliments of the U.S. Embassy in Bahrain" to the Amir and his Ministers, other foreign Embassies, U.S. government agencies, charities, and the like. The deal worked out very well, and as far as I know, this tradition is still being carried on.

Obviously, with Iraq's invasion of Kuwait, the physical security of the Embassy was of utmost importance. We, therefore, put in place at the Embassy the following elements:

(1) The overall security of the Embassy was the responsibility of the resident U.S. Regional Security Officer and his staff. They supervised the effectiveness of all aspects of security at the Embassy, the Ambassador's Residence, the Marine House, and the residences of all Embassy employees;

(2) 24-hour protection of the exterior of the Chancery walls was handled by the Bahrain State Police;

(3) Physical security at the gates and interior areas within the compound was assigned to a very diligent, highly trained team of Gurkhas from Nepal. They had been contracted through a London firm from among recently disbanded British Gurkha military units. Persons seeking U.S. visas or to visit the USIA Library were x-rayed and screened before entry.

(4) The heavy internal doors that protected the sensitive areas within the Embassy were manned by specially trained U.S. Marine Se-

curity Guards.

The Ambassador's four-bedroom Residence was leased from a Bahraini citizen and was adjacent to a Shiite village. Located about a ten-minute drive from the Chancery, it was guarded by four Bahrain Security Police on eight-hour shifts. Fortunately, during my three and a half years in Bahrain we had no serious security problems, thanks to the friendliness of the Bahraini people, the abilities of their Security Forces, and the diligence of the U.S. Regional Security Officer and his staff. However, recently in 2002 during a pro-Palestinian rally a group of some 20 protestors were able to scale the Chancery's outside walls and smashed vehicles.

The Embassy's long-time, loyal ambassadorial driver was Jassim Marhoon, a tall, big-framed, very religious Shiite from the village of Malkiya. We became good friends, and I often visited his home. The Bahrain Government had promised Jassim that he would receive the plot of land adjacent to his relatively modest home. However, through some mix-up in the Ministry of Housing, this piece of land was given to someone else, to the great disappointment of Jassim and his family. Aware of his disappointment, I worked quietly and unofficially to help Jassim, and after about six months of quiet diplomacy the matter was happily resolved in his favor. The Government gave Jassim the adjoining piece of land, and the original "grantee" was given a satisfactory substitute

elsewhere. Jassim and his delighted family immediately built a high brick wall to permanently in-
corporate the newly acquired land into his property.

U.S. Military Relations

When I arrived in Bahrain, the U.S. enjoyed
close, yet pragmatic, mutually advantageous military relations with Bahrain. Since 1947 Bahrain had
been host to U.S. Navy vessels in the Persian Gulf.
U.S. military activities in the Gulf were implemented and controlled by the U.S. Central Command (located at McDill AFB, Florida) with the
Navy's "Commander, Middle East Force," resident
in Bahrain.

The Gulf region contains more than 70 per
cent of the world's oil reserves, on which the economies of the United States and its allies were heavily
dependent. The Command's area of responsibility
sat astride the major maritime trade routes which
link the Middle East, Europe, South and East Asia,
and the Western hemisphere. Ships ply these
routes, and the maritime choke points of the Strait
of Hormuz, the Suez Canal, and the Bab el Mandeb
(which lies at the southern end of the Red Sea) carry
the all-important petroleum products that fuel the
economies of our European and Asian allies and
also the myriad of other commodities that cross
the oceans in world trade.

Central Command's main mission was to

assure access to Gulf oil and the freedom of navigation in international waters. This task was based on the unavoidable fact that the new international system that had replaced U.S./U.S.S.R. bipolarity at the end of the Cold War could not survive without Gulf oil. The industrialized West needed an assured supply of dependable crude oil from the Gulf producers, and it was also desirable that the price of oil, as a function of supply and demand, remained acceptable. The unhindered shipment of oil from the Persian Gulf was the U.S.'s continuing top security concern in the region. It was equally important to all the major industrialized countries that directly or indirectly depended on an uninterrupted supply of crude oil from the Gulf to fuel their ever expanding economies. In this respect, as U.S. Ambassador to Bahrain, I had a particularly good vantage point since Bahrain was a key U.S. military location at the center of the Gulf. It was one of the very few places in the region at that time where the U.S. military presence was accepted. Certainly, the Bahrainis, though modest in numbers, have always been there when the U.S. needed them. As a former chairman of the U.S. Joint Chiefs of Staff (and former U.S. Ambassador to the U.K.), Admiral William Crowe, U.S. Navy, expressed it, "Pound for pound, the U.S. has no better ally in the world than Bahrain." Another former chairman Colin Powell (now U.S. Secretary of State) was a frequent visitor to Bahrain and concurred in that expression (see photo #31).

A key component of the U.S. military presence in Bahrain was the U.S. Navy's Administrative Support Unit, Southwest Asia (ASU-SWA), a support facility for U.S. Navy ships operating with the Middle East Force in the Arabian Gulf. It was located in Juffair, on an original 25 acres of leased land (which since 1991 has been expanded threefold). The Juffair Naval facilities were established by the British as a Naval installation (H.M.S. Juffair) on April 13, 1935. For economic and political reasons, after their treaty expired, the British Forces withdrew their military presence from Bahrain. The United States, through a formal agreement with the Bahrain Government, took over Juffair and established the ASU in 1971.

Gulf War I

Shortly after my arrival in Bahrain Saddam Hussein began pressuring neighboring Kuwait to write off Iraq's debt to Kuwait incurred during the Iraq-Iran war. Saddam also accused Kuwait of using directional drilling under the Iraq/Kuwait border to steal Iraqi crude oil. Iraq also claimed that Kuwait's oil production policy was contributing to the drop in world crude oil prices, with a seriously adverse impact on their essentially bankrupt post-war economy. Iraq was also seeking to gain additional territory to improve its shipping access to the Persian Gulf. At the root of all the rhetoric was their long-standing claim that historically Kuwait was a province of Iraq. The Kuwaitis un-

equivocally rejected Iraq's allegations and territorial claims and refused to negotiate. It was known
that a large contingent of Iraqi troops had been
moved to the Kuwaiti border, but this was interpreted by Kuwait and by the U.S. State Department
as simply a pressure tactic by Saddam to expedite
resolution of his claims against Kuwait. It was as-
sumed that, in accordance with Islamic custom, no
Muslim country would invade another Muslim
country and, tragically, Saddam's threats were not
taken seriously.

April Glaspie, a capable foreign service officer and the U.S. Ambassador to Iraq in 1990, attended a late-night meeting with Saddam in
Baghdad on July 25, 1990, regarding the dispute
between Iraq and Kuwait. In response to Saddam's
question "What is the United States' opinion on
this matter?" Glaspie replied, "We have no opinion on Arab to Arab disputes, like your border disagreement with Kuwait. Secretary Baker has directed my attention to the instruction, first given
to Iraq in the 1960s, that the Kuwait issue is not
associated with America." Saddam chose to inter-
pret her words as indicating the U.S. would not
interfere in internal Arab disputes and proceeded
accordingly. Sadly, she had planned a trip to London for medical treatment for her mother on August 1, 1990, the day before the Iraqi invasion took
place, and she never returned to Iraq.

Due to apparently irreconcilable differences,
talks in Jidda, Saudi Arabia, between Iraq and
Kuwait were broken off by the Iraqis. The Kuwaitis

thought that the talks would be resumed a few days later. They were wrong. On August 2, 1990, Iraqi forces invaded Kuwait. Kuwait City was swiftly captured, and Iraqi armor moved south in pursuit of the fleeing remnants of the Kuwaiti forces and to seal the Kuwait-Saudi border. The Saudis interpreted this move south as a serious threat to their massive oil fields in the Eastern Province. Alarmed, King Fahd sought immediate US. military support to defend the oil fields. President Bush promptly responded. Within days U.S. forces were landing in the Kingdom utilizing the magnificent Saudi port and air facilities. The Kuwait ruling family had fled to Saudi Arabia and later became the government in exile and a strong voice for the liberation of their country.

Activities in nearby Bahrain were immediately placed on war-time footing. USAF F-4G aircraft soon began arriving at Shaikh Isa Air Base at the south end of Bahrain via direct non-stop flights from the U.S.A. with the aid of aerial refueling. The airfield's first construction phase, with the assistance of the U.S. Corps of Engineers, including long runways of 12,500 feet, had fortuitously been completed literally just a few days earlier. The cost of construction was $115 million, paid for by the Bahrainis and Saudis. However, base housing facilities under phase 2 were still unfinished and in any case were only designed to support and house personnel suitable for Bahrain's appropriately modest air force.

Tents and latrines were quickly erected by the U.S. Forces to accommodate initially about 2,600 personnel, later rising to 8,000 when the Marines arrived in full force. The U.S. Air Force's 35th Tactical Fighter Wing (Deployed) arrived in August, 1990, with F-4G advanced "Wild Weasel" aircraft to provide lethal "Suppression of Enemy Air Defenses" (SEAD) and with aerial reconnaissance. They were to fly 3,100 sorties during Desert Storm. Twelve Wild Weasels led the successful initial mass bombing raid on Baghdad in the early hours of the air campaign on January 17, 1991. Throughout the 42 days of the war, F-4G aircraft fired 918 air-to-ground missiles, which effectively silenced the Iraqi radar-guided surface-to-air missile and anti-aircraft artillery. This allowed the other coalition aircraft to conduct combat operations in a vastly reduced surface-to-air threat environment. They departed Shaikh Isa Air Base on June 23, 1991, after ten months of operation in the region. The U.S. Marine Corps also had their superb 3rd Marine Air Wing living in tents at Shaikh Isa Air Base under the command of USMC Major General Royal Moore. This organization provided outstanding air support to the Marine Corps' successful ground operations to liberate Kuwait.

During Desert Storm, there were about 540,000 U.S. troops in the Arabian Peninsula area under General Norman Schwarzkopf's command (see photo #27). Bahrain made a splendid contribution to the U.N. coalition and accommodated 17,000 U.S. military personnel, with 250 U.S. aircraft, at Shaikh Isa Air Base and Muharak Airport, that flew 11,000 sorties against Iraq and Kuwait. In early November, 1990, Secretary of State James Baker III came to Bahrain. On Nov. 5, he asked me to accompany him on an aerial flight to visit the 1st U.S. Cavalry Division in the Saudi desert (see photo #29).

The old U.S. Embassy building in Bahrain was made the headquarters of the large military logistical task force commanded by Lt. General William "Gus" Pagonis to prepare the Coalition offensive for the liberation of Kuwait. It is little known that major base support for this vast undertaking came from Diego Garcia, a tiny island in the Indian Ocean. Although it was over 3,000 miles away from Kuwait, Iraq's invasion of Kuwait was the beginning of the most intense operational period in the island's history. From August 1, 1990, to February 28, 1991, NSF Diego Garcia achieved and maintained the highest degree of operation readiness, providing unprecedented levels of support as a critical logistics staging area.

Direct support required the quick provisioning and topping off of 16 ships of the Maritime Pre-positioning Squadron and Afloat Pre-positioning Force. This enabled them all to get underway within six days. The first 11 ships were en route within a 24-hour period.

Diego Garcia also supported aviation units, conducting over 2,000 combat and reconnaissance sorties over Kuwait and Iraq. Units deploying to Diego Garcia included a Strategic Air Command

Provisional Bombardment Wing, a NavyReserve Helicopter Squadron Detachment providing search-and-rescue support, a full Maritime Patrol Squadron, and a Fleet Air Reconnaissance Squadron Detachment. Photographic Services provided fast turnaround time, despite a 1,000 per cent increase in the aerial film footage development requirements. Equally important, Diego Garcia acted as a cargo and personnel staging base for the Military Airlift Command and aircraft from four other countries, moving cargo and personnel to and from the USN battle groups and other operational forces in the North Arabian Sea. Overall, the number of aircraft supported increased 500 per cent.

Among the most vivid memories of my three and a half years in Bahrain were the Gulf War "Town Hall Meeting" emergency briefings to the understandably nervous American community. The meetings were held in the BAPCO Club Ballroom from September to December, 1990. In those anxious weeks of Desert Shield/Desert Storm there was great concern in the U.S. community about the risks of Iraqi Scud missiles, and biological and chemical warfare. With a full-capacity, very attentive audience I chaired the meetings, with the capable assistance of Vice Admiral Stanley Arthur, USN, then the head of U.S. Naval Activities in the Gulf, and other U.S. military experts in Scud missiles, gas masks, and evacuation plans. "CNN" provided 24-hour-a-day news coverage in our living rooms. The CNN reporters became household names, and in the months prior to commencement of the air campaign on January 15, 1991, it was largely a "CNN" war. We listened to their every syllable. They kept us informed faster than the U.S. official word could reach us through normal Embassy channels. The U.S. military leaders and specialists perhaps perceived the coming conflict in different dimensions — and were not always all that reassuring. One question to an officer from an obviously nervous lady was: "Colonel, what happens if I get hit by a Scud?" Answer: "Ma'am, you'll have a bad day!"

These "Town-Hall Meetings" in the BAPCO Club tried to present convincingly calm and optimistic "situation assessments" to the assembled American community. The air of confidence and steadfast reassurance was aimed at discounting the wild "rumor mill" in the civilian community and easing the very real growing public anxiety. As a result of the meetings, panic in the American community was averted, and we avoided unnecessary evacuation of U.S. civilians from the Island. On the morning of Iraq's invasion of Kuwait, the Japanese Embassy was closed, and the Japanese government ordered the immediate and mandatory evacuation of all its citizens from Bahrain. Even the British had encouraged their citizens to leave. All this upset the Bahrain government and gave them the feeling that they were being abandoned by previously friendly foreign governments. At the age of 22 I had landed in Normandy on D-Day, and had since been involved in many wars. It was clear to me how important it was to assess realistically the situation and to remain calm. Our positive persuasion paid off, and almost all the Americans remained in Bahrain throughout the War. To this day, over thirteen years later, I am still reminded by Bahrain senior officials that they were thankful and appreciative that the Americans stood firmly with them throughout those difficult and often terrifying months.

The saga of the distribution of gas masks will remain for many as one of the more interesting highlights of the days of pre-Desert Storm. British state-of-the-art gas masks were handed out to all British men, women, and children. On the other hand, the American gas masks, left over from World War I, were made available from the U.S. Embassy on a limited basis, to the obvious distaste and voluble protests of the American community.

One of the very emotional and memorable events of my time in Bahrain occurred on Thanksgiving Day, 1990. The BAPCO Club Ballroom was crowded with 250 U.S. Marines and their BAPCO host families. Tables were full of turkey and all the trimmings for this time-honored celebration of life. BAPCO's CEO said to me, "Mr. Ambassador, will you please read the President's Thanksgiving Message, and I will say the grace." I agreed. There was absolute silence in the ballroom as I read the President's Message of Thanksgiving. The words of inspiration from President Bush had a very special meaning for those young warriors who would soon go into their first battle. After the grace a young female Marine came up to the table that I was sharing with a Patriot Anti-Missile Detachment and asked, "Sir, may we sing the national anthem?" I was delighted and responded, "Yes, of course, but we have no orchestra, no music." She smiled happily and replied, "Leave that to the Marines, Sir." I watched her thread her way back across the ballroom, speaking to other Marines on the way. Soon twenty young Marines were up on the stage. They gave a stirring a cappella rendition of "Oh, say, can you see . . ." When they finished there was barely a dry eye in the room, and after a brief silence came the wild Marine roar of affirmation—the same pride and patriotism as their fathers' and grandfathers' before them . . . Semper Fi! I felt an enormous sense of pride being an American and having the honor of representing the President on that very special Thanksgiving Day.

There were some unusual events during those hectic days. The U.S. Central Intelligence Agency found it expedient to centralize many of its wartime regional activities in helpful Bahrain. The number of people involved was large, and the Agency found it necessary to lease a very large walled compound containing a group of houses which were used both as offices and residences. The Agency remained active there throughout Desert Shield/Desert Storm and then quietly diminished their staff.

Another important aspect of the Gulf War was the need to advance our public diplomacy and to expand favorable knowledge of the U.S. viewpoint, both to the Gulf region and to the rest of the

Arabic and Islamic world. In order to do that the U.S. needed to quickly deploy a medium-wave radio-relay station for Arabic language programming for the Middle East and the Gulf. The burning question was, "Where could it best be placed?" Bahrain was the ideal location, and I was asked if Bahrain would accommodate such a politically sensitive radio transmitter.

At the urgent request of the U.S. State Department and the Voice of America, I personally went to see the highly influential Bahraini Minister of Information, Tariq Al-Moyaed and presented my request. Tariq ran a "tight ship" for over 22 years at the Ministry of Information and had very definite ideas as to how Bahrain's image should be projected, particularly toward the rest of the Arab world. Though he was basically pro-West, in the matter of the Iraqi invasion of Kuwait he definitely did not like the idea of Bahrain being host to an Arabic-language extension of the Voice of America. He feared that Bahrain would be viewed negatively in the eyes of Arab and Islamic people, as a "mouthpiece" for the Western world, especially since the Bahraini government would not have control over the content being broadcast. He adamantly refused to approve the proposal. I tried to explain the vital importance that these broadcasts would play in the overall Gulf War. I sought to play on our quite close friendship by addressing him on our normal first-name basis as "Tariq." For the first time in our relationship he snapped back at me, saying, "Address me as Mr. Minister."

"Yes, Mr. Minister," I replied, smiling, and realized that this was not a propitious moment to continue my appeal.

I promptly returned to the Embassy, reported the events to Washington, D.C., and sought their further guidance. Washington quickly replied, as I had anticipated, saying that the matter was a vital priority and should be pursued urgently at the "highest levels."

It was my judgment that the Minister of Information had made up his mind and was unlikely to reverse himself. However, I felt that in the light of our continuing relations I should try again with him so I met once more and made my best appeal. I let him know that this was of vital concern to Washington and that I had been instructed that, if necessary, I was to pursue this request to "the top." Tariq's face flushed, but he would not change his mind, even though he realized I would need to go "over his head" to the Prime Minister or the Amir. I told him that as U.S. Ambassador this was something reluctantly that had to be done in the U.S. national interest.

I promptly met the Amir at the earliest opportunity and made my case, stressing the great urgency of the matter and its importance to the successful outcome of the Gulf War. The Amir listened gravely, and when I was finished, he said, "We will consider the question and will respond promptly." Happily, the answer, which came the next day, was favorable. Bahrain had again proven its sincerity and friendship by permitting the relay station to be established for six months and then allowing an extension of a further five months. This was one of those occasions in which my close personal relationship with the Amir certainly paid dividends.

On November 8, 1990, President Bush announced plans to greatly expand U.S. forces in the Gulf in order to eject Iraqi forces from Kuwait. On November 29, the U.N. authorized the use of the coalition military forces to liberate Kuwait.

The U.S. Department of Defense, Congress, and the media all feared that the Gulf War and Saddam's ruthlessness would result in a high number of civilian and military casualties and might well provoke deadly Iraqi chemical reprisals as had occurred with the Kurds and against Iran. Some media predictions for U.S. military casualties topped 35,000 so friendly Bahrain was requested to accommodate three U.S. military field hospitals, as well as two U.S. Navy floating hospitals offshore (the USN Mercy and the USN Comfort).

The largest of the Naval field hospitals, packed into approximately 750 large containers, was shipped from Japan to Bahrain. As the vessel steamed towards Bahrain with all possible speed considerable concern was being expressed by the Bahrainis about where this hospital would be accommodated. Many persons believed that it would become a target for Iraqi Scud missiles and nobody wanted it "in their back yard." On a day or two before the vessel's scheduled arrival, I had lunch in the guest house in BAPCO with Don Hepburn,

BAPCO's CEO, and told him about the problem. He immediately got up from the lunch table and said, "Come with me, Charles. I'll show you where we can put it." He took me to the proposed location, which was inside the BAPCO company area in Awali, adjacent to the company's hospital. I quickly agreed that the site was perfect. Within two hours Hepburn had obtained the necessary approvals from the Prime Minister and BAPCO's Chairman, Yusuf Shirawi, the Minister of Oil and Industry. By 4 o'clock that same afternoon the SeaBee's were on site, and a fully air-conditioned, fully equipped 400-bed tent hospital was soon in operational readiness.

Other medical facilities in Bahrain included the 47th Army Field Hospital and the 22nd TAC ASF hospital at Shaikh Isa Air Base. Many of the field hospital personnel were U.S. Reservists who had been called away from their civilian medical and dental practices. There were also 28 New Zealand nurses who added an international dimension to the operation. Fortunately, the apprehensions about heavy casualties did not materialize, and the U.S. suffered the incredibly low casualties of 24 U.S. dead and 500 wounded. With lots of spare time, the medical staff spent much of the Gulf War in their camps playing cards and missing their families.

Because Bahrain had rapidly become an essential component for the coalition forces, the Iraqi radio broadcast a threat of Scud attacks on the area. However, Iraqi Scud missiles had a relatively unsophisticated guidance system and were very in-accurate. A number of Scud missiles fell in the sea, short of Bahrain, but four Scud missiles entered Bahrain airspace, three of which were diverted in the air by Patriot missiles. The fourth missile landed in a deserted area of Bahrain where it blew a big hole in the ground, but caused no damage. One Scud hit a military barracks in Dhahran, Saudi Arabia, about 20 miles from Bahrain, killing 28 coalition troops. Given the general inaccuracy of the Scuds, we were never quite sure whether the four Scuds were actually aimed at Bahrain. After the Gulf War, I secured from the U.S military an engine from a crashed Scud and presented it to the Minister of Information, who placed it in the Bahrain National Museum.

Rest and Recreation for Allied Troops

The days for the preparation of Operation Desert Storm turned into weeks, then into months, of sandstorms, choking dust, and almost unbear-able heat and humidity. The morale of U.S. troops deployed in lonely distant desert areas was a grow-ing concern to the Department of Defense. The re-moteness of sandy desolate outposts in Saudi Arabia required that they be continuously re-sup-plied with water, food, and every other necessity. Conditions were also somewhat depressing for the thousands of U.S. service men and women sta-tioned in Bahrain and on board U.S. Navy vessels. Many of these troops were entertained at my Residence and given gifts provided by the USO and hospitality by voluntary organizations. Every day BAPCO hosted 400 U.S. personnel from Shaikh Isa Air Base in the company Club. These were mainly U.S. Marines who, unlike the U.S. Air Force personnel, were denied access to alcohol, but nevertheless the food and the air-conditioning were a welcome relief from tent life on the Base.

Although the Saudis urgently needed our military protection, they declined official requests to provide our troops with Rest and Recreation (R & R) facilities in their country. The Saudi government feared an adverse cultural impact on their strict Islamic principles. At the direct request of the U.S. Department of Defense in a late-night phone call, I actively sought to secure approval for R & R facilities in Bahrain. Agreement was quickly obtained with the help of the Amir, Shaikh Isa, and his experienced Foreign Minister, both of whom appreciated the harsh conditions our troops were undergoing in the deserts.

The hotels in Bahrain were overflowing with Kuwaiti refugees and the stream of official, military, and civilian visitors. The hotel ballrooms and conference rooms were often turned into sleeping areas. I proposed, therefore, that a cruise ship be leased and docked in Bahrain as a housing and floating R & R Center. The Cunard Princess was ultimately leased by the U.S. Department of Defense and anchored in Bahrain. Some officials of the U.S. State Department were concerned that our troops might cause social problems in Bahrain, damaging relations with a valuable ally, and they accepted the R & R proposal with some trepidation. I was informally made to understand that if anything went wrong, "it would be my neck." Since I was not a State Department career officer, I was not unduly concerned. I probably had more faith than they did in the discipline and public behavior of our troops and took responsibility for any adverse consequences. Partially due to our careful planning and implementation nothing went dramatically wrong, and there were no serious breaches of military conduct among the 73,000 U.S. service members who happily participated over the next four months in the shipboard R & R scheme.

Under this program 900 U.S. troops at a time were transported by bus across the Bahrain-Saudi Causeway to the cruise ship from their camps in the desert. They spent three days on board the Princess, and on the fourth day they were returned to their bases. The same buses then brought back to the Princess another 900 service personnel. Thus, R & R was provided for 1,800 people each week. They could relax, drink beer, watch movies, enjoy floor-shows, play games, and telephone home. Since we did not want to prohibit them from going into town, it was arranged to lower the price of the drinks on shipboard to about one-half of the cost in the hotels of Manama. That lured the servicemen back to the ship very quickly and minimized the risk of shore-side incidents. U.S. taxpayers are pleased to learn that the cost of this operation was largely paid for by the Japanese financial contribution to the Gulf War. Many servicemen have since told me what a memorable and enjoyable experience it was to be hosted in such a friendly and tolerant haven. Morale was certainly boosted, and the "Princess Operation" was clearly an important contribution to the physiological readiness of our troops for the forthcoming offensive against Iraq.

Bob Hope's Last Overseas Troop Show

We were delighted to receive in Bahrain our "not-too-secret" weapon, the greatly beloved entertainer Bob Hope. The legendary veteran of some 60 years of troop entertainment toured U.S. military units in the deserts of Saudi Arabia in his usual effervescent style, using the back of an open truck as his stage. This Gulf War effort was the last of Bob's overseas military entertainment ventures, but it was one of his best.

Bob was allowed to put on a full-scale show in Bahrain (with Marie Osmond, Dolores Hope, his wife, and others) to entertain the troops. Bahrain's Minister of Information Tariq Al-Moyaed, attended the performance. I went on stage and told the four to five-thousand patiently waiting G.I.s how much the U.S.A. and Bahrain appreciated their efforts, adding that I was sure the Minister wanted also to express his thanks. Tariq caused great amusement when he took the microphone and exclaimed, "No! I'm here to see Bob Hope!" The crowd roared in approval. This amusing quip resulted in Tariq and me being included in the final TV version of the Bob Hope Gulf War show. That was December 26, 1990, and the show helped enormously to boost morale for those troops in Bahrain away from their families over the holiday season.

On the evening of December 27th, Tariq invited the cast to his spacious residence in Saar. Bob, wife Dolores, Linda (his daughter and competent manager), Marie Osmond, and other performers enjoyed a delightful buffet dinner at Tariq's home. The evening was full of fun and laughter, and, somewhat with tongue in cheek, Bob changed into an Arab thobe and had his photograph taken with Tariq, which was later printed widely in the world press (see photo #30).

Bob's performances in Saudi Arabia and Bahrain were filmed for a television version for the USO and were later widely shown on U.S. television. The show was mostly filmed in Bahrain since the Saudi religious leaders did not condone women entertainers singing and dancing on stage. The TV production showed thousands of our troops relaxing and laughing, temporarily forgetting the anxiety of the imminent coalition counter-attack for the liberation of Kuwait. Bob Hope kindly sent me a two-page letter of thanks on January 11, 1991. We all pay homage to Bob, a great patriot, humanitarian, comic genius, and entertainer, who died at the age of 100 on July 27, 2003.

The Saudi leadership was dismayed at the presence of U.S. service women among our troops in the Kingdom, and they rejected a request for actress Brooke Shields to visit the U.S. troops during the Christmas period. Instead, she was warmly welcomed in Bahrain, to the delight of all at Shaikh Isa Air Base.

Gulf War I's Outcome

On January 17, 1991, the coalition launched a massive USAF-led air campaign against Iraqi targets in Kuwait and Iraq.

Just before dawn on February 24, 1991, the coalition ground campaign began, with the USMC leading the way with a direct advance against Iraqi positions in the south of Kuwait. The Marines were led by the capable Lt. General Walt Boomer, USMC. Simultaneously, a masterful and totally unexpected, fast moving "left hook" ground strategy was launched by the coalition in the open Iraqi desert west of Kuwait utilizing 146,000 U.S. troops as well as other coalition units. One-hundred hours later, on February 28, 1991, the ground war was over. Eighty thousand demoralized Iraqi troops surrendered. The enemy retreated in complete disarray, leaving the road to Basra littered with bodies from their burning tanks and trucks, surrounded by the pathetic booty pillaged from Kuwait City. In the final hours of the battle, Saddam vindictively set on fire 800 Kuwaiti oil wells in February, blanketing the region with thick blinding black smoke which darkened the skies over Bahrain for several months.

It helped the morale of our fine U.S. troops that the highest rating the Gallup poll has ever recorded, thus far, for confidence by the U.S. population in the U.S. military came in 1991, after Operation Desert Storm, when it reached 85 percent.

An often asked question in later years was, "Should the coalition have pushed on to Baghdad to capture Saddam and totally destroy the Iraqi Republican Guard?" However, the objective set by the U.N. was to free Kuwait, not to occupy Iraq. If our armor had swept into Baghdad, we would have been seen by the rest of the world as a bully, the world's sole super-power, exercising our superior military power in the annihilation of a Muslim state in order to control their oil production. In addition, the U.S. then did not want to undertake the many problems that occupation and restoration of Iraq are now causing as a result of Gulf War II. Nonetheless, in retrospect, one could reasonably argue that the coalition forces could have insisted that Saddam personally sign a surrender agreement. This would have lowered his status in the eyes of his countrymen — and in the rest of the Arab world. A few days after the signing of the Peace Agreement with Iraq, General Norman Schwarzkopf told me privately that he had agreed to permit the Iraqis to continue to operate their helicopters in Iraq because he had no instructions to the contrary. "I hope I have done the right thing," he added. As we now know, Iraq used these helicopters with devastating effect to brutally subdue the attempted Shiite uprising in the South.

Saddam showed himself to be incredibly reckless as well as totally ruthless. He invaded both Iran and Kuwait. He launched Scuds against Tel Aviv even though he knew Israel already had nuclear weapons. It was only American appeals to Israel to stay out of the fighting that saved Baghdad from massive retaliation. Despite his recklessness, he did not dare to use his chemical weapons against the coalition forces in the Gulf or against the Israelis. The threat of Iraqi chemical and nuclear attacks was taken so seriously that U.S. Secretary of State, Jim Baker, bluntly warned the Iraqis that the coalition would immediately retaliate in kind. The Iraqis apparently heard and understood this message, and no such attacks were made. However, just in case, many troops and civilians carried gas masks throughout the war. Some political analysts continued to counsel vigorous deterrence methods because they believe that an oil-rich and relatively technically advanced country such as Iraq may ultimately try to join the expanding nuclear club.

Following the end of Desert Storm, the United Nations created the U.N. Special Commission (UNSCOM), charged with overseeing the dismantling of Iraq's weapons of mass destruction. Because of the proximity of Bahrain to Iraq, and with the Bahrain government's willingness to help, UNSCOM selected Bahrain as its Regional Headquarters. Its large staff of experts drawn from many nations shuttled back and forth to Iraq from

Muharraq Airport utilizing their U.N. aircraft. UNSCOM occupied the old U.S. Embassy building, and UNSCOM officials were very appreciative of the Embassy's assistance in cutting through the normal bureaucratic red tape to obtain approval for them to locate in Bahrain, thus leaving the team members free to focus on their increasingly difficult task in Iraq.

On April 5, 1991, the U.S. authorized Operation Provide Comfort to protect Iraqi Kurds from Saddam's brutal repression. On August 26, 1992, the U.S. established Operation Southern Watch to protect Shiite Marsh Arabs from Iraqi fixed wing and helicopter attacks. Unfortunately, despite U.S. expectations to the contrary, Saddam remained in power until the U.S. and British military action in April, 2003.

On a less dramatic note, despite all the emphasis on the war effort I made sure that we never lost sight of the Embassy's responsibility to promote U.S. commercial and trading relationships in Bahrain. Having been U.S. National Export Promotion Coordinator and Deputy Assistant Secretary for International Commerce during the Nixon/Ford Administration, I knew the great importance of trade and commerce to both countries. I actively used my contacts in Washington and elsewhere to facilitate commercial interaction wherever possible.

In the less frantic months that followed the end of Desert Storm, I was able to devote some of my personal time at the Residence to updating my earlier book, *Turkism and the Soviets,* first published in 1957. I was fortunate to have the able assistance of Mrs. Joyce Barnes for the typing and editing of the revised text. Without her outstanding secretarial skills I doubt that the project would have been completed. The book was subsequently published by Praeger in 1993 under the new title *The Turks of Central Asia,* which was more relevant to the post-war era.

On June 12, 1991, after 18 months in Bahrain, Ambassador John H. Kelly, then Assistant Secretary of State for Near Eastern and South Asian Affairs, prepared my Performance Evaluation, which said, in part:

> . . . you quickly established strong and productive relations with key Bahrainis including the Amir, the Prime Minister, the Crown Prince, and the Foreign Minister. Indeed, your relations with the Amir are more cordial than those enjoyed by many of your predecessors.
>
> These personal ties have enabled you to advance vital U.S. interests. During the Gulf crisis, for example, your frequent meetings with senior Bahraini leaders assured the smooth transition from the relatively small U.S. peacetime military presence in Bahrain to the large wartime one. You were able to persuade the GOB that Bahrain would be the most suitable place for R & R facilities for the hundreds of thousand of U.S. troops in

the theater. And thanks largely to your persistence, and seemingly endless demarches, you convinced Bahrain's cantankerous Minister of Information to permit the VOA to establish a transmitter in Bahrain and to broadcast some programs in Arabic. We are fully aware how much the VOA is in your debt.

Remembering the short "appreciation period" from the countries aided by the U.S. in the past, which seems to have followed the end of many wars, I encouraged the State Department to take quick formal diplomatic action following the successful end of the Gulf War. On October 27, 1991, a new U.S.-Bahrain Agreement on Defense Cooperation was signed by the effectual Bahrain Foreign Minister Shaikh Mohammed bin Mubarak Al-Khalifa and myself in the presence of the then U.S. Deputy Assistant Secretary of State, Richard Clarke (see photo #35). It was an important document, which has shaped our relationship ever since. It subsequently helped to make possible the establishment ashore of the Headquarters of the U.S. Fifth Fleet with a resident USN Vice Admiral and his staff in Bahrain. The leased land area in Juffair has now been expanded from what it was in 1990. The U.S. has completed extensive new barracks (which has eliminated the need for the U.S. Navy to put replacement and transient personnel in expensive Manama hotels) as well as headquarters buildings at a cost of over $40 million of U.S. government funds. Bahrain has understandably preferred that there be little publicity about this important arrangement.

President Bush invited Shaikh Isa for a State Visit to Washington, D.C. in appreciation of Bahrain's generous cooperation throughout the Gulf War. Each year the U.S. President is able to accommodate only six or seven Heads of State for an Official State visit because the security and logistics for large entourages are mind-boggling. Each Official State Visit normally includes a stay in the Blair House, and this too requires major administrative preparation across the street from the White House. A small country like Bahrain may necessarily wait for years before an invitation for an Official State Visit to Washington is feasible.

On October 15, 1991, President Bush warmly welcomed the Amir to Washington in a formal ceremony on the White House lawn, complete with military band, guard of honor, guests, and speeches (see photo #32). An impressive array of guests included senior U.S. and Bahrain military, diplomatic, and civilian personnel. President Bush made a gracious welcoming address, and Shaikh Isa responded. The party then moved into the White House for a simple but elegant lunch.

Well before the visit of the Amir to the White House, Bahrain's Office of Protocol in the Foreign Ministry began to consider what gifts would be appropriate for the Amir to present to the U.S. President and his wife. After careful consideration it was decided that the President would be given a uniquely elaborate date palm-tree made of 8.5

pounds of 21-carat gold, which alone was worth about $60,000, and adorned with 749 "dates," which were natural pearls from the waters around Bahrain, all hand-crafted by Bahrain's Al-Mannai goldsmiths (see photo #33).

Mrs. Bush was presented with a beautiful pearl necklace of 133 natural pearls, the largest being 8.5 mm., set in 18-carat gold with a center-piece made up of 3.5 carats of diamonds (see photo #34). When I asked Mrs. Bush what she thought of the gift, she understandably said, "I cried." She cried, of course, because the gifts had to be handed in as U.S. government property. However, they are today displayed for public viewing in the official President Bush Library in Houston, Texas. The Amir's visit was a glittering success and did much to further enhance the long and beneficial political, military, and economic relationships between our two countries.

In mid-1992 General Joseph Hoar, USMC, visited Bahrain after succeeding General Schwarzkopf as CINC, U.S. Central Command. He was graciously received by the Amir, Shaikh Isa, and by the Prime Minister, Shaikh Khalifa. Shaikh Isa kindly took General Hoar, myself, and other U.S. military officers for a brief cruise on his new private 218-foot, Italian-made yacht, which replaced the "AWAL."

In view of Diego Garcia's vital logistical role in preparation for Desert Shield/Desert Storm, I was delighted to have the opportunity to visit the island in March of 1992. Thanks to the U.S. Navy, I

was able to travel on one of the U.S. Navy char-
tered flights that left each week from Norfolk, Virginia, stopped in Naples and Bahrain, and finished
its flight in Diego Garcia, before making the return
flight to Norfolk.

In 1965 with the formation of the British Indian Ocean Territory (B.I.O.T.) Diego Garcia came
under the administrative control of the British government of the Seychelles. In 1976, the Seychelles
gained independence from England, and the
B.I.O.T. then became a self-administering territory
under the East African Desk of the British Foreign
Office. The Crown's senior person on the island is
the British Representative, who acts as both justice
of the peace and Commanding Officer of the Royal
Naval Party 1002. With the formation of the
B.I.O.T., a formal agreement was signed between
the governments of the United Kingdom and the
United States (circa 1966) making the island available to satisfy the defense needs of the two governments.

Until 1971, Diego Garcia's main source of
income was from its profitable copra oil plantation.
At one time, copra oil from here and the other "Oil
Islands" provided fine machine oil, and fuel for
European lamps. During the roughly 170 years of
plantation life, the coconut harvest on Diego Garcia
remained fairly constant. The plantation years
ended with the arrival of the U.S. Navy Seabees
and the start-up of U.S. military construction. Following the overthrow of the Shah of Iran in 1979,
Diego Garcia saw a dramatic build-up. In 1986,

Diego Garcia became fully operational with the completion of a $500 million construction program. Its geo-strategic location and full range of facilities make it the last link in a long logistics chain that supports a vital U.S. Naval presence in the Indian Ocean and North Arabian Sea. The U.S. Navy Support Facility (NSF) is the host U.S. command on the island. As such, it provides common services for all tenant commands and fleet support for afloat units in the Indian Ocean.

Following my visit to Diego Garcia, I took a month's leave, from April 22 to May 22, 1992, and traveled by commercial airlines from Bahrain to Singapore, Bali, and California, Las Vegas, Columbia College, Washington, D.C., London, and back to Bahrain. In Singapore I met with my long-time friend, Kwek Leng Joo, Managing Director of City Developments Ltd. (CDL), and stayed at their lovely Orchard Hotel. Many years before I had spent a very interesting three months as an IESC real-estate development consultant to CDL in Singapore and with his brother the resourceful Kwek Leng Beng. We celebrated Kwek Leng Joo and Alice's twelfth wedding anniversary. I also had an orientation visit with CALTEX's Managing Director, Cliff Hon, and made a courtesy call on the U.S. Ambassador Robert Orr.

From there I went on to the Bali Hilton Hotel on Nusa Dua beach and then onward to San Diego. I enjoyed a splendid black-tie dinner at the University Club given by the delightful and irrepressible Dr. Judson and Rachel Grosvenor, and also went to the Regency Club in West Los Angeles for a wonderful reception hosted by Armand and Sima Fontaine, acquaintances from my days on the California State Contractors License Board. On May 12, I spent an enjoyable day with dear friends, Reed and Rita Sprinkel, on their yacht, the "Viking Princess," which had been an official vessel during the exciting America's Cup yacht races off San Diego (and on which I later had many very enjoyable visits) (see photo #75).

I next traveled to Kansas to see my cousin and his wife, Peter and Adelaide Sipp, and their talented daughter, Polly Sipp Ford. Thanks to her and to Dr. Donald Ruthenberg, I was pleased to receive an Honorary Doctor of Public Administration degree from the prestigious Columbia College in Columbia, Missouri. While there I gave the commencement address and was happy to see Solange Herter, lovely wife of Dr. Fred Herter, former President of AUB. She was at Columbia College to donate valuable, historic papers related to Russia, which had been collected by her father.

This was followed by a three-day consultation at the U.S. State Department in Washington, D.C., a brief stop in London, and then on to Bahrain. I had completed an enjoyable "around the world" in 30 days.

In April of 1992, Ambassador Edward P. Djerejian, then Assistant Secretary of State for Near Eastern and South Asian Affairs, issued a very complimentary Performance Evaluation, which said:

Your experience over the last two and one-half years, and the close relationships you have formed with the senior most princes and leading Bahraini officials, have enabled us to move smoothly through the post-war adjustment period into a new era of bilateral cooperation. During my visit to Manama in January, 1992, I was impressed by the evident warmth of your relationship with the Amir, the Foreign Minister, and other top GOB officials. In a part of the world where personal contacts are the *sine qua non* of diplomacy, these personal relationship have served U.S. policy interests well.

While many examples of your substantive knowledge could be cited, one which especially leaps to mind is your assistance to the UN Special Commission (UNSCOM) overseeing dismantling of Iraq's weapons of mass destruction. UN officials have expressed their gratitude for the Embassy's assistance, and your ability to call senior GOB officials directly, cutting through bureaucratic red tape, enabled the UN team to concentrate on its assigned task. In another case, your close relationship with the Amir and your knowledge of how the GOB works was vital in VOA's being granted a five-month extension for its Arabic-language broadcasts—a key U.S. policy objective, enabling us to give the lie to Saddam's propaganda.

Taking advantage of a bilateral relationship which was strong to begin with, you deftly championed U.S. interests in several fields where there was a potential for disagreement with the GOB. The best example of your leadership is in the area of human rights, where in spite of GOB perturbation over the Embassy's contacts with the families of detained suspects, you continued calmly and logically made our case. The increasing awareness the Bahrainis accord to the importance of world opinion on this emotional topic testifies to your persistence. Human Affairs Bureau has told me of its pleasure over GOB receptiveness to a dialogue and urges the continuation of your worthwhile efforts.

Given the postwar climate of budget austerity and its impact on resources and personnel management, your stewardship of Embassy Manama has been careful and pragmatic, even when this meant passing up opportunities which could have expanded the Embassy's capabilities. All of our embassies in the Gulf have faced hard choices at a time when few additional resources are available, and you have used what you had in an exemplary manner.

Aside from the day-to-day business of running an embassy, I have also noticed the skill with which you managed a stream of visits (including my own). The professional way you ironed out details in Bahrain made the Amir's October, 1991, State Visit one which State Department protocol called "the smoothest in a long time." This was especially important in view of the close friendship between the President and the Amir, and the White House let us know it was pleased.

Your grasp of U.S. policy objectives and how best to pursue them was demonstrated on more than one occasion. For example, your enthusiastic efforts in behalf of the Department's goal of supporting U.S. commerce in the Gulf led to an extremely successful bilateral conference in Manama which awoke many Washington offices to the opportunities for trade with Bahrain. The inquiries we continue to receive from U.S. businessmen interested in Bahrain speak for themselves.

Your reporting on your contacts with members of the ruling family and senior GOB officials was excellent, and several times alerted the Department to subtle shifts of opinion or future areas for concern. Likewise, the extremely close relationship you developed with U.S. military officers made negotiation of a military cooperation agreement relatively easy, as did your ability to act as a conduit between the GOB and the U.S. military — a true test of your intellectual skills, which you passed with flying colors.

Several times in the past year we called on you to undertake tasks which were not congenial but where your interpersonal skills showed to the best advantage. In asking an antagonistic Minister of Information for an extension for VOA broadcasting, a task which must have been personally a difficult one, you struck exactly the right note and, in spite of the Minister's intransigence, laid the groundwork for a successful appeal to the Amir. Likewise, in dealing with the Foreign Minister's insistent repetition of his request for our endorsement of Bahrain's claim to the Hawar Islands, your attitude of being an attentive listener while repeatedly making the point of our neutrality and desire for a peaceful solution was right on target.

With the bilateral relationship flourishing, I suggest that you urge your officers to report on signs of disaffection as well. Last year's memcons on contacts with the families of detainees were excellent examples of what can be done. By spreading out such contacts over time and not doing too much at once, you should minimize any negative official reaction, which in any event you will know best how to handle. Your own reporting based on high level contacts assures that we know more about their own view of the context in which indications of discontent may arise.

I fully share the President's great confidence in you. Knowing that the U.S. Ambassador in one of the Gulf's smallest but nonetheless most complex societies can carry out the toughest tasks assigned to him in minimum time and with maximum efficiency and panache is very reassuring. Embassy Manama's relationship with Washington has been completely rebuilt during your tenure, and the efficiency, productivity, and high reputation of the Embassy and of the officers who have served under you are testimonials to the job you have done.

As you know, we do not expect the financial stringency currently affecting the Department to disappear in the next few months or years. This means, unfortunately, that we cannot give you all the resources we would like you to have, but the skill with which you have managed affairs so far assures us that Manama will continue to keep up the fine practices you have established since your arrival.

We share the opinion of you expressed by the Amir, one whose warmth has seldom been matched when heads of state commented on the jobs done by their U.S. Ambassadors. Your performance in Manama has been beneficial to both U.S. policy goals and to private U.S. citizens in the region, and I am fully confident that it will continue to be so. In short, keep up the fine tradition you have already established.

In January, 1993, after the elections and the change in the White House, President Clinton's staff instructed that the politically appointed U.S. ambassadors should depart their posts by March 1 at the latest. The Bahraini government then officially requested the State Department to extend my tour of duty until a newly appointed ambassador could arrive. All such requests were denied so I made plans to depart Bahrain on March 1, 1993.

On February 11, 1993, Don and Roma Hepburn organized a wonderful farewell party at Al Dar in Awali, BAPCO's company compound. It was a formal black-tie sit-down dinner attended by about 55 friends and dignitaries. Don gave an eloquent and laudatory speech, which I greatly appreciated.

Bahrain's Amir, Shaikh Isa bin Sulman Al-Khalifa, hosted an elaborate farewell dinner on February 18, 1993. He honored me by awarding Bahrain's "First Class Order" (Bahrain's highest decoration). He kindly cited me for ". . . outstanding services during the Gulf War operations and for successful efforts in enhancing relations between Bahrain and the U.S. . . ." I was honored and felt pleased knowing that I had done my best to significantly strengthen the relationships between two nations I so greatly admired.

The following day the Foreign Minister, Shaikh Mohammed bin Mubarak Al-Khalifa, gave a luncheon in my honor for 56 dignitaries, including ministers, foreign diplomats, and other guests. I have long admired him, and his kind gesture truly warmed my heart.

That evening, the Minister of Information, Tariq Al-Moyaed, arranged a farewell dinner at the unique Al-Sawani restaurant with a similar number of guests. The disagreement between us during the war time had long since been forgotten. He referred to me as "a real pal."

On completion of my duties in Bahrain, at the recommendation of Deputy Assistant Secretary NEA, Ambassador David Mack, I was given the U.S. State Department's "Foreign Affairs Award for Public Service" on March 10, 1993, in Washington, D.C. It was presented by Assistant Secretary of State for Near Eastern Affairs, Edward P. Djerejian, in the presence of the Bahraini Ambassador and officials of the State and Defense Departments. It was described as the U.S. State Department's highest award for a non-career diplomat.

The citation stated that it was being given "in recognition of outstanding achievement from 1989 to 1993 as Ambassador to Bahrain. Ambassador Hostler's performance was praised as meeting the highest standards of the Department of State and of U.S. diplomacy." Noting that the Embassy had reported an unusual outpouring of recognition and affection for the Ambassador upon his departure, Djerejian stated, "Your performance during Desert Shield and Desert Storm met the standards of American diplomacy in getting the job done—and done well—regardless of danger and distractions."

The Secretary of Navy awarded me the Navy Commendation Medal, saying, " . . . in a volatile and consistently changing political environment, Ambassador Hostler showed tremendous insight and skill, safely navigating U.S. and Bahraini relations through a period that included the Iraqi invasion of Kuwait and Coalition Operations Desert Shield, Desert Storm and Southern Watch . . . Ambassador Hostler's distinctive accomplishments, unrelenting perseverance, and steadfast devotion to duty have reflected great credit upon himself and the U.S. Department of State . . ." The medal was presented by the competent Vice Admiral D. J. Katz, Commander, U.S. Naval Forces Central Command.

After my departure from Bahrain and as a tribute to my relations with the Bahrainis, I was asked by the Government of Bahrain to be their Honorary Consul General in the Western U.S.A. For me to accept this offer first required that written approval be obtained from the Secretary of the U.S. Air Force (because I am a retired USAF Colonel), and then from the U.S. Secretary of State. This was accomplished so that, since 1993, I have had the pleasure of filling this post on a voluntary basis. At that time, I was the only Honorary Consul General for Bahrain in the world (one has since been appointed as Honorary Consul in Hong Kong). Bahrain is a great and proven friend of the U.S.A., and I am honored to represent them in this fashion.

For me, three and a half years of service as the U.S. Ambassador to the State of Bahrain was in every respect a wonderfully satisfying professional and cultural experience. It was destiny, the point of convergence of all my past lifetime of experience — academic, U.S. intelligence, military, political, and business. All were intensely focused on the full spectrum of international affairs in the U.S. national interest, both in peace and in war at the vitally important energy center of the world.

Shaikh Isa died in March, 1999, and was succeeded the same day by his eldest son, Shaikh Hamad bin Isa Al-Khalifa (see photo #28). Shaikh Hamad, born January 8, 1950, had been the Crown Prince and founder and Commander-in-Chief of the Bahraini Defense Forces (BDF). He had attended for a time the British Military College at Sandhurst. He especially enjoyed raising Arabian horses and was kind enough to invite me quite often to his homes and yacht (the M/V Jameel, at Safriyah). Shaikh Hamad and I worked together well and pleasantly during the Gulf War, and he took particular interest in military matters and in ways to develop and improve the BDF. His open-mindedness and close understanding of the military helped strengthen Bahrain. When I was in Bahrain, I understood that Shaikh Hamad had four wives (though according to local custom, I never met them). Now King Hamad has encouraged a more liberal approach to such matters, and his wife HH Shaikha Sabeeka is Chairwoman of the Supreme Council for Women and speaks frequently at public conferences.

King Hsamad's eldest son, Shaikh Sulman bin Hamad Al-khalifa, is now the Crown Prince. I first met Shaikh Sulman while he was attending the American University in Washington, D.C. He is a bright, forthright, and intelligent young man (born October 21, 1969). I took him for a visit on June 8, 1992, as the guest of honor, on the U.S. Carrier "Independence." Shaikh Sulman showed a great deal of interest and handled himself very well in his interactions with the crew. I was very impressed with this then 22-year-old young man, and believe that some day he will be very effective as King of Bahrain if he succeeds his fine father. Later Shaikh Sulman attended Cambridge University in England for an advanced degree. He succeeded to his father's earlier position and is currently the Commander-in-Chief of the Bahrain Defense Forces.

Bahrain is now one of the most politically open societies in the Gulf, though during the time I was there (1989-1993) it did not have formal democratic institutions. The ruling Al-Khalifa family has taken direct action to address these questions, and Shaikh Hamad has wisely initiated plans for democratic reforms and elections, which led to Bahrain becoming a Constitutional Monarchy (see photo #28). The King, Shaikh Hamad, on February 15, 2002, impressively announced his approval of the plan that creates a bicameral legislature. The ruler appoints the members of one of the two elements of the legislature. Municipal elections occurred on May 9, 2002, with national legislative elections on October 24, 2002. Men and women were allowed to run for office. President Bush announced on October 25, 2001, that Bahrain had been accorded Major Non-NATO Ally (MNNA) status in recognition of the long-standing ties between the U.S. and Bahrain.

Chapter Ten
New Ventures and Commitments (1993 - 2003)

Upon leaving my fulfilling post in Bahrain on March 1, 1993, for the journey back to the U.S.A., I felt that at the age of 74 years careful consideration should be given as to where next to make my home. Friends residing in Southern France, Ulf and Chris Styren, who lived near the lovely town of Le Garde-Freinet, above beautiful St. Tropez, and Brigadier Ivor and Dorothy Hollyer, who lived in the delightful Algarve in Portugal, both kindly invited me to visit and consider those areas as a place to seek a residence.

Four or five days were spent pleasantly exploring each of those beautiful locales. In spite of their beauty and charm, I came to realize that it would be hard to surpass the climatic, social, and business advantages of the San Diego/Southern California region. I headed homeward through Washington, D.C. where I was given retirement benefits from the U.S. State Department and a pleasant farewell. There is certainly truth in the saying of writer George Moore, "A man travels the world over in search of what he needs and returns home to find it."

In San Diego County, I drove about La Jolla, Del Mar, and elsewhere, and finally focused on the pleasant village-like town of Coronado, just across the bay from the city of San Diego. I was fortunate to find there a newly completed set of condominiums built directly on the bay, called "Coronado Point Condos." The view from these buildings is unimpeded and spectacular. Many sailboats and large ships (naval and commercial) navigate elegantly nearby frequently, and San Diego city is sparkling across the bay. I was entranced and went immediately to the real estate broker. "Sorry," he said, "The condo you want has already been signed for by two prior contingent buyers." I realized that through his technical lingo he was saying that the earlier buyers had signed offers that were variously contingent on their being able to sell their existing residences, so I made it clear that I was prepared to buy immediately without any reservations. In the end, it was sold to me, and I have reveled in the view and the property's quick appreciation in value.

It was good to be again in the Southern California area near long-time friends like Milton and Peg Shedd (Milt was a fraternity brother at UCLA), Stan and Phyllis Aylmer (Stan was also a fraternity brother), Patsy Schmidt Nayfack (schoolmate and fraternity "date" at UCLA), George and Mary Ann Wentworth, David and Victoria Collins, Geoffrey and Kay Beaumont, Captain Ted Wilcox, USNR, Richard (and Marge) McManus, Frank and Tillie De Vore, Colonel Bob and Mary Porter, Stan and Sue Collier, Colonel and Mrs. David Yorck, and the Baloyan family in Tijuana.

My good luck continued in that time period by meeting my lovely companion, Ms. Chin-Yeh Rose. She is a beautiful, charming, intelligent lady, born in Taiwan, who amazingly has my same birth date, December 12, although she is 30 years younger than I. She came from a loving and nurturing family where education was strongly emphasized. Her elder sister Lei Chen obtained a scholarship in the U.S.A. and earned a Ph.D. in biochemistry, and later earned an M.D. in oncology. Her elder brother Richard Lei also was offered a scholarship and earned a Ph.D. in electrical engineering. Her younger brother, Captain T. K. Lei in Taiwain, is a leading figure in the international squid fishing industry. He obtains quotas from many countries to fish in their waters and handles refueling, transferring catches, and providing crews. He is building a fish processing and storage plant in Northern China to further expand that business. Chin-Yeh enrolled at Columbia University in New York after graduating from a college in Taiwan. After spending two years in New York, she married and later divorced in San Diego. She earned a B.S. in accounting from San Diego State University. After working several years for large firms, with her last job as a controller, Chin-Yeh started an import and export business in 1985. Her endeavor took her to many parts of the world, which helped to build up her confidence and independence. Shortly after we met in 1993, Chin-Yeh gradually diminished her international trade business due to our busy schedule. I am impressed with her zest in wanting to learn and how she manages to retain knowledge. Her incredibly good memory has helped me in my investment strate-

meals, and local wines. As historian Daniel Boorstin has said, "The traveler is active; he goes strenuously in search of people, of adventure, of experience. The tourist is passive; he expects interesting things to happen to him. He goes sightseeing." Thus, Chin-Yeh and I have enjoyed traveling at almost every opportunity averaging five major trips each year. Our busy voyages over the years have taken us to many exciting and interesting places.

People to People International (PTPI) "Mission in Understanding" (MIU) Travels

It has been a great pleasure to be asked by PTPI to lead a number of "Mission in Understanding" delegations. Each one was unique and memorable in its own way. I have truly enjoyed them all. Chin-Yeh has accompanied and assisted me on each of the delegations (with the exception of the first one in 1983).

The first PTPI group I led occurred 20 years ago when I was chairman of the California State Contractors License Board. Thirty-six persons traveled to Russia and China from August 1 to 21, 1983, to interact with their counterparts and t learn how building contracting took place in those Communist and very different countries. This voyage (and many of the following trips) was arranged by the very able Marc (and Sandy) Bright, who is now V/P Special Operations for PTPI.

Upon returning to the U.S.A. after being U.S. Ambassador in Bahrain, I was again happily involved with PTPI. I widened their travel destinations to include the Middle East and led a delegation of 34 persons to Morocco (Rabat, Casablanca, Fez, and Marrakech), Jordan (Amman, Petra), Israel (Jerusalem), Bahrain, and Saudi Arabia (Hofuf Camel Market and Dhahran Aramco Exhibit) January 11-30, 1995 (see photo #41). Bahrain was not accustomed to receiving large groups of touristic travelers, particularly the Protocol Department of the Foreign Ministry, who kindly involved themselves in handling our itinerary in that country. We did not know exactly what to expect when we arrived at the airport late at night. After a short wait at the VIP lounge to get our passports processed, we walked out to face 13 beautiful black limos. Our delegates had the chauffeurs and limos at our disposal for the many days we stayed in Bahrain. The Amir of Bahrain, Shaikh Isa, received all of us at his private palace the next morning at 8 a.m. As far as I know, this was one of the few times the Amir had ever received tourists. I believe he did it because of my efforts to contribute to U.S.-Bahrain relations during the Gulf War and because we genuinely liked each other. I remember during our private meetings he often with his kind and gentle demeanor encouraged me to seek a lady friend so my work would not consume my life totally. I still remember vividly the warm and approving smile on his face when I brought Chin-Yeh to visit him the first time in February, 1994.

Due to the success of our prior delegation, I led another PTPI group of 36 people on the same route, except that Saudi Arabia was not accessible because of an explosion in Riyadh. This trip occurred November 2-19, 1995 (see photos #43, #44, #45, and #46).

From October 34 to November 11, 1997, I led a 32-member delegation to the Persian Gulf. This trip included Bahrain, Abu Dhabi, Oman, and Kuwait (see photo #57).

From March 28 to April 14, 1998, I led a group of 22 persons to Egypt (Cairo and a cruise on the Nile), the Sinai Peninsula, Jordan, and Israel (Jerusalem) (see photo #58).

My next PTPI trip took place from October 22 to November 6, 1998. We visited the Amazon River, Brazil, and Argentina (see photo #61).

A very unique PTPI MIU involved leading a group of ten persons to Central Asia, where we visited Uzbekistan (Tashkent, Samarkand, Burhara, Khiva, Urgench) and Turkmenistan (Ashgabat). We traveled from September 5 to 18, 1999.

With a special license from the U.S. Treasury Department, I was allowed to lead the very first PTPI delegation of 35 U.S. citizens to intriguing Cuba and the Bahamas (Nassau). We traveled from May 22 to June 2, 2000 (see photo #69).

Our next PTPI adventure was to China. We led a PTPI group of 21 members to the historic Silk Road in western China. Chin-Yeh's fluent knowledge of Chinese came in handy during this trip, which occurred September 2-15, 2000 (see photo #70).

From November 17 to 26, 2002, we led an 18-person PTPI group to Ecuador (Quito and the fascinating Galapagos Islands) (see photo #78).

Two more trips are scheduled for the near future. On the first we will lead a group of 18 persons to Viet Nam and Cambodia November 14-25, 2003. Then we are planning a trip to Iceland and Greenland in June of 2004.

Other Personal Travels after 1993

The enterprising owner of Far Fung Travel, Kathleen Fung, asked me to lead two groups to some very interesting places in the Middle East. On the first of these I led a travel party of 18 people to Bahrain and Yemen April 10-27, 1997. Prior to this trip I had traveled to Yemen five times for the International Executive Service Corps (IESC) on voluntary assignments (see photos #53, #54, and #55).

Then from April 21 to May 9, 1999, I joined Kathleen Fung and her ten-member group in Damascus, Syria. Lebanese President Emile Lahoud received us at the Presidential Palace in Baabda, Lebanon. We had lunch at Marquand House at the American University of Beirut as guests of President John Waterbury (see photos #63 and #64).

One especially memorable occasion was traveling to Normany and receiving a French Commemorative medal on the 50th anniversary (June

6, 1994) of the D-Day Landing (see photo #38). Jacques and Eleanor Chevignard and their friends provided wonderful hospitality to accommodate us in Caen, Normandy.

Another remarkable trip involved the 50th anniversary of the Slovak Uprising (which occurred on August 28, 1944). Ambassador Julian Niemcyzk (an OSS veteran and close friend), Jeffrey Jones, the President of the Veterans of OSS, and I, along with several other OSS members, were invited by the President of Slovakia in August, 1994, to be part of a distinguished group which dedicated a plaque for OSS members killed in Palumka, Slovakia, in WWII (see photo #39). The heroine, Maria Gulovich, who risked her life to help those brave OSS members, also joined us there.

I was invited to be a guest lecturer on the new cruise ship M/S Rotterdam VI (Holland American Lines) as a part of their 98-day world cruise during March/April of 1999. Chin-Yeh and I embarked in Mumbai (Bombay, India) and sailed to Abu Dhabi (UAE), Doha (Qatar), Muscat (Oman), Republic of Djibouti, Safaga (Egypt), Aqaba (Jordan), Suez (Egypt), entered the Suez Canal, Port Said (Egypt), Ashdod (Israel), and debarked at Haifa (Israel). I was required to give only three lectures during 17 days of cruising. It was fun to be grouped with well-known entertainers and celebrities. The entire trip was indeed delightful.

Besides leading delegations, Chin-Yeh and I have traveled independently to many places in the

U.S. and abroad. Some involved Board of Directors meetings, but mostly they were for personal pleasure over the past ten-plus years. We went on some rather adventurous discoveries ranging from camping in San Ignacio, Baja California, Mexico, for whale-watching/touching (see photo #79), snorkeling at Australian Great Barrier Reef, to one-month long globe-trotting trips, and also on board numerous relaxing cruises throughout the world. Chin-Yeh has been a great travel companion, and we both enjoy visiting places, observing different cultures, and broadening our horizons. I hope I will be able to sustain for future years the difficulties of traveling while having a good time. Mark Twain had a keen perspective when he said, "Travel is fatal to bigotry, predudice and narrow-mindedness." How true! (See photos #42, 47, 48, 49, 50, 51, 52, 56, 59, 60, 67, 68, 71, and 73.)

Our busy and interesting voyages over the years have taken us to Taipei, Bangkok, Bahrain, Burgundy, Caen, Evian, Milan, Nice, Monte Carlo, Paris, by yacht from Seattle to San Juan Islands, Vancouver, Stuart Island (Straits of Georgia), Victoria (Vancouver Island), Vienna, Bratislava, Banska Bystrica, Athens, Antiparos, Paros, Mykonos, Malta, Venice, Florence, Pisa, Rome, Aruba, Cartagena, Colombia, San Blas Islands, Limon, Costa Rica, Grand Cayman, Rabat, Casablanca, Fez, Marrakech, Amman, Petra, Jerusalem, Hofuf and Dhahran (Saudi Arabia), Playa del Carmen and Cozumel (Mexico), Ocho

Rios (Jamaica) , Salomo (Spain), Barcelona, Zaragoza, Madrid, Toledo, St. Petersburg, Moscow, Ankara, Cappadocia, Konya, Perge, Kale Sunken City, Pamukkale, Ephesus, Kusadasi, Canakkale, Istanbul, Antwerp, Brugge, Knokke, Amsterdam, Basel, Brittnau, Zofingen, Lucerne, Ballenberg, Garmisch, Zurich, Liechtenstein, Geneva, Mont Blanc, Singapore, Semarang, Surabaya, Bali, Kuala Lumpur, Penang, Phuket, Honolulu, Yemen, England, Wales, Ireland, Fairbanks, Seward, College Fjords, Valdez, Glacier Bay, Juneau, Ketchikan, Vancouver, Kuwait, UAE, Oman, Basseterre, St. Kitts; Fort-de-France, Martinique; Port of Spain, Trinidad, Roseau/Cabrits, Dominica, St. Thomas (USVI), Half Moon Bay (Bahamas), Egypt, Sinai Peninsula, Jordan, Helsinki, Copenhagen, Oslo, Bergen, Stockholm, Amazon (Brazil), Cuba, Chile, Argentina, Uzbekistan, and Turmenistan.

Consular Corps

Having been appointed by the Government of the State (now Kingdom) of Bahrain as their Honorary Consul General (for the Western U.S.A.), I began those duties in San Diego, California, in 1993. Bahrain had become the host to the U.S. Fifth Fleet, and approximately 50% of the many U.S. Navy vessels which operate in the Persian Gulf and Southwest Asia come from the large U.S. Naval Base in San Diego.

My consular activities involve largely representation and promoting trade and tourism for

Bahrain. There is also a pleasant cross-border social environment with nearby Mexico. In the years 1996 and 1997 I was elected as President of the San Diego Consular Corps. The Corps has many pleasant and talented members including Randall Phillips (representing Japan), George (and Alison) Gildred (Chile), William F. (and Suzan) Black (U.K.), Dr. James (and Karen) Clements (Malawi), Oswald Gilbertson (Norway), Mrs. Maria Olson (Spain), and Mrs. Ella (and husband Jean-Pierre) Flores-Paris (Honduras). For many years I celebrated Bahrain National Day by giving a large annual party (see photo #62).

There are 21 countries which maintain consular posts in San Diego. Mexico has an active career consulate general in San Diego with about 40 full-time employees because of the busy border crossing at Tijuana only 15 miles away. With the growth of *maquiladoras,* tourism, and heavy trade with the U.S., Tijuana has grown to a population of over two million persons. Baja California has its own Consular Corps representing 18 countries, including a large and busy U.S. Consulate General in Tijuana.

Philanthropy

As I have grown older and my capability to donate has increased, I have taken particular interest in helping a number of organizations, including the Hubbs-Sea World Research Institute, San Diego State University, the Council of American

Ambassadors, the San Diego Natural History Museum, and People to People International. However, my warmest charitable feeling was toward the American University of Beirut (AUB) in Lebanon. From 1953 to 1955, as mentioned earlier, I attended this fine university, which has given wonderful years of service to the Middle East since 1866, and I received a Master's degree in Middle East Studies. It was long my desire to leave a bequest to AUB, and in October, 1980, I included AUB in my trust. I give credit to my beloved Chin-Yeh Rose, who, along with AUB's Presidents, Dr. Fred Herter, and Dr. John Waterbury, convinced me to make a pledge and begin the gift of $11.7 million while I was still living. Thus began the concept which today is the building of the Charles Hostler Student Center.

Chin-Yeh and I were invited to AUB when the project was ceremoniously announced in Beirut on February 27, 2001 (see photo #72). The four-building Student Center will house student recreation and activity functions, including an indoor swimming pool (the first swimming pool ever to be built at AUB), health and fitness facilities, a basketball court, and an international-standard track and field area, spectator seating, a 300-seat theater/auditorium, office space, and food services. Its prominent Lower Campus location will help to transform the public edge of the Mediterranean Corniche, and link it to the AUB Beach and Green Field.

Vincent James Associates and James Carpenter Design Associates presented the concept design for the Hostler Student Center, which won the jury competition in early October of 2002. They accompanied Dr. John Waterbury and Steve Jeffrey to visit me in San Diego on January 2, 2003. I appreciated them showing a slide presentation on their winning project among international architects. The ground-breaking ceremony is tentatively scheduled for April 5, 2004, which we plan to attend. I can imagine just how fulfilling and satisfying that moment will feel—a 24-year dream come true. In addition, the most gratifying feeling is that this act has inspired others to contribute to AUB, and that is what philanthropy is all about. On May 26, 2001, Queen Noor of Jordan kindly presented me the AUB Distinguished Services Award at the AUB Alumni Meeting in Chicago (see photo #74).

San Diego State University (SDSU)

The city of San Diego is fortunate to be the home of a number of fine universities. They include the University of California, San Diego, the University of San Diego (a private Catholic university), and San Diego State University, which has a significant history and at least 34,000 students.

In 1999 I was honored to be made an Adjunct Professor of Political Science associated with SDSU's Institute on World Affairs. This Institute is headed by Professor George Bergstrom, who has had a distinguished background in world affairs including long connections with Oxford University.

At SDSU, I am happy to be in contact with fine persons like President Stephen L. Weber, Dean Paul Strand, Professor Harry Polkinhorn, and Dean Paul Wong. Among other projects at SDSU, Chin-Yeh and I were pleased to be involved as charter donors for the beginning of SDSU's new Center for Islamic and Arabic Studies. This Center will play a useful role in bringing greater understanding in Southern California of the significant role of the world's 1.2 billion Muslims. This matter deserves careful study and attention particularly following the horrific and devastating events of September 11, 2001, in the United States (see photo #77).

Sixtieth Anniversary of D-Day Normandy Landings

The British Broadcasting Channel (BBC) began a major $3 million historic research filming project in the year 2003 to produce two 90-minute documentary films, partnered with the Discovery Channel and other international TV producers. Their worthy objective was to recognize in June of 2004 the sixtieth anniversary of the D-Day Landings in Normandy and to feature the exciting, relatively unknown, then-top secret deception program, which probably saved the lives of thousands of Allied troops in Europe. This involved the Allies' XX (Double Cross), counter-espionage, and Ulta deciphering programs.

A great deal of advance research was done by a thorough BBC analyst named Dan Parry. During his preliminary work, Dan had contacted the legendary Geoffrey Jones, long-time leader and President Emeritus of the Veterans of OSS. Geoffrey recommended Dan get in touch with me because of my long service in OSS/X2, CIA, and in counter-espionage work. This began a fruitful exchange of material with Dan and the BBC. When Dan heard that Chin-Yeh and I planned a month-long visit to Portugal and Spain in 2003, he made arrangements for the BBC to send a production unit to Madrid. On May 20, 2003, we met with the talented and pleasant BBC team composed of Producer Tim Bradley, Director Richard Dale, Tim Goodchild, and two camermen at the Ritz Hotel. Earlier that day my good friend from Newpoert Beach, California, and now U.S. Ambassador to Spain George (and Julia) Argyros kindly invited us for lunch at the embassy Residence (see photo #80).

Then, on March 21, the resourceful BBC team arranged a filming at the legendary Horcher Restaurant where German spies (including agent Garbo) in WWII had met with German officials from the nearby German Embassy. We lunched at La Magella Restaurant and then went to a room at the Ritz Hotel where they did filming and interviewed me in detail for several hours about my Normandy experiences with the deception and counter-espionage program. We ended up the day filming in the beautiful and famous Parque de

Retiro, where many clandestine meetings with German agents had occurred. I understand that the two 90-minute documentary films will be released on June 5 and 6, 2004, for the celebration of the sixtieth anniversary of the Normandy Landings.

It is satisfying to know that this important WWII XX program, as well as the WWII work of OSS's X2 personnel, will finally be brought to the world's attention on the sixtieth anniversary of D-Day. This brings a happy feeling that the work and courage of our Allied compatriots are at last being recognized. I look forward to standing on Utah Beah with Chin-Yeh Rose at my side on June 6, 2004, if "God is willing."

I miss the more active and challenging life that had involved government and international affairs. The current problems that are troubling Iraq and other parts of the Middle East make me wish I was still age-eligible to utilize my long area experience to help in seeking solutions. Nevertheless, this is not a prospect, so I am happy to travel as much as I can.

I thank Chin-Yeh and other close friends for encouraging me to write my memoirs. As I am completing this book, my thoughts turn to those whose paths I have been blessed to cross and whose friendship I deeply cherish. While it seems that the busy pace of our lives precludes exchanging notes on a regular basis, I hope that this book will serve the curiosity of those who care to know more.

Every life is unique, and no one can know his or her fate in advance. When I look back over the course my life has taken, I see a richness of professional and personal experience I could never have imagined. Each choice along the way directed me along an unfolding path that has become, in memories recalled sometimes with fondness and at others with mixed feelings, who I am. This path continues to beckon me onwards. Most recently, to my good fortune, Chin-Yeh and I were married on February 1, 2004. Warm wishes and blessings sent from friends gave another surge of energy and enthusiasm to extend and enrich my exciting life journey of 84 years. As Joseph Addison said in 1711, "Those marriages generally abound most with love and constancy that are preceded by a long courtship."

1. 1921, Illinois. Charles at age two.

2. About 1930, Illinois. Charles' parents: Catherine and Sydney Hostler.

3. 1930, England. Attending Coatham School in Redcar at age 12.

4. 1931, Somewhere in the Midwest on the way to California. Charles' parents driving from Chicago to San Francisco with their belongings in the midst of the Depression.

5. 1940, Los Angeles. At UCLA (in ROTC) at age of 20. Graduated in January, 1942, one month after Japanese attacked Pearl Harbor.

6. March, 1942, California. Charles as a California Highway Patrol officer.

7. March, 1942, California. On the same day, Charles changed
uniform preparing for duty as a 2nd Lt. in U.S. Army Air Force.

8. 1943, Washington, D.C. Undergoing OSS training.

9. 1944, England. Receiving "Parachute Insertion Training" at British Special Training School #51 in Ringway.

10. March 14, 1945, Germany. During Allied troops movement into Cologne.

11. April 21, 1945, Florence, Italy. During Italian campaign in WWII with Ponte Vecchio in background.

12. May 26, 1945, Italy. Charles (center) at Villa Torre
Sarceno, Isle of Capri, with Kermit Roosevelt, Jr. (with
glasses), who later led CIA overthrow of Mossadeq in Iran.

13. October 28, 1945, Rumania. Hunting near Alexandria,
Rumania. (L to R: OSS Agent Frank Stevens, George
McDonald, and Charles).

14. May 10, 1946, Rumania. L to R: Rumania's first Communist Prime Minister, Petru Groza, King Michael, and Russian Generals reviewing parade.

15. September, 1948, Turkey. Charles and three others on a one-month U.S. military reconnaissance of 5,500 miles by jeep through Eastern Anatolia, Armenia, Soviet frontier, and Iran (at beginning of Cold War).

16. 1955, Pentagon. Colonel Charles W. Hostler in uniform.

17. December 13, 1960, Antiparos, Greece. Mayor Roussos (in center reading proclamation) of Antiparos Island welcomes Charles and his son bringing "message in a bottle" gifts.

18. January 24, 1961, Jordan. Late King Hussein of Jordan with inscription to Charles: "With our best regards and wishes".

19. 1973, California. Charles in the center as founder and chairman of Board of Irvine National Bank, with members of Board of Directors.

20. October, 1974, Tunisia. Charles as Deputy Assistant Secretary of Commerce meeting with U.S. Ambassador Talcott Seelye and Tunisian Prime Minister Nouira and Undersecretary John Tabor on the terrace of Ambassador's residence in Tunis.

21. January, 1976, Ghana. Accompanying U.S. Ambassador Shirley Temple Black (beloved child movie star) at Ghana International Trade Fair when Charles was Deputy Assistant Secretary of Commerce (International Commerce).

For Charles
Hostler
Silver Jubilee visit
of HM The Queen
to Cleveland (Eng).
Cecil Crosthwaite
HM Lord Lieutenant of
Cleveland.
14 July 1977

22. July 14, 1977, England. Charles' uncle, Lord Lt. Cecil Crosthwaite, receiving HRH Queen Elizabeth in Middlesborough.

23. June 1, 1978, England. Charles' uncle, Lord Lt. Cecil Crosthwaite, receiving HRH Prince Charles of Wales in Cleveland/Yorkshire on 250th anniversary of birth of Captain James Cook.

24., October 18, 1989, Washington, D.C. Secretary of State, James Baker (on right) officiates at Swearing in Ceremony as Charles becomes U.S. Ambassador to Bahrain, aided by David Ransom, who later also became U.S. Ambassador to Bahrain.

To Ambassador Charles Hostler
with High Regard – Best Wishes, G. Bush

25. March 28, 1990, Washington, D.C. President George Bush (Sr.) welcomes Ambassador Hostler at White House.

26. July 4, 1990, Bahrain. Official opening of new U.S. Embassy in Bahrain by His Highness, the Amir, Shaikh Isa bin Sulman Al-Kahlifa, and Ambassador Hostler (29 days before beginning of Gulf War).

27. September, 1990, Bahrain. General Norman Schwarzkopf and Ambassador Hostler in joint planning session with Bahraini Minister of Defense, Shaikh Khalifa bin Ahmad Al-Khalifa, and his staff.

28. September, 1990, Bahrain. Shaikh Hamad in center (now King of Bahrain, then Crown Prince) with Amir Shaikh Isa, U.S. Secretary of Defense Richard Cheney, U.S. Ambassador Hostler, and USMC Major General Royal Moore.

29. November 5, 1990, Saudi Arabia. Secretary of State, James Baker, visits 1st U.S. Cavalry Division during Gulf War, accompanied by Ambassador Hostler.

30. December 27, 1990, Bahrain. Comedian Bob Hope, Bahraini Minister of Information, Tariq Al-Moyaed, and Ambassador Hostler enjoying dinner at Minister Al-Moyaed's home, a day after Bob's last performance for the troops.

31. May, 1991, Bahrain. Colin Powell, then Chairman of Joint Chiefs of Staff, with inscription to Charles.

32. October 15, 1991, Washington, D.C. Official State visit of Amir of Bahrain to White House.

33. October 15, 1991, Washington, D.C. State gift from the Amir of Bahrain, Shaikh Isa, to the President of U.S.A., George Bush, Sr. The "Palm Tree" was hand-made in 21-ct. gold with 3,824 grams of weight and 32 inches in height on a marble base. This masterpiece has 749 Bahraini pearls which weighs 72 grams symbolizing the dates hanging from the palm tree. It was crafted by Bahraini goldsmiths and is in the care of George Bush's Library.

34. October 15, 1991, Washington, D.C. State gift from the
Amir of Bahrain, Shaikh Isa, to Mrs. Barbara Bush. The "Pearl
Necklace" was hand-made in 18-ct. gold with 51.3 grams of
weight and 133 pearls (the biggest pearl's diameter is 8.5 mm
and the smallest 5.5 mm). The center mother-of-pearl piece is
decorated with 3.505 ct. of diamonds. It also is in the care of
George Bush's Library.

35. October 27, 1991, Bahrain. Signing of U.S.-Bahraini
Agreement on Defense Cooperation with Foreign Minister
H.E. Shaikh Mohammed bin Mubarak Al-Khalifa.

36. June, 1992, France. Ambassador Hostler giving speech in French at Confrerie des Chevaliers du Tastevin at Chateau du Clos de Vougeot in Burgundy.

37. June 4, 1994, France. Chevaliers du Tastevin remembers 50th Anniversary of D-Day, with Grand Chamberlain Jacques Chevignard, Chin-Yeh Rose, and Eleanor Chevignard (in red dress next to Charles).

38. June 6, 1994, France. Receiving French Commemorative Medal, awarded at Abbaye de Dames in Caen during 50th Anniversary of Normandy D-Day Landing.

39. August 28, 1994, Slovakia. 50th Anniversary of Slovak Uprising during WWII and the dedication of plaque for OSS members killed in Polumka, Slovakia. U.S. Ambassador to the U.N., Madeline Albright, and Secretary of the Army, Togo West, were present. (L to R: President of Veternas of OSS, Jeffrey Jones; Ambassador Julian Niemcyzk, and Charles).

40. September 7, 1994, Malta. Prince Henri Paleologo and Princess Françoise in Malta as Chin-Yeh Rose became Dame of Order of St. John, Knights of Malta.

41. January 26, 1995, Saudi Arabia. Long-time friends Mary Ann and George Wentworth joined Charles' first People to People International delegation to the Middle East. Photo was taken after visiting the impressive Saudi Aramco Exhibit.

42. July 21, 1995, Red Square, Russia. Charles (with Chin-Yeh's help) as International Executive Service Corp (IESC) Consultant in Moscow.

43. November 9, 1995, Morocco. Visiting the over 1,000-year-old leather tanning process in Fez.

44. November 12, 1995, Jordan. In front of the famed "Treasury" with Jordanian Camel Corps Troopers in Petra.

45. November 19, 1995, Jordan/Israel. L to R: Charles, Chin-Yeh Rose, Marta and Ambassador Tom Stroock at the Allenby Bridge on the Jordanian side waiting for permission to cross toward Jerusalem.

46. November 11, 1995, Jerusalem. Leading People to People International delegation to the Holy Land. Joined by friends Ambassador Tom and Marta Stroock, Victoria and David Collins, and Arlene Kieta.

47. April 29, 1996, Turkey. Charles and Chin-Yeh touring historic Ephesus.

48. June 21, 1996, Switzerland. Visiting Maryse and Willi Zimmerli at their chalet with their grandson Guillaume in Ayer.

49. February 26, 1997, Indonesia. Borobudur Temple near Semarang. The temple was constructed out of volcanic rock during the 8th and 9th centuries and later was abandoned and buried under ash and tropical growth until the 1800s.

50. March 6, 1997, Thailand. Visiting the reclining Buddha in breathtaking Phuket.

51. March 19, 1997, California. Lunch at Ritz Carlton Hotel in Laguna Niguel with Count and Countess Oswald and Brigitte Voorbraeck (in the center) and Victoria and David Collins.

52. March 20, 1997, Coronado. Friends at Charles's home. L to R: Charles, Prince Henri, George Wentworth, Chin-Yeh Rose, Mary Ann Wentworth, Ginette Jaramillo, Princess Françoise, Peter Jaramillo, and Brigitte Voorbraeck.

53. April 15, 1997, Bahrain. L to R: Admiral Tom Fargo (then Commander of the U.S. 5th fleet headquartered in Bahrain, now Commander of U.S. Pacific Command), Chin-Yeh Rose, Charles Hostler, CEO of Investcorp, Nimr Kirdar, and Mubarak Kanoo (the Kanoos have been a prominent Bahraini merchant family for over 100 years).

54. April 18, 1997, Yemen. On a rooftop, in the capital Sana'a.

55. April 24, 1997, Yemen. Yemeni military escorting our group from Sana'a to Marib because of numerous tourist kidnappings.

56. August 26, 1997, Glaciar Bay, Alaska. Cruising the inside passage of Alaska.

57. November 5, 1997, Oman. After Arabic food in a tent, we joined the musicians at Tent Village at the side of the magnificent Al Bustan Palace Hotel.

58. March 31, 1998, Egypt. Camel riding at Pyramids in Giza.

59. August 21, 1998, Norway. Visiting the unique Vigeland Sculpture Park in Oslo, Norway, during Scandinavia trip.

60. August 21, 1998, San Diego. Good friends Jan and Dick Pauley joining the Hubbs-Sea World Research Institute's annual picnic. Charles has been a supporter of this worthy institute for nearly 40 years.

61. October 29, 1998, Brazil. Spectacular Sugar Loaf in the background, Rio de Janeiro.

62. December 15, 1998, San Diego. Bahraini National Day Party given by Charles at his residence. Consul of Sweden, John Norton, and a long-time friend, Afife Baloyan, from Tijuana, Mexico.

63. April 25, 1999, Syria. In the courtyard of Umayyad Mosque in Damascus. Women are required to cover their hair and body before entering.

64. April 30, 1999, Lebanon. Charles and Chin-Yeh visiting Baalbek, the "open-air museum" of ancient ruins.

65. September 19, 1999, Uzbekistan. At the Mosque that Timurlane built for his eldest wife in Samarkand.

66. September 17, 199, Turkmenistan. People to People International delegation farewell party in Ashgabat.

67. February 27, 2000, Fiji. Native Fijians preparing Kava Kava drink, which we tasted.

To Charles
Best Wishes *Bush signature*

68. May 15, 2000, San Diego. President George W. Bush (Jr.)
at dinner with Charles and Chin-Yeh, Rancho Santa Fe.

69. May 27, 2000, Cuba. In front of the picture of Castro and
Hemingway at Finca Vigia where Hemingway lived and which
is now a museum.

70. September 13, 2000, China. Wearing Kazakh garb at the Heavenly Lake, Tien Shan Mountains in Xingjian Province, China, along the ancient Silk Road. Xingjian is predominantly Muslim and has many ethnic groups from Central Asia.

71. September 18, 2000, Taiwan. Touring Kinmen Island (in closest vicinity to China) with Chin-Yeh.

72. February 28, 2001, Lebanon. Announcement of "Charles Hostler Student Center" at American University of Beirut, with university president, Dr. John Waterbury.

73. May 5, 2001, Florence, Italy. Revisiting the famous Old Bridge, Ponte Vecchio, 56 years later, with Chin-Yeh.

74. May 26, 2001, Chicago. Queen Noor of Jordan presents Charles with American University of Beirut Distinguished Service Award (L to R: Ali Ghandour [Trustee], Chin-Yeh Rose, Naguib Halaby [Queen Noor's father], Queen Noor, Charles Hostler, and Mrs. Halaby).

75. June 7, 2001, San Diego. Guests of Reed and Rita Sprinkel on their beautiful "Viking Princess" yacht cruising the Mexican Coronado Islands.

76. September 8, 2001, Denmark. CEO of People to People International, Mary Eisenhower (President Ike Eisenhower's granddaughter) presenting Charles with Eisenhower Distinguished Service Award in Aalborg.

77. May 16, 2002, San Diego. L to R: Charles Hostler, San Diego State University (SDSU) Dean Paul Strand, SDSU President Stephen Weber, and Mirza Al-Sayegh, Chairman of Maktoum Foundation of Dubai during Mirza's visit to SDSU regarding the new Center for Islamic and Arabic Studies.

78. November 22, 2002, Ecuador. Face to face with a giant tortoise in the fascinating Galapagos Islands.

79. March 25, 2003, Mexico. Awaiting a small boat for Gray Whale watching in San Ignacio, Baja California. The mother whale pushes the baby whale close to our boat so we can touch the whale. An extremely thrilling experience.

80. May 20, 2003, Madrid. U.S. Ambassador to Spain (and California friend) George Argyros and wife Julia receive Charles and Chin-Yeh for lunch at Embassy Residence.